But They Spit, Scratch, and Swear!

Call For A Free Resource Catalog
School-Age NOTES
P.O. Box 476
New Albany, OH 43054
1-800-410-8780
www.schoolagenotes.com

But They Spit, Scratch, and Swear!

The **Do's and Don'ts** of Behavior Guidance with School-Age Children

@ **by Mary Steiner Whelan**

A-ha! communications

Published by **A-ha!** communications
3044 12th Ave. S.
Minneapolis, MN 55407
steinerwhelan@yahoo.com

ISBN 0-9679925-0-8

The author acknowledges these sources for epigraphs:

Evans, Mari, ed. *Black Women Writers*. New York: Doubleday, 1984.
Toni Cade Bambara quotation.

Bombeck, Erma. *The Best of Erma Bombeck*. New York: Galahad, 1987.

Casablanca. Dir. Michael Curtiz. Warner Brothers, 1942.

Craft, Juanita Jewel. *A Child, the Earth, and a Tree of Many Seasons: The Voice of Juanita Craft*. Dallas: Halifax, 1982.

Elkind, David. *The Hurried Child: Growing Up Too Fast Too Soon*. Reading: Addison-Wesley, 1981.

Evershed, Jane. *Jagadamba*. Minneapolis: Jane Evershed Card Collection, 1994.

Frankl, Viktor. *Man's Search for Meaning: An Introduction to Logotherapy*. Trans. Ilse Lasch. New York: Simon, 1984.

Jackson, Michael, and Lionel Richie. "We Are the World." USA for Africa. Columbia, 1985.

Kim, Tae Yun. *The Silent Master: Awakening the Power Within*. San Rafael: New World Library, 1994.

Milford, Nancy. *Zelda: A Biography*. New York: Harper, 1970.

Moore, Virginia. *Virginia is a State of Mind*. New York: Dutton, 1942.

Neill, Alexander S. *Summerhill: A Radical Approach to Education*. London: V. Gollancz, 1969.

Perry, Bruce. D. "Childhood Trauma, the Neurobiology of Adaptation, and 'Use-dependent' Development of the Brain: How 'States' Become 'Traits.'" *Infant Mental Health Journal* 16 (1995).

Steiner, Jean, and Mary Steiner Whelan. *For the Love of Children: Daily Affirmations for People Who Care for Children*. St. Paul: Redleaf, 1995.

Simon and Garfunkel. "The 59th Street Bridge Song (Feelin' Groovy)." Columbia, 1966.

Stories throughout the book cited to Jean Steiner and Mary Steiner Whelan are from *For the Love of Children: Daily Affirmations for People Who Care for Children*. St. Paul: Redleaf, 1995.

To John and Mark, my brothers.

I love you.

Table of Contents

List of Illustrators

The illustrations in this book were done by persons in the school-age care community: children, parents, teachers, supporters. Thanks to each of them for lending their talents to this book.

LaNaya A. Olson

Vicki Bliss

Vicki Bliss

Chapter opening illustrations by:

Mallory Anderson

Vicki Bliss

Zahkyia Taqui Holley

Lindsey Miller

Catherine Moriarity

Aneesa K. Nathim

LaNaya A. Olson

Carly Schumacher

Holly Welch

Thanks also to all the people who submitted drawings. We wish we could have used all of your art. Your time and enthusiasm are greatly appreciated.

Preface

With a lot of support from my friends and family, in 1998 and again in 1999, I did volunteer work with women and children in Africa. When I left for Kenya and Uganda, I had some fear that when I saw the conditions of children there, I would begin to think that the problems children face in school-age care programs here would seem insignificant. Instead, I became more committed to helping our children in any way that I can. It became clear to me that there is absolutely no reason why children in the United States and other "developed countries" shouldn't be happy and have the resources they need, the attention they deserve, and the loving guidance of adults that is necessary for healthy development.

With our enormous resources, instant access to information, a glorious infrastructure, high levels of education, and lots and lots of money, there should be no suffering children in our society. Certainly, there should be no children who do not have their physical and emotional needs met. That means that we need to look at our communities, our distribution of goods, our differential between schools in communities with different income levels, and our means of providing basic human needs for everyone in our land. We need to allocate time, resources, and money, for justice and care for all families and therefore for all children.

School-age programs should not have to beg for funds when they care for children for a great part of their waking hours. Programs for school-age children shouldn't be hidden away in basements or cafeterias with pushed-back tables. There shouldn't be high student-staff ratios. Well-meaning staff shouldn't lack the training that they need while struggling to help raise our country's children.

Children in school-age programs should have highly trained, loving people caring for them. They should have the support staff that they and their families need. They should have the equipment, the tools, the sunlight, and experiences that will allow them to grow into empathetic, responsible, capable, and healthy adults.

Staff in school-age programs should be well paid, receive excellent benefits, and have access to education and support. They should be respected as extremely valuable people in our society. They should have everything they need so that they can concentrate on helping children to be fully alive adults.

If our society would turn itself around and change its assumptions about what is important, about who counts, we would begin to raise healthy children. Our children would be healthy enough to be empathetic toward other people in the world. As adults, they would be able to live fulfilling lives while they helped resolve the economic inequities that perpetuate the problems of African children and their families, and of peoples who suffer as some Africans do.

Many children in Africa suffer from hunger or are dying of diseases that we long ago overcame. They have no shoes, clothing, clean water, or strong homes. Their education is pathetic or nonexistent. Their parents are sick, exhausted, and depressed. They are also intelligent, resourceful, and loving. With little or no income, they try to teach their children, hoping the whole time that they will just stay alive. And, no, they are not happy that way. They wish for a way of life that would meet their very basic needs and allow their children to thrive.

The current imbalance of resources means that there are thousands of people whom I have met who haven't even heard of computers. How are they to make it in a competitive world as they "develop" as new democracies?

We must talk, write, petition, educate, change our lifestyles in this country so that a land so wealthy as ours has no needy children. We have to get for children what they need—including values that count all others as important.

We need to vigorously support efforts to improve school-age care, where millions of children become who they will become. There is no reason not to. That will be a big step in raising children who will be able to work for justice for all the children in the world community.

If you and your schoolagers would like to set up connections with African children, or if you have any other things you would like to discuss with me, please contact me:

Mary Steiner Whelan
3044 12th Ave. S.
Minneapolis, MN 55407
651-642-5116

Acknowledgments

I wrote this book on three continents, using eight computers.

Many people gave me places to write and computer guidance. Thanks to those who shared their space:

- Linda Hucke, who took me into her pleasant home as I transitioned.
- Dorothy Johnson and her hosts Roz and Mark Anderson, who made available a retreat home by a lake in northern Minnesota. Its peacefulness inspired me to keep writing.
- Jadini Beach Hotel in Ukunda, Kenya, who helped me because I was writing a book about children.
- Innkeepers in Playa del Carmen, Mexico, and my family and friends, who allowed me to use parts of our vacations for writing and to use them as sounding boards.
- My parents, Matt and Jean Steiner, who let me use their townhouse and Power Mac.
- Those who patiently helped me with computers, which seemed to have it in for me: Hetal Dalal, John Steiner, Majhid Nathim, Kathy Olson, Sue Baldwin, Aaron Schumacher, Deb Schumacher, Aaron Leisen. Special thanks to Elijah Omolo and Walter Odhiambo in Mombasa, Kenya, who, in the midst of personal hard times, helped me find a computer that worked.

Thanks also to:

- My roommates, Rosemary Schaffer and Shawn Whelan, who let me know when it was time to go for a walk or think about things in a new way.
- Kevin Whelan, substantive and managing editor, who encouraged me, kept a low profile, and maintained a high energy level.
- Cathy Spengler, design and production, who worked her magic on a tight and complex timeline.
- Andrea McCready for excellent copyediting.
- Tim Uren for careful data entry.

- Joe Whelan for supporting me to go forward with this project. Thanks also for pickup and delivery services.

- Sue Baldwin for listening, consulting, and caring.

- My mentors, especially Sister Mary Alcuin Stack—Aunt Mary— and Roz Anderson, for trusting me and asking me to stretch my mind and my beliefs.

- To all the people working each day with schoolagers—thank you for making a difference in children's lives.

- To my friends and family, who respected the time it took to write this book.

- To each of my children, Kevin, Sarah, and Shawn, for being resilient and resplendent people: thank you for loving me as I learned, often with difficulty, to shift my paradigms about parenting and life. You mean the world to me.

Introduction to Behavior Guidance:
How to Use This Book

As I begin to write this book, I can see before me thousands of people. Most of them are staff and caregivers who work daily with school-age children. Others supervise programs. Some train staff. A fortunate few are students learning about the School-Age Care (SAC) field before they work in it. Parents, principals, base commanders, grandparents, board members, community leaders, and other interested people fill in the picture.

Some people's faces shine with hopefulness. Desperation casts shadows on others. Many faces sag with fatigue. Some look puzzled.

Those folks clutching on to hope read the title of the book. Their hearts race. They say out loud, "At long last, I'll know just what to do with Janet or Andre or in the gym or when a kid looks me in the eye and says, 'You can't make me!'"

The people mired in desperation open the book reluctantly. They assume it's the same old thing. "It's no use. Either kids today are rotten or I'm incompetent. I'll read it if I have to, but I can tell you that no book is going to help."

The tired and the puzzled shrug and ask someone to tell them how this bundle of pages is possibly going to make their lives easier.

I would like to write a book that could be a quick fix for everyone.

I would like to say to the hopeful, "Yes, this book does have all the answers." I want to hold my hand out to the desperate and say, "The kids are not monsters. You have many skills, and this book will make it all better." To the tired I want to give renewed energy and to the puzzled, solutions.

Alas, I can't guarantee anything. This book will not tell you exactly what to do in every situation with every child. There is no single "right" way to deal with a child's behavior. I don't have all the answers, so neither does this book. But I hope it will help.

I say these things with some humor but also with an awesome sense of responsibility. The people who will read this book deal with tens of thousands of children each day. Each child comes with her or his own history, culture, and personality. So do all of you. So do I. What you do and say will affect each child in some way forever. As you put your professional skills into practice, you change kids' lives. One way or the other. You either help them become stronger and more fully human or thwart their growth. Nothing that you do with children is neutral. You help shape children's todays and determine their tomorrows. Who they are now and who they will become is, in part, your responsibility.

By writing this book I am sharing that responsibility with you. I wish I knew more. I wish I could read all the latest research. That I could visit every program that exists. That I could talk personally with each of you about your concerns. That I could know each of the children in your care.

Of course, I can't do all that. I wish I could. I can promise you that I will use my knowledge, my experience, my intuition, my heart, and the high esteem that I hold for both you and the children, to attempt to honestly and respectfully help you. I can tell you that if you read this book and do the exercises with an open heart and mind, you will deal differently with children, and it will help. Much of what I know, I've learned from people like you and from the children themselves. I am humbled and honored to be a part of your work.

Discipline, or behavior guidance, or whatever the popular term may be, is often the most difficult part of what we do. It is also often the most important. It can open for children the world of possibilities that live within them for self-control, competency, self-respect, creativity, integrity, resiliency, and self-worth. Or, behavior guidance can close down children's hope, their empathy for others, and their positive sense of self. Discouraged, abandoned children either act in or act out. Secure, nurtured children inter-act.

The way we guide children's behavior can diminish behavior problems and give children roots and wings. Or our actions and reactions can perpetuate the cycle of misbehavior and punishment that leaves children floundering and afraid.

Although it often helps to approach our work with humor, our jobs are very serious. I join you to take look at what we do and how we do it. To keep what we do well and to be willing to change what may be harmful. Neither you nor I will ever be fully equipped to do what we are already doing. But we do have good intentions and some skills that work. We can continue to learn and make progress. And we can have some fun along the way.

I hope this unique book written especially for school-age care professionals will help. It briefly examines historical influences and school-age development issues. And, true to its mission, most of it deals with behavior guidance. As I wrote the book I began to understand more and more clearly that in order to effectively guide behavior, we need to take a journey into ourselves, the children's needs, and relationship building. For this reason, the book contains many stories from my personal experiences—and asks you to reflect on many of yours.

The essence of our work is to relate to, respect, influence, and guide children. This book is really about hearts and minds—yours and the children's. Once we look into our hearts and think about what we find there, we can implement behavior guidance practices that work to change behaviors.

Because this book delves into complex human relationship issues, I created a style that is not the typical textbook or training format. This book will probably be used in trainings, in classrooms, and by individuals. Whatever the setting, it is not a book that can simply be read. It is an interactive book that you *do*. It is intended to generate personal reflection and increased understanding that will enhance the art of working with children. It is a book to be lived. The book asks you to think, to feel, to change, to shift paradigms, to affirm and question yourself and your practices.

Please be open to trying things that you have not tried before. The exercises are not busywork. They are integral to the learning that can spring from doing this book. Many of the exercises assume that you are currently working in a school-age care program, because I think that most readers will be in some way involved in those programs. If you are not, I believe that the book can be helpful to anyone working with school-age children or who is preparing to. Use your creativity to apply the exercises to your setting or family, or make up a setting. Please do not skip the exercises. Many of the lessons from the book will be yours alone. That is one of the powerful elements of your work. Only you can bring to children what you have to give. Like your fingerprint, your influence on a child's life is unique.

It is also important to discuss with others the ideas, insights, and struggles you experience while you work with this book. We benefit from interacting with others to clarify, strengthen, challenge, and apply our thinking. Practice, revise, read again. By the time you complete this book the corners should be tattered. There should be writing everywhere, words written down in its pages that only you could write because they come from and are about you and your relationship with children.

The journey through the book will assist you with the most dynamic, and personal, part of your work—behavior guidance. The way that you handle guiding children will affect who they are and will become. In a fast-paced world such as ours, you may be the only person children can connect to long enough to believe in themselves. I hope that each of you will some day hear the words, "You changed my life." Because you do change lives daily, in ways large and small. The work you do is complicated. But it is worth it, because you and the children deserve to be together in meaningful ways that enrich all of you.

The book is divided into two sections. The first section talks about the history and makeup of school-age programs and kids' development. These issues influence your work with schoolagers.

The second section contains the do's and don'ts that I have practiced as a school-age care teacher, supervisor, director, and consultant. I have traveled around the country talking about these practices, learning about them from you and from the children. They are about how we guide, talk with, and help children. I hope that they make a difference for you. I believe that the principles respect children and adults, and that they are practical enough to implement and complex enough to be effective. Their application will reduce the number of discipline problems you have. They are not easy in some ways. However, they gradually become as easy as walking or talking as you understand and practice them.

I hope that doing this book will be enlightening, invigorating, challenging, and fun. I hope that it will make your job easier and more fulfilling. I thank you for the children whose lives you will impact in positive ways. I'm right beside you as you journey towards learning how to do behavior guidance—even though the children might "spit, scratch, and swear."

Section 1
School-Age Care & Behavior Guidance

Chapter 1

What Is This Thing Called Behavior Guidance?

by Aneesa

Tell every child they have a purpose on this planet.

May the birthright of every child be to have a wise caretaker,

Who understands the fine line between discipline, and the

> *Breaking of a spirit, and how to mend one, and*

The need for understanding and freedom of expression—

> *Without fear of physical attack…*

…For the great spirit of the child grows in the garden of complete love,

> *Giving seed to a sure sense of self,*

And a fearless child becomes a wise and loving elder,

And every child that flourishes with love, respect and encouragement

> *Gives roots to a future without limitations on love.*

≈ Jane Evershed

What is behavior guidance? It is…

- The one topic that will always fill a workshop room at a conference
- The most difficult thing you do
- Consequences
- An art
- The most important thing you teach
- Rules
- Discipline
- The single biggest reason that people leave the school-age care field
- A matter of opinion
- A science
- A nightmare
- Punishment
- Group management
- The number-one cause of burnout
- Self-discipline
- Impossible
- Problem solving
- Rewards
- Behavior modification
- Time-outs
- Conflict resolution

Prosocial skills　　Essential
Time consuming　　Complicated
Confusing　　Exhausting
Control　　Frightening
Empowerment　　Fascinating

Behavior guidance brings to mind all the terms listed above. Behavior guidance has also been known, maybe by the most people and for the longest period of time, as "discipline."

Every five to ten years there is a new, "more correct" term for what you all know is the trickiest part of your job. Words to describe things are important. They can change the way we think about things. I was going to try to make up a better term, one that better sums up what this book tells you about behavior guidance. But for most of you, doing your work from day to day, the words don't matter.

What matters is how to cope with discipline. How to guide children's behavior so that your program has some semblance of order. So that you appear and feel competent. So that you can get on with what you want to experience with the kids. So that you are not so tired.

Therefore, for the purposes of this book, we will use the familiar terms "behavior guidance" and "discipline," just so that we all know what we're talking about. You will come up with a better, more complete definition—one that works for you and the children—as you work with this book.

Punishment and Control or Teaching and Relationship?

Discipline is often equated with punishment. It is not punishment. Punishment and control are ways that some people have tried to manage kids—and adults for that matter—for years. If you woke up one morning, rubbed your hands together with evil glee, and said, "Aha, I have it! I will work in school-age care so I can punish children!" please raise your hand now.

I'm sure you didn't raise your hand. That isn't why you got into this field. There are many reasons people find themselves working with school-agers. But wanting to punish kids isn't one of them. Quite the opposite: one of the reasons most people get involved is that they like children. And yet, how much time do you spend in a day or a week doing something to children that could be called punishment? Children see and feel it as punishment when they are constantly being corrected, being yelled at, having activities taken away from them, being lectured, or being ignored because they do not behave as expected. If you are doing these things regularly, you spend too much time punishing, when punishment is not what you want for yourself or for the children.

How Do Children Cope with Power-Based Discipline?

Dr. Thomas Gordon does an exercise with adults in his workshops. He asks them to recall the specific ways that they themselves coped with power-based discipline when they were young. Here is the complete list that several adult groups formulated:

- Resisting, defying, being negative
- Rebelling, disobeying, being insubordinate, sassing
- Retaliating, striking back, counterattacking, vandalizing
- Hitting, being belligerent and combative
- Breaking rules and laws
- Throwing temper tantrums, getting angry
- Lying, deceiving, hiding the truth
- Blaming others, tattling, telling on others
- Bossing or bullying others
- Banding together, forming alliances, organizing against the adult
- Apple-polishing, buttering up, soft-soaping, bootlicking, seeking excessive flattery from adults
- Withdrawing, fantasizing, daydreaming
- Competing, needing to win, hating to lose, needing to look good, making others look bad
- Giving up, feeling defeated, loafing, goofing off
- Leaving, escaping, staying away from home, running away, quitting school, cutting classes
- Not talking, ignoring, using the silent treatment, writing the adult off, keeping a distance
- Crying, weeping, feeling depressed or hopeless
- Becoming fearful, shy, timid, afraid to speak up, hesitant to try anything new
- Needing reassurance, seeking constant approval, feeling insecure
- Getting sick, developing psychosomatic ailments

- Overeating, excessive dieting
- Being submissive, conforming, complying, dutiful, docile
- Drinking heavily, using drugs
- Cheating in school, plagiarizing

Thomas Gordon, *Discipline That Works: Promoting Self-Esteem in Children*
(New York: Penguin, 1991)

When I first read this list, I noticed that many of the coping mechanisms are behaviors that we often say are the most difficult to deal with in school-age children. I had to ask myself, "Which came first? Are we inciting, or at least reinforcing, the behaviors that we most want to eliminate? Even, maybe especially, with the words that we use with children?" We often think of power and control only in the case of physical discipline with children. And yet we have each felt the pain of the look, the word, the body language that takes away our power and leaves us using behaviors like the ones in the list above to cope as best we can.

Also, although not all the behaviors the adults listed would be viewed as behavior problems when children use them, most are unhealthy behaviors. We certainly do not want to promote these destructive coping mechanisms in another generation.

Which of the behaviors in the list above did you use to respond to power when you were a child?

What controlling behavior on the part of adults promoted these behaviors?

Which behaviors do you often see children in your program exhibiting in response to control?

What do you see the adults in your program doing to promote these behaviors, perhaps unintentionally?

_____

_____

Give an example of a time when you observed children reacting to a teacher or other adult who was lecturing, forcing them to apologize, or threatening them:

_____

_____

Give an alternative solution to the problem that the adult was trying to address with the child:

_____

_____

Changing the Way We Think about Discipline

I imagine that what you want for children is the opportunity to learn how to interact with people in cooperative, respectful ways. You want them to be able to learn how to resolve conflicts in a healthy, not a harmful, manner. You want them to respect themselves. You want children to behave in ways that honor who they are and who others are, in ways that allow people to feel safe. You want children to feel safe. You want them to follow the rules of society that keep people from getting hurt. You want them to think and feel, judge, and then act. You want children to think for themselves, rather than merely following others. You want them to learn how to face challenges, not hide from them through misbehavior or self-destruction. You want children to stand up for themselves and their beliefs without stepping on others. You want them to help build a community and to be vital members in it. You want children to learn many ways of acting, of thinking, of being, that promote fairness for all.

Learn—that's what you want children to do. In order for them to learn, you will need to teach them. You will have to guide them with example, direction, information, dialogue, relationship building, assistance, practice, and support during their trials and errors. With your help, they will learn the complex set of skills that it takes to be contributing citizens of the world.

Wow! That is a huge task. But it is more like what you hoped to do, isn't it? You'd prefer to be a teacher, a guide, and a mentor, rather than a punisher.

It's time to change the way we think about discipline. The model that many of us have is one of punishment and control. Often we act upon it simply because it is so familiar. Many of us were brought up in homes and went to schools where that model was in place. Even if we don't realize it, our actions towards children spring from the way others dealt with us and those around us. It takes thought and intentional changes in our actions towards children to work with them in ways that will help them change their behaviors but will not be punitive.

The punishment and control model is still the one most commonly used to discipline children. We have already established that punishing children is not what you want to spend your time doing. In addition, punishment and control aren't working. If they were, discipline wouldn't be such a huge problem. If the model worked, you wouldn't find yourself saying, "I've done everything. I've put him on time-outs. I've talked till I'm blue in the face. I've pulled him out of gym. I've taken away his supplies. I've made him do pushups in the hall. I've promised him rewards. I've tried it all, and nothing works." The most familiar model doesn't work. Punishing and controlling is not effective, and it is not what you want to do with kids.

Now is the time, then, to change the way we think about discipline.

Old model: Use punishment and control to make kids act appropriately.

New model: Teach, guide, and build relationships to encourage children to act appropriately.

Giving Discipline Enough Time

One outcome of changing the way you think and act around discipline is that one change leads to another. If you shift from punishing children to control their behavior, to guiding their behavior and helping them build relationships, you will find yourself making at least one more shift.

The punishment and control model often leads one to believe that discipline is something that wastes time, stealing valuable hours from the learning activities of a school-age program. Once the children are under control, the old model says, you can get on to what is really important. So, you try to "fix" behavior quickly and move on.

When you shift to the teaching-relationship model, you strengthen your belief that helping kids learn how to behave so that they and others feel secure and respected is the most vital thing you do. You are making another shift:

Old model: Behavior guidance is an unnecessary, aggravating waste of time.

New model: Behavior guidance (guiding children to self-discipline through relationships) is the most important thing you do with children.

When you start to act on the new model, you will begin to give discipline more time. Instead of being frustrated because you had to take time to deal with behavior guidance, you will feel proud that you helped kids develop the skills they will use most frequently throughout their lives. You will plan on building relationships with the kids and allowing kids to make choices. You will include in your schedules activities, games, books, dramatic play, and discussions that address guidance issues. And you will slow down the program's pace so that you have time to be the guide you want to be when kids need to learn discipline.

Not that behavior guidance is easy. It is not. It is crucial and it is complicated. At different times it involves preventing problems, taking immediate action, using new techniques, letting go of techniques, being strong, giving choices, taking risks, changing attitudes, being firm, being understanding, having rules, being flexible.

You already know that behavior guidance is not punishment and that it is vital to a child's and society's well-being. You also know that it is multifaceted. You may have suspected that it is even more complex in school-age care than in other places. You are correct.

In the process of working through this book, you will develop your own definition for behavior guidance. It will take the rest of this book and more for you to know which of the words that opened the chapter (see pages 3 and 4) you want to keep and which others you want to add. Your definition of behavior guidance will change, sometimes daily.

You are to be commended for taking on the task. It is difficult. It is also creative, emotional, and at times even fun. By learning, thinking, and practicing, you will relax into your own style of behavior guidance. You will be able to adapt it for the children and the situation before you, and be successful.

What is behavior guidance? What is behavior guidance in school-age care? You will tell me on page 366. I'll stay with you during your journey to a definition. Good luck! And good for you for getting started. For trying to figure out how to "…understand the fine lines between discipline and the breaking of a spirit, and how to mend one."

Write a definition of behavior guidance as you understand it now:

_____

_____

_____

_____

_____

At the end of the book you will compare the definition above to your new definition.

Please write your notes, thoughts, or stories here:

Chapter 2

The New Kid on the Block

by Zahkyia

Sharon runs a school-age care program in a public school building. Most of the staff in her program have college degrees. They spend many extra hours planning, bargain shopping, and attending workshops. Their program was one of the first ones in the nation to be accredited by the National Association for the Education of Young Children.

One day in the teachers' lounge, Sharon prepared a fruit tray for a group of legislators who were coming for a tour of the school-age program. She overheard two of the elementary teachers talking. "Those day care kids are so nasty," one teacher said. "Mothers should stay home with their kids."

"What amazes me," said the other, "is that Sharon has a master's degree in education. Don't you think she'd want to get an important job?"

≈ Jean Steiner and Mary Steiner Whelan

From time to time there's a new kid in every community or neighborhood. The other kids watch her carefully. They whisper among themselves.

"We got along just fine without her."

"Look at how dumb she is. She doesn't know the rules."

"Who does she think she is, anyway? Coming here with her new ideas and upsetting things."

"She's probably going to take some of my stuff—my friends or my toys or my place on the block."

At some point somebody's mother or big brother or grandmother says, "Just give her a chance. You might even get to like her."

And so, somewhat begrudgingly, they let her in, little by little. Some kids like her and some don't. But she's here to stay, and eventually she becomes a part of the world they live in.

School-age care is like that new kid on the block. It hasn't been around very long. The founding programs are celebrating their twenty-fifth year or so. It used to be that children stayed at home, mostly with their mothers, before and after school, on school holidays and breaks, and during summer vacation. Dad went to work. Mom stayed home. All was right with the world—or so it seemed.

And then for lots of reasons, mothers started working outside the home, in greater and greater numbers. Children stayed at the neighbors' or with extended family. When kids got old enough, depending on the community's definition of "old enough," they were awarded the house key. Sometimes they wore it around their necks on a shoestring or a chain. They were called the "latchkey" kids.

Those models seemed to work for a while. But as the number of children going home alone or to take care of siblings increased, some people noticed that children were getting hurt or were scared. Police reports showed that juvenile crime increased after three o'clock in the afternoon and during school breaks. Employers noted that productivity decreased during the same times, as phones rang in the workplace and parents settled sibling rivalries or diagnosed unseen illnesses.

Concerned individuals began a few programs in recreational facilities, in schools, in child care centers, and in family child care homes. There were no guidelines or special licensures. School-age children just started coming in groups into existing institutions for child care when school wasn't in session. Like the original kids in a neighborhood, the folks in the established institutions viewed these children, and those who provided care for them, with the suspicion given to the new kid on the block. People said things among themselves.

"Mothers should stay home with their children. I/My wife stayed home and raised our kids. It worked fine."

"They don't know what they're doing with those kids. Just baby-sitting, that's what it is. Those kids talk in the halls and don't even walk in lines. No sense of rules."

"Now they're trying to say that kids need to choose their activities instead of just doing what they're told. They don't need all that staff. Just plug in a video and keep them quiet till their parents pick them up."

"They're not educators. What are they doing using the gyms and computer rooms? They have to pay their own way, that's for sure. None of our educational tax money should pay for those kids."

But eventually, somebody's mother, big brother, or grandma who happened to sit on the school board or the parks and recreation board said, "Just give them a chance. You may find they help the community."

And so, in many cases begrudgingly, the institutions let school-age care in. Some grew to appreciate it, and some didn't. But it was here to stay and became part of the world they live in.

What does this history of school-age care have to do with behavior guidance? Being the new kid on the block brings its problems. The problems spill over into the programs and affect what we do with the children.

School-age care attempts to meet children's needs in ways that are often different from the more familiar structures, for many reasons:

- Program hours: early morning to early evening, all day during summers and school breaks

- Age groups: not cute preschoolers, but five year olds to twelve or fourteen year olds

- Purpose: socialization, life-long learning skills (not "school")

The long hours, loud voices, and high activity levels of schoolagers, along with the relaxed atmosphere in which children make choices, can seem disruptive in settings that were designed to meet other needs. Some of the discipline issues in school-age care result from trying to fit a program that is appropriate for schoolagers into an environment that isn't compatible with the scope and purpose of school-age care.

Please read the following challenges and suggested solutions that other programs have found helpful. Then come up with other suggestions that you think might work. Even if you don't have the specific problem or are in a different setting, do the exercise anyway. It may bring up related issues in your setting or in settings where you will work in the future. Relax; be thoughtful, creative, and positive!

The Challenge

You are the lead teacher of a new school-age care site in a school district. The site is located in a parks and recreation building. The parks and recreation department is not too happy to have another program in the building. They already have a complicated schedule to jostle. However, the school district and the city decided that's where school-age care will be housed. There isn't much going on in the building during the hours your program operates, and yet the building supervisor wants you to use only one gym and a few basketballs. He figures kids love basketball, so what's the problem? You know that kids will get bored the first day with no other options and there will be discipline problems galore. What do you do?

Suggestion

Take the supervisor out for lunch. Ask him to collaborate with your program on a series of enrichment classes that your kids can attend for a nominal fee and that are also open to the public. Tell him that you will provide half of the staff. Include community field trips and service projects involving all ages of people. Remind him that the city and other funders love collaborations and intergenerational programming. Tell him you'll let them put the feather in his cap if he'll also let you use that classroom next to the gym. Suggest the chocolate torte and pick up the tab!

Your Ideas

1. _____

_____

2. _____

_____

3. _____

_____

The Challenge

You are a teacher in a school-age program located in a public school building. The principal says that the children will walk in silence and in straight lines "in my school, no matter what time of day." The current mandate of the school district is that the principal of each building has the last word. No matter what you believe about how children can best grow into independent people and learn to act appropriately in informal situations, you are stuck with the principal's rules. What do you do?

Suggestion

Explain to the children that the principal is in charge of the building. Like it or not, you are going to have to abide by his rules in the halls. You know this is the kids' time out of school and that they would like to be more relaxed and independent. Ask them to suggest ways and times that they can meet those needs. Write down and implement as many of their ideas as possible.

Your Ideas

1. _____

_____

2. _____

_____

3. _____

_____

Exercise continued on next page

The Challenge

You are the school-age room's staff person. Parents see after-school care as an extension of the school day for their school-age children. They want you to make sure that their kids get their homework done before they get picked up in the evenings. You think that children should have some time to unwind. You also dread power struggles that will probably result if you demand homework right after school. However, parent fees pay for your program, and with schoolagers becoming a larger segment of the child care market, you can't afford to make parents too unhappy.

Solution

Talk to the center's director. Get her support to set aside some space for doing homework (keep looking—there is some, somewhere). Inform the parents that for the sake of their children's health there will be a designated time for an afternoon snack and active play. After that time their child is free to choose the homework space. However, whether the child chooses the option or not is between the parent, the child, and the classroom teacher. You are happy to provide the space and, when possible, a staff member or volunteer to answer questions and assist the kids with homework.

Your Ideas

1. _____

_____

2. _____

_____

3. _____

_____

The Challenge

The school that houses your school-age program teaches 500 children during the 5½-hour school day. During that time the children use approximately 28 different areas, not including offices and teacher space. Your program can use the cafeteria, in which you care for 144 children for 5½ hours a day. The space allocation doesn't make any sense to you. But, at least for now, that's how it is.

Because you and the other staff believe that children need to have privacy, make choices, and have a stimulating environment, you have a problem. Without any space division, children will see a great opportunity to run the length of the cafeteria. The noise will get intense without spaces for children to function in small groups. Those who want to work alone will be disrupted.

Suggestion

Enlist the help of families, friends, parents, friendly faculty, and children. Together go to garage sales, scrounge, and raise funds to get roll-out shelves, floor pillows, small collapsible tables, equipment, and carpets that will define areas. Make friends with that school food service worker who has some storage room she doesn't have to use. Practice setting up the space until you have it down to a science, and that dull cafeteria can be turned into interest-based learning centers in fifteen minutes flat!

Your Ideas

1. _____

_____

2. _____

_____

3. _____

_____

Exercise continued on next page

The Challenge

You vowed that you would never take schoolagers in your family child care home. However, you don't want to lose the preschoolers to the child care center down the street that takes all ages. The parents say, "Just let the older ones help you with the little ones. It will be good for them." You know that the novelty of helping will soon get old. You also feel that the older kids need to have their own activities. You don't want to spend a lot of money on expensive electronics and other entertainment toys. What to do?

Solution

Have Big Kids' Time every Thursday afternoon. Help the kids plan next week's activities. Long-range projects like garage sales, plays, painting refrigerator boxes, car washes, backyard tenting, and making gifts will each involve the kids for at least a week. Put up a list of supplies needed for the plans. Tell the parents to sign up for what they will bring. Use fundraising money from car washes and other events to have a pizza party, give to charity, buy the little kids something special, or buy a new toy for the Big Kids' shelves, which are way too high for the little kids to reach.

Your Ideas

1. _____

_____

2. _____

_____

3. _____

_____

These challenges illustrate just a few ways that the very newness of school-age programs can influence behavior guidance issues. The complications that schoolagers bring to another institution's way of doing things—or your own—can create discipline problems before the kids even show up for the day. You have to look at existing influences on your program, including rules and systems that were put in place for different ages of children or for other educational programs. You need to analyze and formulate workable, creative solutions so that your program operates in ways that encourage, rather than impede, appropriate behavior.

Even though you are the new kid on the block, you can do it.

Please write your notes, thoughts, or stories here:

Chapter 3

The New Neighborhood

Creativity
Empathy
Teamwork

Self-confidence
Problem solving
Leadership
Communication

School Age Care

by Zahkyia

I've always wanted to live in a neighborhood with you.

≈ Fred Rogers

As school-age care has grown, it has become the new "neighborhood" for hundreds of thousands of children.

You may have been a child in one of the old neighborhoods or communities. What did neighborhoods do for kids when they really lived in them? A neighborhood provided an informal network of friends, parents, and other adults; the school, the mosque, synagogue, or church; and perhaps a corner store, a park, or an alley for socialization. There were boundaries and rules. Even if they were unspoken, kids knew what they were. They knew, for example, that there were certain yards you'd better not hit the baseball into. That they went indoors when the street lights came on. That they always spoke politely to the woman at the register in the grocery store. That Mr. Marvin would tell their mother whatever he saw them doing. That the place between the neighbors' garages, or the barn, was a safe place to discuss otherwise forbidden topics. That they could go into a friend's house if his mother was home.

Children quickly learned what breaking the rules or overstepping the boundaries meant. If the baseball went into the Nelsons' yard, it was lost, and the next time the children played ball in the alley, the police would show up and tell them to get out. If they didn't speak politely to the store clerk, she would shag them out. If they spoke about forbidden topics within earshot of an adult, they'd be forbidden for a month to see the friend they had been whispering to. If they acted up when they went to town, the news of their behavior seemed to miraculously get home to their mom on the farm. What they did at the 4-H meeting could determine whether they could play after their work was done on Saturday.

Children also learned what their community valued. They learned the roles the community believed in for men and women, for people old and young, from their culture and other cultures. They learned what was esteemed: rural or city living, competition or cooperation, material possessions, education, manual labor, monogamy, religion, differences, sameness. They may have learned things like these:

- If they cheated at games, other kids didn't want to play with them.
- If they dared to be different where everyone was supposed to be the same, they were ridiculed.
- If their family was too educated, they were snobbish.
- If their family didn't have a car, they were poor, and not good enough.
- If their parents were divorced, they weren't a real family.
- Old people were treated with respect.
- Gay people weren't okay.
- Babies were the community's treasure.
- Lying was okay to cover for a friend.

...and a million other lessons. Every neighborhood had its own examples of values and rules and consequences.

As they got older the kids would sometimes be on their own to explore their options, to form their values, to learn from the mores of their community. Whatever children learned there—in their neighborhood, on the way to school, after school, during the holidays and long summer days—stuck with them unless something jarred it hard enough to be reconsidered.

The old way wasn't necessarily the best system. Some things kids learned were helpful; some needed reexamination. However, whether or not it worked for children and for the community, it's a thing of the past.

Now that all the adults in the majority of families are working, most children go to child care or school-age care. Children are in their neighborhoods only after dark and for parts of the weekends. Many kids live in two or more homes in different communities. Often schools, places of worship, friends, shopping, recreation, and relatives are not near the children's homes. This is a huge change, especially for school-age kids' development, because they are not learning from their neighborhoods the way they were twenty or thirty years ago. Now, school-age care *is* the neighborhood for a large number of children.

This role puts a great responsibility on you. Add up the hours that a child enrolled in a school-age care program spends there. It is often more hours than they are awake at home and almost always more time than they spend in school. And yet school is usually seen as the major part of children's lives once they enter kindergarten. The questions most often asked of children over the age of five are, "How's school?" "Do you like school?" "What grade are you in?" Seldom if ever does an adult ask, "What are you doing in the school-age care program?" Even the name of our field is *School-Age* Care.

Needless to say, school is very important. However, it is not the only place where children learn. To demonstrate this fact using your own life, take a couple of minutes to do this exercise:

Think of a typical weekday in your life. Thinking, thinking, thinking....
What skills and/or facts that you learned or wish you had learned as a child do you need to draw on daily?
Make a short list:

1. _____
2. _____
3. _____
4. _____
5. _____

After each skill or fact write *L* if you learned it as a child. Write *W* if you wish you had learned it as a child.

If you acquired these facts and skills as a child, where and/or from whom did you learn each of them?

1. _____
2. _____
3. _____

Exercise continued on next page

Think of your relationships in various parts of your life.

What skills and/or facts that you learned or wish you had learned as a child help you develop healthy relationships?
    Make a short list:

1. _____

2. _____

3. _____

4. _____

5. _____

After each skill or fact write *L* if you learned it as a child. Write *W* if you wish you had learned it as a child.

If you learned these skills or facts as a child, where and from whom did you learn each of them?

1. _____

2. _____

3. _____

    When people do this exercise, the skills that typically show up are things like

Self-confidence	Problem solving
Negotiation	Decision making
How to access information	Conflict resolution
How to get along with people	Empathy
Self-motivation	Leadership
Teamwork	Integrity
Communication	Authenticity
Creativity	

    Very rarely do people respond to the questions by saying that every day they need to remember the capitals of the states or the definition of a parallelogram. The places where they learned and the people who taught them are not limited to the classroom and elementary teachers. There is, of course, another whole list of things that people didn't learn as children and had to acquire later on, sometimes through painful experience.

The education that children get in school is an important part of development. But there are many other important sources of learning, which are even more important in an era when information changes so quickly that what we learned yesterday can be obsolete next month. People need to know how to relate, create, solve problems, make decisions, get along with others, think, judge, and act. It is vital to a democracy that the people in the country know how to analyze information, work for the common good, and make responsible choices. Twenty years ago, children learned some of these things through interactions with the adults and institutions in the old neighborhood. Where do they learn them today, if not in school-age care programs?

Although they have to function as the new neighborhood for thousands of children, school-age programs often feel isolated from the rest of the community. This isolation is often evident before the program even begins! For example, I sometimes consult with programs that are starting up. The building I enter may be a preschool, elementary school, parks and recreation facility, or some other community institution. I meet the person who is setting up the school-age program, who often has at least one other full-time job. "I'll show you the space we are going to use for the schoolagers," she says.

I can almost predict where I will be taken: to a room in the basement with no windows, or a room that used to be used for storage, or a cafeteria, or a space that will be shared with the band. My guide is often proud of the space because she has lobbied long and hard to get a school-age program at all.

"We'll paint these walls and use something to try to divide it up."

"It has potential," I say. It does have potential, because the committed, enthusiastic person working on it brings potential and makes it work.

What the space says, of course, is that school-age care is coming into being but is not fully accepted as yet. Under these conditions, it is easy for you as school-age care staff to feel isolated and left out.

Part of your job, then, is to connect with the wider community. Children spend a great deal of time with you. But you are not the only adults in the children's world. Link up with community resources. Let them know that you are there and that you want them to be involved with the children. Try the Red Cross, public health nurses, the police department, fire department, local businesses, nursing homes, hospitals, and the chamber of commerce. Visit neighborhoods that are in some way different from the one in which the program is located. Learn and talk about the differences. Find projects that join together the rich and the poor; the old and the young; various cultures; urban, suburban, and rural people. Think of partnerships that you can build. Maybe it's as simple as a field trip or a guest speaker. Or it might be a financial partnership. The newspaper might give your kids a monthly column about being a kid today. The kids might volunteer at the Red Cross. The local bowling alley might give free bowling time. The mayor might recognize your program.

All of these efforts build what sociologist James S. Coleman calls *social capital*. "Social capital in the community exists in the interest, and even the intrusiveness, of one adult in the activities of someone else's child" ("Social Capital, Human Capital, and Schools," *Independent School* Fall 1988). Coleman is talking about children's relationships with, networks with, knowledge of, and respect from and for others in the community.

You are one of the people helping the child build social capital. It is important that during the hours children are in your care, they do not feel that they are being warehoused somewhere out of sight until their parents come to get them. They can, and should, be assets to the community.

Introduce the other people in the neighborhood to the children in your care. You and the children will feel less isolated and more valuable as your program both contributes and is valued. Children can invest their social capital in ways that will make them more competent people. They will convert it into human capital. "Human capital...refers to the internal capacity that the social capital helps the child develop within him or herself to perform functions of value—strength, knowledge, and skills to earn a living as well as the skills and wisdom to create a home and family life and to participate in the community" (Harold W. Watts, "Investing in Children: Closing the Real Deficit," *News and Issues* Summer 1995).

Those children whose behaviors are sometimes challenging are probably those who don't feel connected to the wider community, who don't feel valuable, who haven't any social capital to invest in themselves. As you help them build relationships in the wider world you will see their self-esteem rise and their behaviors improve.

Tyler has a hard time relating *to just about everyone. He is aggressive and belligerent. He has a couple of friends in the school-age program. If they aren't around, he stays by himself, defying anyone to even talk to him. If other children do talk to him he strikes out verbally or physically.*

The program Tyler attends is located in a small town, one of those towns that used to be a general store and a gas station until urban sprawl turned it into a bedroom community. There is now an ugly strip mall almost in the center of town where grassy fields used to be. The school-age care teacher, Lee, has made a connection with the town. She got them to agree that the school-age care kids could put large pots of flowers along the median that divided the road in front of the strip mall. She got the local landscaping company to donate the pots, dirt, and plants.

She announces the project to the kids. They are excited about the idea. Then she says, "I will need two people to help coordinate this project. One will work with the landscape company and one with the town officials to figure out how to get this done. I think that Kim would be a good choice to work with the town. Are you willing, Kim?"

"Sure," Kim replies. "But I will need everyone's help."

The other kids give her a round of applause.

Lee looks at Tyler sulking in the corner. Okay, Lee, she says to herself, give it a try.

"And I would like Tyler to be the coordinator with the landscape company," she says out loud. In her head she says, Please let him say yes, *I think.*

To everyone's surprise Tyler shrugs and says, "Why not?"

The other kids give a fearful smattering of applause.

The group decides what they want the coordinators to ask the town and the landscape company. When can they plant? How will they transport the pots? Will the mayor come to a community party to celebrate the plantings? Will the geraniums and petunias they want to plant be too expensive to donate? Will the plants survive in the middle of the street?

Lee gives Tyler the phone number for the landscaper, Harold. He is to get the information and report back to the group. Tyler agrees to call Harold, although he says, "I've never used the phone to call someone important before." Lee sees his hand shaking as he presses the numbers.

"I think we need a face-to-face to settle some of these questions," Harold tells Tyler. The following week Harold arrives at the school-age program in a large pickup truck to take Tyler to his company for a tour and a meeting. "Cool," the other kids say as they watch Tyler ride away.

The relationship grows. Harold and Tyler become partners. Tyler reports back to the group. Tyler's reports become more confident, echoing with Harold's booming voice and business sense.

The project is a huge success. The community paper runs a front-page story. Harold and Tyler pose together for the accompanying photo. The pizza shop in the strip mall provides pizza and the city band plays. Harold gives a speech thanking lots of people, "…especially Tyler, a young man with a good head on his shoulders."

Tyler has become almost a different person. In his final report to the group about the project, he says, "Don't be afraid to do hard stuff. It makes you feel pretty good." The other kids give him an enthusiastic round of applause. Hanging his head down a bit, he sits back down. "Thanks," he says, with a small smile that starts somewhere deep in his heart.

🌀 🌀

Not all of your liaisons with the wider community will have such dramatic results. But you will see changes in individual children and the group as they learn the skills necessary to have a meaningful place in the world.

Write down two projects that would link the children in your program to the community.

_____

_____

_____

What community groups would be involved?

_____

_____

_____

What might the children learn from the involvement?

_____

_____

_____

What would the children contribute to the community?

_____

_____

_____

How would the project help decrease behavior problems?

_____

_____

_____

What is the first step that you need to take to make one of the projects a reality?

_____

_____

_____

On what date will you take the first step?

_____

_____

_____

There has clearly been a shift in our society. Much of the responsibility and joy of helping children develop vital skills and learn values now belongs to you, the adults in school-age care. A part of that responsibility is reaching out and including the whole neighborhood.

Chapter 4

Getting to Know the Neighbors

by Zahkyia

Won't you please? Won't you please? Please, won't you be my neighbor?

≈ Fred Rogers

Who are the adults who live in the new neighborhood of school-age care? Who are the people children see before and after school, and during non-school days, for recreation, value formation, role modeling, boundary setting, and learning who they are and how to socialize? Of course, those people are you. You are in charge of the new neighborhood in which so many children will grow up.

You have accepted the obligation to facilitate the development of the whole child. To teach children through who you are, how you treat them, how you structure your programs, what information and learnings you make available, and what you value, so that children will become the people they deserve to be, the adults our world needs.

Many researchers tell us that what a child believes by the time she is nine, she believes for a lifetime. If a child is greedy, she will remain greedy. If a child is racist, she will remain racist. If a child is sexist, she will remain sexist. Unless there is a life-altering occurrence. Guess whose job it is to help form those belief systems and to provide the life-altering events. Yours!

Those are high expectations. But if you don't do it, who will? In partnership with parents, who are often stressed and don't have enough quality time with their children, you are an essential element of positive development in the lives of children.

Parents

Before we look more closely at who you are, let's talk about parents. You as a school-age care provider are the new neighborhood. Your closest neighbors are the children's parents. Neighborhoods for children in school-age care are often less defined by location than by people. The people with whom children interact most frequently are you and their parents. If you are a good neighbor to parents, children will trust you more. There will be less stress in children's lives. And, as in the old neighborhood, children will know that your concerns and their parents' concerns are linked.

It is easy to look at parents these days and judge that they aren't taking enough time with their children, that they are too lenient or too strict, that they don't even care. I firmly believe that all parents at some level want the best for their children, even if their parental love is drowning in a sea of problems or history that you may or may not know about.

Even if I am wrong, if there are some parents who truly don't love their children, there are no children who do not care for their parents. No matter what the parents are like, no matter how they treat the child, there is a hard-wired connection between children and their parents and other primary caregivers.

You do not have to condone everything that a child's parent does, but never speak against a parent to a child. Children feel insecure if they believe that they are in a place where the people do not like their parents. Neither should you tell parents that their children are bad. Parents, usually already carrying a bundle of guilt, hear this statement as a message that they are bad parents. In either case you can create thick defensive walls between you and the people you want and need to work with.

From the beginning of your program each season make it very clear that you and the parents are partners in their children's lives. Make it clear, also, that they are the primary people in their children's lives. Tell them through newsletters, bulletin boards, calls to them at home just introducing yourself, invitations to talk to a group of kids about what they know or do. (Not only parents who are doctors and dentists should be invited to speak—bricklayers, restaurant servers, garbage collectors, farmers, bus drivers, and factory workers are all interesting.) Offer potluck nights or cheap meal nights for the parents and children every other month so.

Above all, talk to parents about their children in positive, caring ways, even if the topic is improving a child's behavior. The best way to get a parent to be an ally is to be one yourself. An ally doesn't wait to pounce on a parent when she walks through the door after a long stressful day. A long list of the child's misbehaviors presented in this way, followed by, "Something has to be done," will either get the child punished or make the parent angry at you. Neither result will help the discipline problem. Much better to ask when you can call parents or talk to them for fifteen minutes.

Or to put concerns in writing and ask them to reply in writing. If writing is not an easy thing for the parents, you can offer to meet them somewhere off-site for an informal discussion. In some cases, you may want the program to hire an interpreter. Sometimes just a walk around the block with a parent is a relaxing way to express your ideas and to listen to theirs. Some programs have comfortable chairs in the classroom or in a teachers' room that invite informal discussions.

You do not have to inform parents of their children's every misdeed. Most can be taken care of at the time they occur and then be forgotten. I certainly wouldn't want anyone following me around all day and then reporting to my mother, "She ate the dried-out Easter candy at one o'clock. She didn't make her bed. She snapped at her friend when she interrupted her writing. She didn't do the dishes until five minutes ago. She really wasn't working all day—she watched Oprah."

Parents should know how things are going in general. Be sure to let them know on a regular basis about the positive things their child does. Don't surprise them with a pile of serious behavior problems that have been going on for months. Forget the small stuff.

Many children who do not do well in school-like settings have parents who didn't either. Parents are often intimidated by institutional settings and people who look or act like teachers. They may also have different cultural expectations than yours of how children should behave with teachers, or what a parent's role in education is. When you meet with parents, if you see that they are nervous or uneasy, don't overwhelm them with buzz words from the educational field. Don't surprise them with an appearance by the psychologist. Keep the conversation at an equal level. Speak about the positive things you see in the child and the family, even if you have to search for them. Tell them that you want the best for their children, that they are the experts on their children and you want to learn from them. Tell them that you also hope that they will learn from your view of their children in another setting.

On the other hand, if the parents come in treating you like a baby-sitter and start spouting large words at you, pull up every professional term you know to let them know that you are knowledgeable. These parents are also intimidated, in all likelihood, because their child is less than perfect and they believe that it is their fault. Once you have established your professional role you can start talking at a more emotional and personal level about their child's welfare.

There will be parents who absolutely will not work with you. There are parents who simply are not functioning. But that is not true of most parents. With steady, respectful, and patient attempts you will begin to have parents who are allies in your work with their children.

Think of one way that you are going to involve parents in your school-age care program. Write it down.

_____

_____

_____

What are the barriers to success?

_____

_____

_____

How will you overcome them?

_____

_____

_____

Staff in School-Age Programs

So who are you, these important people in children's lives? You are a diverse group of people. Some of you have college degrees, some don't. You are young and old. City and rural dwellers. Progressives and conservatives. Women and men. From many cultures, religions, and belief systems. You speak different languages and with differing accents. Your diversity is good for kids. In the new neighborhood they will meet different kinds of people. They will learn to assess different points of view, different ways of looking at the world.

There are some things that you have in common. Probably not one of you said as a child, "When I grow up I want to be a school-age care provider." Most likely you had never heard of such a position. If you had, there certainly was not an educational track to learn how to become a school-age care professional. The first certificate and degree programs in school-age care are just getting up on their wobbly legs. While school-age care tries to figure out exactly what a profession is and how to become one (a necessary but lengthy process), you are taking care of the children. You didn't think that you would be in this field but here you are. How did that happen?

Some of you got degrees in other fields. You couldn't find a job so you took a position in a school-age program until you could get a "real" job. There are folks with degrees in philosophy, literature, biology, psychology, and dozens of other areas serving as staffers. Others of you have elementary or secondary education degrees. Perhaps you hope the position will give you an inside track into a school district.

Some of you wanted to move from a routine sort of job into something more meaningful. Some of you do it because you "love kids." You may be working your way through high school or college. Some of you like the part-time hours. Maybe you burnt out on another job and thought it would be fun to work with children. Others of you don't have a clue how you got here. You join your degreed colleagues to try to figure out how to do this work that you do each day. All of you quickly figured out that although what you know is somewhat helpful, school-age care often requires its own skills and knowledge, much of which you don't have.

Each day you run into challenges. If you are new to school-age care or have been here awhile, you can sometimes lean back on the "I never wanted to do this in the first place" excuse for being stuck with the problems in front of you. It is sometimes helpful at that point to assess why (or if) you should continue this work. It is important that what you do meets some of your own personal needs. Not just because the job is a good thing to do, or it works for your family, but because it is somehow a fit with who you are.

Try this exercise. Do it even if today isn't a day when you are in doubt about your job. It may come in handy later or you may be able to help someone you work with.

When you were a child, what did you want to be when you grew up?

1. _____

2. _____

3. _____

What personal dreams attracted you to those jobs?

1. _____

2. _____

3. _____

What skills and beliefs do you have that would help you be successful in those jobs?

1. _____

2. _____

3. _____

Which of your dreams, skills, and beliefs do you use in your school-age care job?

1. _____

2. _____

3. _____

Which dreams, skills, and beliefs are missing or underused?

1. _____

2. _____

3. _____

What are some ways that the missing dreams, skills, and beliefs can be woven into your work?

1. _____

_____

2. _____

_____

3. _____

_____

I hope doing this exercise helped you discover that there is a connection between you and the kind of work you are doing. Maybe it wasn't all just an accident, after all! And maybe the connections are part of the reason that you are so often good at what you do.

When you are feeling discouraged, you can't see clearly that what you do is complex and interesting enough that many of your skills and beliefs are, or can be, incorporated into what you do. It could be beneficial to do this exercise in a staff meeting or a performance review so that others can help redesign parts of your job to affirm the strengths that you bring to your work.

You can, of course, make changes on your own to find more fulfillment in your work. When you recognize that your work meets your needs and is helpful in your own development, you approach it with more energy and enthusiasm.

You certainly do not want to be in a job that doesn't offer any personal satisfaction. You also owe it to the children you work with to be reasonably happy in your work. Many discipline problems don't come from the children, but from the adult's inability to give the job the energy it deserves. Kids need adults who can help them learn how to cope and thrive.

Learning From the Past

Established: One element common to school-age care staff is that you didn't plan to go there. Once you *are* there, once you are working in the school-age field, you draw on your past experiences, and the beliefs about yourself that they generate, to do your work. Everyone, no matter in what field, does this to some extent. However, if your job requires certain skill training and value analysis, you learn to override or relearn some of your past experiences. As emerging professionals, school-age care staff have inadequate pre-job training and education for working with children in school-age care settings. Your actions are deeply influenced by your past experiences and beliefs about yourself.

Being with children, unlike working as a surgeon or carpenter, for example—will bring you back to the feelings that you carry about yourself from your childhood. In turn, those feelings have a huge effect on your work with children. Because of this, you need to be aware of what you carry with you from the past.

When I was a new elementary teacher, *I had a boy in my class who had multiple problems. Kyle's uncle abused him regularly. His family was poor. He had trouble staying focused and loved to talk very loudly at times when it was important to be quiet. But Kyle was a charmer. His shock of disheveled red hair and crooked-toothed smile won my heart. I poured my soul into trying to help him academically and emotionally. The high point of my year was the day in June when Kyle opened his report card and exclaimed, "This is the first time I didn't get any fails!" I felt that I had made a significant difference in that child's life. I thought I would be one of those people he would always remember.*

In August, I was setting up my classroom for the next school year. Some neighborhood children were in the halls, hanging around as they tend to do that time of the year. I heard a child ask my star student who his teacher was last year. "I can't remember her name," Kyle responded. "But she has a big nose." I was deflated. All that I did for him and he only remembered my nose?

◉ ◉

In fact, my nose is a vulnerable topic. It is rather oddly shaped and the message I received from many people as I grew up was that my nose stood between me and prettiness.

I also learned as a child that I shouldn't be proud of what I did. I could always do better. I shouldn't get puffed up by my accomplishments. Without knowing it, that little boy had reached way down into my self-esteem issues. I thought I must not have really helped him. That my appearance probably interfered with my ability to teach. That I might as well not try so hard to make a difference. And that certainly I had no cause to feel good about my work. I couldn't laugh it off, really, although when I told the story I made it sound as if I had. I took at least a little of that thinking into the next school year.

I was reminded of that story, and of the feelings it aroused in me, many years later.

This summer I was playing *with some gentle waves in the ocean. A sparkly little girl about seven years old, whom I had seen at the hotel, noticed me. She made her way towards me with her younger brother following her. She was the talker of the pair. He splashed and watched. She told me all about her life. That she was on vacation with her grandparents whom she hadn't seen for a long time. That it was hard to talk to them because they were too busy doing things to listen. Her family had been living in another country for a few years and she was having trouble making friends. She was often lonely for her dog they had to leave behind. She talked for about half an hour until her grandmother called her in. "It was nice talking to you," I said.*

"Thank you for listening," she said. "Most grownups don't. I want to talk to you again." I felt good about the fact that I had given up a bit of my own solitude to listen to her. I figured we probably would see each other at the hotel. Maybe I would have another chance to be a listening adult for her.

The next day I was in the ocean again. The girl and her brother headed in my direction. I waved at them. "Ahh, she is coming back for more of my adult affirmation of her self-worth," I thought to myself.

Her little brother waved back. "You shouldn't wave at strangers," she chided him, and moved them both in a different direction.

◉ ◉

This time I really did laugh it off. I knew that children are present mostly in the now. The impact we might have on them is woven into the synapses of their brains and the sense of self-worth in their hearts. Whether or not she remembered me, the fact that I listened to her helped her in some tiny way. I didn't feel bad about feeling good. I silently thanked her for reminding me again about how kids function. I realized that at this minute she had another developmental need that she thought deserved attention. For some reason she needed to assert her status as big sister.

The knowledge and skills that I had acquired from experience and class work in the years since I started teaching overrode the feelings about myself from the past. What I knew about children helped me not to take her actions personally. Her actions affirmed my ability to work with children rather than diminishing it. I would even have been all right if she told her brother not to wave at strangers with odd noses!

In order to be effective in our behavior guidance with children, we must continue to identify those points that make us weak rather than strong and do something about them. If we don't, we are likely to reenact the way that we were treated as children or be immobilized by our own bad feelings.

It always seems amazing to hear that children who were physically abused are more likely to abuse their own children. Why would that not be the last thing they would ever do to someone else? It is not as simple as mimicking the behavior that you saw as a child. It is more about the feelings that the mistreatment, which could have been unintended, caused you to carry about yourself. If your childhood was not perfect (no one's was), take a look at the negative things that you learned from it about yourself. And then, do your best to change those beliefs. You deserve it. So do the children that you are working with. Doing this work will allow you to interact with the children in ways that will promote their growth in self-discipline.

Try this exercise to begin the process of becoming aware of issues that might block your ability to discipline effectively:

Identify a negative belief that you have about yourself. Write about how it makes you feel, not where it came from, as honestly as you can.

Now search your childhood to see where that belief came from. Who taught you to believe it? Who reinforced the belief? Give as much detail as possible. Details will make the memories more real.

_____

_____

_____

_____

_____

_____

_____

How has this belief negatively affected the way you live? Give a specific example.

_____

_____

_____

_____

_____

_____

How do you think this belief might interfere with the way you deal with children and behavior guidance issues?

_____

_____

_____

_____

_____

_____

Exercise continued on next page

Pretend that you are the person or persons who taught you this belief about yourself. Write a letter from them to yourself as a child. Tell the child that you are sorry about the way you made her feel. Tell the child that the messages you gave were not true. Let the child know that it will not happen again. Tell the child how capable she is.

_____

_____

_____

_____

_____

_____

_____

Now as your adult self, write an affirmation that replaces the old belief. Here are some examples:

"I can be proud of what I do."
"I am beautiful."

_____

_____

_____

Repeat the affirmation out loud until you feel yourself really believing it. Copy it onto another piece of paper. Put the affirmation somewhere where you can see it. Say it over from time to time. At least several times a week. Repeat this exercise when you see yourself reacting to children in a way that you don't feel good about.

Psychologist Alice Miller says, "The more you were beaten, in any way and repressed it, the more you will beat your children in some way" (*Banished Knowledge: Facing Childhood Injuries* [New York: Doubleday, 1990]). You will often find that you are reenacting the adult role that hurt you. You don't want other children to grow up feeling like that. The first step is to feel good about yourself so that you can effectively nurture and teach others. I promise that as you continue to uproot the old bad feelings, your success rate in discipline issues with children will improve.

The Supervisor's Role

Often staff react to the crisis caused by multitudinous discipline problems by making more rules or tougher consequences for the children or by adopting yet another canned discipline program. Supervisors often respond to staff members in the same way when programs go through difficult times around discipline. We need to recognize that the solutions are not all about the children. There is also a staff crisis, not only in finding staff but in their ability to do what is expected of them. Staff for the most part are trying to do the best they can with what they have and what they know. One essential ingredient of a peaceful, cooperative program is staff that are being supported in striving for their own healthy development.

Therefore, if you are a school-age care supervisor or director, you have an important role in helping staff with these self-development issues. Your role includes nurturing staff. You need to provide access to education. Staff members need training and information that will give them new knowledge and skills to draw on. Supervisors need to help staff assess their personal strengths and weaknesses. You can support staff in their attempts to change their belief systems. The staff who are the least effective, the harshest, are probably dealing at some level with harshness from their own past.

You may feel that this work of nurturing staff and assisting them in doing their own personal work is not your job. You have a tough position and helping staff improve their ability to work with children by encouraging them to work on their own issues may seem unnecessary. However, until the time when there are adequate numbers of staff trained in school-age care, and until the salaries are high enough to retain those people, supervisors need to promote the well-being of current staff members, so that staff members can more effectively promote the well-being of children.

Even after working conditions improve, staff will need education and nurturing. The business world is becoming aware of the need to attend to employees in a holistic way. Many current management models include ways that managers and supervisors can establish systems that help employees find their strengths and improve themselves based on self-knowledge. This role for management is even more important when the goal is not only productivity but also influencing children's lives.

Here are some ways you can support staff to become better at working with children by examining their own issues. If you are not a supervisor, perhaps you can suggest some of these ideas to your supervisor.

- Have the staff take the Myers-Briggs Type Indicator assessment (Consulting Psychologists Press, Inc., 3803 E. Bayshore Road, Palo Alto, CA 94303). This assessment is enjoyable to take. It helps staff understand themselves and each other better. It opens up conversations among staff members. This is also a good resource for supervisors because it gives insight into the personalities of the staff members. Include some of the exercises from this chapter in staff meetings or staff evaluation times.

- Work with this book together as a staff or include its completion as part of the orientation process.

- Talk to staff members about their lives as children in informal, positive ways. Take your staff's lives outside of work into consideration. You shouldn't be their counselor or their mother, but you can be a considerate, interested supervisor.

- Work with them in the same way that you ask them to work with children—give them respect, attention to their concerns, and information where needed.

- Ask the staff to do self-evaluations, sharing strengths as well as recommendations for growth. You might be surprised at how well staff members get to know themselves and become better able to work as a team.

- Remember their birthdays, give them a small bonus on their anniversaries, and listen, listen, listen.

- Read *The Visionary Director*, by Margie Carter and Deb Curtis (St. Paul: Redleaf, 1998), and use the techniques suggested there.

Your time as a supervisor is limited. Your salary and working conditions are no better than your staff's. You did not expect to grow up to have the position that you have today, either. I recommend that you find support for yourself as well as your staff. If there is not a directors' group in your area, you might think about starting one. Some groups meet monthly. They may have speakers each month on relevant topics such as staff development, budgeting, recruiting, and retaining staff. There is often a large block of time built into the meetings for supporting one another. An organization that can provide some support is the Early Childhood Directors Association, 450 N. Syndicate St., St. Paul, MN 55104. Although not exclusively for directors and supervisors of school-age programs, it offers a newsletter, conferences, and other assistance that might be helpful. Join the National School Age Care Alliance, 1137 Washington Street, Boston, MA 02124. They publish a newsletter, organize national and state conferences, and offer educational opportunities. They are a valuable resource for people involved with schoolagers.

I also recommend that you work with this book for yourself, not only with your staff in mind. Take care of yourself as you care for others. You will be more effective and less likely to burn out as you do your essential work. If you are able to give staff the assistance they need, you will see improvements in the program, perhaps especially in the area of behavior guidance. Happy, understood, empowered people are less likely to become angry with others. They have more energy to think about their actions and reactions. You will be proud of the results of your role in building a program that is more supportive to staff, children, and supervisors.

Admitting Your Strengths

In addition to examining childhood beliefs, it is imperative that all the adults, staff, supervisors, and parents in the new neighborhood are aware of the talents and strengths they bring to the children.

Do the exercise on the following pages to prove to yourself that you have what it takes to do this work:

Make a word collage in the space below using words that describe
your strengths. Use bright-colored inks or crayons if they are available.
Decorate with symbols that represent your work with children.

Now, from your collage, choose a word you think children would most frequently use to describe you. Write in a child's voice and tell why this characteristic is so important to the children. Here's an example:

"Gina is funny. We think it's great that Gina is so funny. It helps us relax…"

_____

_____

Choose a word from the collage (it can be the same word) that you feel is most helpful to you in the area of behavior guidance. Explain why this quality is so vital. Give specific examples of when this quality was useful in a guidance situation.

_____

_____

_____

_____

_____

Next, try completing these sentences:

Kids respect me because I…

_____

I respect myself. When in a discipline situation, I…

_____

School-age care is a complicated, demanding job. If you don't think so, you probably don't understand it. If you do understand it, you are probably often tired and confused. Sometimes because the children are in the programs for short time periods, often only two or three hours at at time, you think that you can just live through it. Maybe you can. But the children deserve more from you. They want you to love them, to laugh with them, to guide them, to respect them, to talk to them, to listen. To do all of that, you need to take a look at yourself. You have to do the hard work.

You love school-age children or you wouldn't do this work. Or at least it wouldn't make much sense to do it. You can often earn more at a fast food restaurant. If you don't want to put your all into the work, if you don't like the kids, you should get out. There is no doubt that this job is not for everyone.

The kids know if you put your mind and your heart into the job. They will respect you for it. You will have fewer discipline problems as you continue to learn more. The kids will sing their song, although maybe never loud enough for you to hear it, "Please won't you be my neighbor?"

Please write your notes, thoughts, or stories here:

Chapter 5

Who Are the Children?

by Catherine

We are the world. We are the children.

≈ USA for Africa

After reading the first few chapters of this book, you've confirmed that you have skills and talents to take on school-age child care. You started looking at ways that your own needs, life experiences, and strengths influence how you function with children. Before delving into the specifics of behavior guidance, it's vital to focus on the children in school-age care.

What are they like? How do they grow and develop? What makes them tick? How do you learn more about them?

There are at least three methods of gathering more information about school-age children: traditional academic learning, observation, and reflection on one's own experience as a child.

Traditional academic learning can involve taking classes, attending workshops, reading books. The fact that you are reading this book demonstrates that you take advantage of formal learning resources.

A second way to learn about children is by observing them, paying attention to how they behave in the program, how they interact with other children and adults, what they enjoy or dislike, and what is easy or hard for them.

A third way to gather information about children is to think back to when you were one. Your own experience as a child can shed light on how the children around you are learning and why they might be behaving the way they do.

Each of these ways of learning has value. One enhances the others. This chapter briefly presents developmental information in general and specific to different ages within the school-age years. Chapter 6 explores observing children and reflecting on our own childhoods as ways of gaining insight into school-age children.

School-Age Development

Let's begin with what others tell us about school-age children—academic knowledge that is available about schoolagers.

Go into any local bookstore. Look in the child development section. You will find an abundance of books on babies and preschoolers. There will also be quite a selection of titles about dealing with teens. Between the potty training phase and curfew stage there is an informational abyss.

Where are the school-age kids, the kids between five and twelve? In school! In our culture's psyche they are nicely tucked away: toilet trained, tying their own shoes, learning their times tables. They aren't out in the family car, dating, or drinking beer yet. Relatively speaking, they aren't much trouble to their parents or the rest of the world. Because they are fairly invisible, and society decided that learning lots and lots of facts is almost their only developmentally appropriate task, they don't get studied much. You know, of course, that they aren't in school most of the time and that their developmental tasks are complex and confusing, and essential.

Although it's not as extensive as it could or should be, there is information concerning school-age kids' development. The following summaries are compiled from books, handouts, newspaper articles, workshops, and research studies. The summaries give a general overview of four areas of development and of each age between five and twelve years. Please remember that not all the characteristics are true for every child.

Children's development is commonly divided into four areas: cognitive, social, physical, and emotional. Although these categories are somewhat simplistic and are at times divided differently for research or curriculum design reasons, they are a place to begin. Some programs are good at meeting one of the needs but not others. Some do a good job of meeting three out of four. Whatever the variation, if a program fails to meet children's needs in any of these four areas, the imbalance will pop up. How? You're right, in behavior problems.

Cognitive Needs

Cognitive needs are those based on children's need to think, to use their minds. School-age kids learn very quickly. They have tons of energy for learning, although as they get older many of them do not like school. Given the right environment, many children can concentrate for long periods of time on projects that interest them. They need time and space to discover and explore their interests.

They can memorize easily. They love to categorize and classify things. They enjoy games, especially those that tap their capacity to memorize and strategize. They are bound by rules and the concept of fairness. They may spend considerable time deciding and debating the rules of a game or the process of a project.

They understand the concept of justice. They can identify actions that are racist, or sexist, or in some other way biased. They can identify stereotypes.

School-age children are tied to physical reality in many ways. They may fantasize from the concrete and create stories about adventures or alien creatures, for example. But they are not usually interested in abstract symbols or ideas. They like to invent things that work, plays that can be enacted, songs that get sung, adventures and mysteries that turn into games or books.

They understand the concepts of time and money. They live in the now although they have the capability to remember the past and see value in planning for the future. They can evaluate themselves, others, and events.

They also need to build intellectual independence by testing out their own thinking. Because of their zest for learning and challenging their own and others' thoughts, they get bored easily.

Unrecognized cognitive needs of school-age children can lead to behavior problems.

Read the following scenario to identify the unmet cognitive needs that may be part of the problem.

Chester and Demi are playing chess. They have spent quite a bit of time setting up the board, agreeing on the rules, and deciding who gets to go first. It is the end of the day. The children have agreed to play until one of their parents comes, and to finish the game tomorrow if their parents come before the game is completed. One staff person is putting chairs up on the tables. The kids grumble that there is too much noise. The staff person says that she has an appointment after work so she has to get her work done. Still grumbling, the kids go back to their game. It's Demi's turn to make a move. She holds her hands over her ears and ponders the move for a full five minutes. As she makes the move, her mother comes to pick her up. "How was your day, honey?" she asks.

Exercise continued on next page

"Put the chess pieces away, now," says the staff person. "Hurry, your parents have a lot to do. You could end the game right now if you take back the move that you just made and do this instead." The staff person picks up a chess piece, undoing Demi's move, and makes a move of her own. "See, you nailed him. The game is over."

"Stupid!" yells Demi. Scattering the chess pieces on the floor, she says to her mother, "This place is for babies. I don't know why you make me come here."

There may be many things going on in this scene. For this exercise, please look only for unmet cognitive needs. Refer to the preceding list if you wish. For example: Children need the right environment to concentrate on their interests. The children expect that the room will be quiet this time of the day. They have established a plan to play their game during that end part of the day because it is quiet. The staff person interrupts the quiet to meet her need to leave early, which means that the children's cognitive need for space and time to concentrate on their game is not being met.

Give three examples of other ways that the children's cognitive needs are not being met:

1. _____

_____

_____

_____

2. _____

_____

_____

_____

3. _____

_____

_____

_____

How could these problems be avoided? For example: The staff person could do other things that she needs to get done and not disrupt the children by noisily closing down the room. Or, she could discuss her problem with the children and come up with a way to solve it, such as helping them find a quiet place to play. Or, she could arrange her schedule so that she has time to do her cleanup after the children leave.

Describe changes that could be made to avoid the problems you found:

1. _____

_____

_____

_____

2. _____

_____

_____

_____

3. _____

_____

_____

_____

Social Needs

Social needs are those based on children's needs to interact with others. Friends, friends, friends are almost everything to schoolagers. Acceptance by friends, often to the exclusion of others, is crucial to them. This need is often manifested by children having one or two best friends. Children also form groups to distinguish themselves from others. In their attempts to secure a place in a group, children can get boastful, loud, aggressive, and argumentative. Children who cannot or choose not to behave in these typical ways may become withdrawn.

Children enjoy secrets among peers. They need privacy for their friendships. They also need time and space to be alone. The pressure of having to act in a way that is acceptable to their peers can get tiring. Sometimes they need to retreat and engage in younger children's activities—fantasy play, talking to themselves, snuggling with a stuffed toy.

Kids love to get reactions from adults for their use of vulgar terms, their lack of personal hygiene, or anything else that adults find gross. However, relationships with adults other than their parents become important during the school-age years. They are testing adults' authority as they work on being independent thinkers. At the same time, they want adults to respect them. The children want to be able to confide in adults and discuss problems in almost an adult way. They desire increased responsibility. They want to have opportunities to try out adult roles. They look to adults for validation.

School-age children are becoming sensitive to others' needs. They are able to empathize at times. They are sometimes able to look beyond their own needs to please or comfort others. They are definitely moving out of the little child's world-view, in which they and their parents were the center. They now live in a place that is full of other people. And they are busy searching for their niche in that new world.

Unrecognized social needs of school-age children can lead to behavior problems.

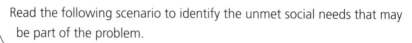

Read the following scenario to identify the unmet social needs that may be part of the problem.

Jeff, Sid, and Corie huddle together next to the playground fence. The playground is actually an open field with a few swings. The staff are at the other end of the field playing kickball with most of the other children.

The three boys are all wearing their peewee football team jackets. They are scratching football plays in the sand. Intermittently, they laugh and argue about the plays they are inventing. Jimmy wanders by the group. He is alone as usual. They laugh, not at him, but a little more loudly than they would if he weren't there.

"What are you dumb jocks doing?" he sneers.

"None of your business," retorts Sid without looking up.

The threesome laughs again.

"Well, then, you won't mind if I do this!" he says, as he drags his foot through their sandy diagrams.

"You major nerd!" screams Corie. "Let's get him!"

Chasing Jimmy and shouting demeaning names, the three boys throw large handfuls of dirt at him. His clothes and hair are filthy.

As the boys get closer to the kickball game, one of the staff people sees the chase and the clouds of dust aimed at Jimmy. She also hears the bad language. She stops the kickball game, saying, "We can play again after I take care of those troublemakers."

Some of the kickball players start cheering on the three boys. Jimmy starts to cry.

The staff person blows her whistle and shouts, "Get over here you three."

"He started it," Jeff yells.

"All of you, close those potty mouths now. Sit against that wall until your parents get here. Then we'll see what you have to say."

There are many things going on in this scene. For this exercise, please look only for unmet social needs. Give three examples of ways that the children's social needs are not being met.

1. _____

_____

_____

_____

2. _____

_____

_____

_____

3. _____

_____

_____

_____

Describe changes that could be made to avoid the problems you found.

1. _____

_____

_____

_____

2. _____

_____

_____

_____

3. _____

_____

_____

_____

Physical Development

School-age children's physical developmental needs are closely tied to their social and emotional needs. Please remember that physical needs at this stage can vary from one year to another. Physical development can also differ significantly from child to child.

Children are growing taller, heavier, and stronger. They are challenged to learn coordination and other physical skills. They need to develop large muscle skills for sports and games and walking down the hall without tripping over their growing feet. They are working on developing small muscle skills for craft, computers, and art. Physical abilities give them both self-esteem and a sense of independence.

School-age children have a high energy level that can be sustained for long periods of time. They need to be able to expend their energy and learn how to channel it in positive ways. Lack of physical exercise will inhibit proper growth and will leave children feeling pent up on the one hand and sluggish on the other. When the children tire, they become very tired. They need to learn their bodies' signals so that they do not become exhausted. They need to get the proper amount of sleep to renew their energy.

Children are less aware than adults of the effects of heat or cold on their bodies. They are often frightened when they feel pain.

They need to eat nutritious food, not foods with empty calories that don't give them sustained energy. This growing phase requires the nutrients that promote the growth of healthy muscles and bones.

They are becoming aware of their physical appearance. Self-care skills need to be developed so that children are healthy and feel good about their appearance. Children's acceptance by peers is often based on appearance. There may be times when children are a bit over- or underweight during these years. They need to learn that their appearance is not the only source of self-worth.

Children begin to mature sexually, which causes changes both outwardly and inwardly that can be confusing and embarrassing. They need to understand these physical changes so that they can learn to deal with them in positive ways.

Physically, children in this age range are dealing with many changes and high expectations that can often be at cross purposes. They generally believe the judgments and information that they receive from peers about their physical abilities, appearance, and changes. However, trusted adults to whom the children speak honestly can have an influence in the kids' assessment of their friends' opinions. Generally those adults are not their parents. Schoolagers often believe that parents treat them as younger than they are, don't understand, or don't have an objective point of view.

Unrecognized physical needs of school-age children can lead to behavior problems.

Read the following scenario to identify the unmet physical needs that may be part of the problem.

The first through fifth graders all come to the cafeteria for snack after school. Buses arrive over a one-hour period of time, from three to four o'clock. All the children get snack at four o'clock when the aide arrives. Until then they are to sit in their assigned places. They are free to engage in quiet conversation or begin their homework.

Heather, Maria, and Alyssa arrive at a quarter after three. They share secrets from the day for a while. Then they begin to play catch across the table. One thing leads to another and soon they are chasing each other around the cafeteria.

Shelley, the staff person, stops them without making too much of a fuss. She seats them in three separate corners of the room and tells them each to be quiet. They have forfeited their right to have snack, she tells them.

Alyssa says, "Doesn't bother me if I don't get those two dinky graham crackers. That snack is for babies anyway."

The girl sitting next to her chides, "Fat as you are, missing snack won't make no difference."

Shelley shrugs her shoulders and walks away.

After everyone has snack they head to the gym. Alyssa refuses to play red light, green light.

"Listen," Shelley says. "We all play this game for a half an hour. Stop your pouting about snack and get moving."

Exercise continued on next page

There may be many things going on in this scene. For this exercise, please look only for unmet physical needs. Give three examples of ways that the children's physical needs are not being met.

1. _____

_____

_____

_____

2. _____

_____

_____

_____

3. _____

_____

_____

_____

Describe three changes that could be made to avoid the problems you found.

1. _____

_____

_____

_____

2. _____

_____

_____

_____

3. _____

_____

_____

_____

Emotional Needs

Emotional needs are dramatic at this age. They cause much confusion for the adults who work or live with schoolagers. They are also confusing to the kids, although the kids don't want to admit it.

Often children are still learning to recognize and label feelings. Some children have learned to name their feelings since they were very young. Others have not had the kind of help from adults that they needed to be conversant about their feelings. In either case, as children develop they become more able to sort out the complexity of their feelings and their reactions to them.

As they continue to develop and learn, they may have difficulty explaining their emotional states. As a result, they will sometimes work out their anxieties, fears, and feelings through their actions. They may withdraw or act out. They may punish themselves or others. They may say "I don't know" when asked questions about how they feel, and it will be an honest, not a flip, answer. Children need adults to continue to give them language and nurturing to learn more about identifying and handling emotions.

School-age children often have strong feelings that can overwhelm them. This is especially true in the areas of fairness, justice, honesty, and right and wrong. Powerful feelings emerge in situations that they feel affect their peers' view of them. Emerging sexual feelings are also confusing.

School-age children are developing a sense of their personal strength. However, when feeling incompetent they often don't have the tools to analyze or cope with those feelings. Therefore, they are often self-conscious and self-critical. They are particularly vulnerable to put-downs or criticism from others, which may reinforce their own critical view of themselves.

Building skills, and being able to accomplish concrete tasks that peers and adults recognize as successful, adds to their self-esteem. Children need accurate recognition, not artificial praise. They sense insincerity immediately and take it as a sign that they are not competent so the adult had to make something up.

They can get upset quickly and appear to get over it quickly. They need to know that they can count on adults to be in control of situations when they are not. They need limit setting that also respects their need to develop independent thinking. They also need adults who can recognize the difference between an emotional situation which really did pass quickly and one that didn't get identified or dealt with.

While struggling for selfhood, children need reassurance that they can retreat into the protection of caring adults who will encourage them to take risks again when they feel safe.

Unrecognized emotional needs of school-age children can lead to behavior problems.

Read the following scenario to identify the unmet emotional needs that may be part of the problem.

Steph is a first grader. She wears dirty and sometimes torn clothes. Her emotions are very near the surface. When upset she either physically attacks another child or runs down the school hall to hide. Staff want to help Steph. But she takes up so much time that they are hoping the director will dismiss her from the program. Their faces grimace when Steph enters the room and they heave a sigh of relief when she leaves for the day.

Strangely enough, her best and only friend is Brittany. Brittany's wardrobe is a child-size version of the latest designer clothes. She is very quiet, compliant, smart, and responsible. She could be in the first graders' version of a clique. But she talks very little to anyone but Steph.

On the afternoons that they are both present the two girls are allowed to go to the housekeeping corner by themselves. As long as there is no loud commotion, they do not have to participate in any other activities. Once in a while, staff hear some sexually explicit words coming from that corner. But they decide that Brittany will put the conversation on the right track.

Unfortunately, Brittany only attends three days a week after school. Steph comes every day before and after school. Brittany's bus arrives twenty minutes after Steph's. Steph usually escapes from the snack table and goes outside to wait for Brittany's bus. The staff sort of ignore the fact that she is gone. They can see her from the window. The fifteen minute interlude can often be a very trying one. And they only get this reprieve three days a week.

One cold fall day, just as Brittany's bus is pulling up, the school principal notices Steph sitting on the steps outside. She brings Steph to the after-school room.

"Did you have any idea where this child was?" she asks.

"No. But it's impossible to keep track of her. She's always running away. She's real trouble."

"I can't believe the lack of control you have. If I had any choice you and these children wouldn't be here at all. Don't let this happen again." The principal huffs away.

"Now do you see what you've done? How many times have we told you not to go out there? You will not be allowed to play with Brittany for the rest of this week."

Steph spits at the staff person and squirms out of the hold on her arm. She darts down the hall, out of sight.

Brittany came in during the principal's lecture and has been watching for the last five minutes. She shuffles over to the housekeeping corner. Hiding under a quilt, she sobs quietly.

"Shhh. It will be all right," a staff person says. *"This will give you time to play with the nice girls."*

There are many things going on in this scene. For this exercise, please look only for unmet emotional needs. Give three examples of ways that the children's emotional needs are not being met.

1. _____

_____

_____

_____

2. _____

_____

_____

_____

3. _____

_____

_____

_____

Exercise continued on next page

Describe three changes that could be made to avoid the problems you found.

1. _____

_____

_____

_____

2. _____

_____

_____

_____

3. _____

_____

_____

_____

Ages and Stages

Children are busy creating themselves. They do it one day, one week, one year at a time. The terms "Terrible Twos," "Terrific Threes," and "Feisty Fours" ring familiar. There is danger in accepting these terms too literally. All two, three, and four year olds are not alike. Nor is any preschool or school-age child exactly the same from one day to the next. However, the tag lines do acknowledge that there are developmental phases that can be looked for in the overall development of children. Six year olds have some needs that differ from those of ten year olds. Children express their creation of self differently at twelve years than they did at five. If you aren't aware of the differences you might talk to a five year old the way you talk to a twelve year old. Or you might structure activities or rules for ten year olds the same way that you structure rules and activities for a six year old.

　　If expectations are the same for sevens as they are for elevens, the kids' needs won't be met. They may not understand what the problem is, but they will react.

How will you see those reactions most often?

You said it before I even finished the question, didn't you?

In behavior problems, of course!

If we know, for example, that seven year olds often tell tall tales, then we can accept their stories as appropriate for their age. We can enjoy sharing their stories without concern that they are "liars" or out of touch with the truth. If we are aware that ten year olds may fear being different, we can be more sensitive to their desire to wear the same kind of shoes that everyone else does. If we know that five year olds often need an audience, we will feel freer to watch their antics or listen to their jokes without concern that they are seeking undue attention.

If we have a sense of the spirit and characteristics of a specific age group, then we can enjoy them more. We are more able to say, "She is such a delightful six year old," because we know that she is displaying characteristics that are developmentally appropriate and that are helping her move on to the next age. We will be less likely to be concerned, for example, that she is not as docile as she was at five, because we know that six year olds are learning to exert their own independence by displaying more defiance than they did the previous year.

Knowing the characteristics does not mean, of course, that we don't deal with the issues that arise. Just as we help a two year old learn how to appropriately express anger, so we help the six year old seek independence in ways that are respectful to herself and to others. But we can relax a bit, seeing her actions as healthy parts of the process of developing as a person.

Please spend a few minutes reviewing some of the characteristics of each age. The following clusters of characteristics of each year from five to twelve may be helpful. The lists here are compilations of characteristics from developmental studies and observations. They are not all inclusive. Nor are the listed traits true of every child in a specific age group. However, such an overview does give a sense of how children may appear, and what they may fear, do, and need, at a given age—and can help us to know what to expect as common issues in each age group.

Feel free to have fun adding words to describe the kids in an age group with which you are particularly familiar. At the bottom of the page for each age group there is an exercise for you to complete that may help you get a better sense of children of a particular age.

Five Year Olds

They are
Friendly
Helpful
Cooperative
Sometimes bossy with peers
Worriers
Showoffs
Procrastinators and dilly-dalliers
Funny
Slapstick comics
Outgoing

They fear
The dark
Loss of mother/nurturing figure
Getting lost
School
Masturbation as bad
Being mocked

They may
Name call and insult peers
Protect personal belongings
Identify stereotypes
Seek praise
Tell jokes (that they think
   are very funny)

They need
Approval, acceptance, and love,
   especially from parent figures
Opportunities to return to
   younger behaviors
Information clarified, given in
   different ways and more
   than once
Self-image boosts
Exploration of their own
   cultural identity
An audience

Please complete this thought with a couple of sentences:

Having reviewed the characteristics of five year olds, I think I would (or would not)
enjoy working with them because...

_____

_____

_____

_____

Six Year Olds

They are

Active

Accident prone

Competitive

Jealous of siblings and peers

Aggressive, physically and
  verbally

Generous

Compassionate

Lonely

Defiant

Sensitive to disapproval

They fear

Thunder and lightning

The supernatural: ghosts, goblins

Embarrassment

Being left out

Change

Death

They may

Tease others

Magnify small problems

Use shock words

Think and behave rigidly

Have tears and temper tantrums

Be greedy

They need

Guided opportunities for
  increased independence

Reassurance that they
  are loved

Strategies for decision making

To explore culture and beliefs
  of peers

Reassurance and discussion
  about fears

To clearly understand
  expectations

Please write a few words to complete the following sentence:

Based on the traits listed about six year olds, I think some challenges in the area of discipline with six year olds might be...

_____

_____

_____

_____

because...

_____

_____

_____

_____

Seven Year Olds

They are

Moody and sulky

Pleasers

Modest

Thoughtful

Moving from fantasy to reality

Empathetic

Adventurers

Tellers of tall tales

Aware that gender and physical
traits remain constant

Intensely involved in activities

Less aggressive than sixes

They fear

New situations

Disruption of routine

Disapproval from peers and
parents

Highly organized competition

Lack of privacy

Own inability to handle pressure
from adults

They may

Have idols

Be unhappy and pensive

Engage in attention-getting
behavior for long periods
of time

Name call

Enjoy dramatic play

Resent interruptions

They need

Short, clear messages regarding
expectations

Uninterrupted periods of time
for activities

Recognition from peers and
parents

Increasing opportunities for
long-term responsibility,
such as pet care

Privacy

Realistic toys and tools

Please complete the following sentence:

Having reviewed the characteristics for seven year olds, I would include the following in my program plans for them...

_____

_____

_____

_____

Eight Year Olds

They are

Independent

Collectors

Sexually curious

Developing own interests

Impatient

Critical

Sensitive but cry less

Appreciative of humor

Cheerful

Lonely without interactions
with friends

They fear

Fewer things, in general

Racism against own group

Staying alone for periods of time
that seem too long

Failure to perform and meet
own expectations

Enemies

Losing special friends

They may

Be critical of self and others

Be impatient

Enjoy scary stories

Get feelings hurt easily

Begin to resent parental authority
but be more respectful of
other adult authority

Like to catch people making
mistakes

They need

Information about faraway
places, differences among
people, similarities among people

More responsibilities with
concrete rewards and
consequences

To remain close to family

Genuine acknowledgment
of accomplishments

Reassurance regarding their
own abilities

A close friend

Please complete the following sentence:

After reviewing the characteristics of eight year olds, I think that it might sometimes be challenging for me to work with them in the area of behavior guidance because…

_____

_____

_____

_____

Nine Year Olds

They are

Curious

Rebellious

Hero worshippers

Independent

Dependable

Loyal and protective

Aggressive, verbally but less physically

Not as interested in creative pursuits

Humorous

Engaged in sex-segregated play

They fear

Fewer things, in general

Loss of dignity or propriety

Differences in physical traits

Being treated unfairly

Being seen as liking the opposite sex

They may

Dislike interruptions but will resume an activity afterwards

Push aside parents' and other adults' ideas

Vehemently demand personal rights, especially in the area of fairness

Scare each other, engage in spying and hiding

Develop a strong belief in themselves

Express a variety of emotions

They need

Adult protection and understanding

Opportunities to be needed and useful

Clubs, groups, organizations to join

To be treated fairly

Safe ways to test independent thinking

Longer periods of time for activities

Please complete the following sentence:

After reviewing the characteristics of nine year olds, I think I would enjoy working with them in the area of behavior guidance because...

_____

_____

_____

_____

Ten Year Olds

They are

Happy, seldom sad

Practical jokers

Rarely in tears

Not able to take jokes about
themselves

More shy if they have had
a tendency to be shy

Secret tellers

Into cliques

Able to understand racism,
sexism, ageism

Empathetic

They fear

Not doing well in school

Being late

Not being able to understand
homework

The rapid changes in their
bodies, especially the girls

Being ridiculed

Being different

They may

Tell puns and riddles

Not get angry easily

Rebel at authority

Want to be part of a team
or gang

Start worrying about the
opposite sex

Do the unexpected

They need

Responsibilities

Regulations that they help
make and/or understand
reasons for

Adults to talk to

Stable relationships

Reassurance regarding their
scholastic abilities

Opportunities to be helpful
to others

Please complete the following sentence:

After reviewing ten year olds' characteristics, I think it would be important that I
cultivate the following traits in myself so I could work effectively with ten year olds…

_____

_____

_____

_____

Eleven & Twelve Year Olds

They are
Able to show respect to authority
Physically developing quickly,
    especially the girls
Interested in exclusive relation-
    ships with the opposite sex
Interested in social order being
    maintained in family, school,
    community
Interested in world events,
    ancestry, geography, history
Aware of cultural and political
    values
Confident in some of their skills
    and their ability to learn
Unpredictable at times
Anxious to be seen as behaving
    correctly
Eager to be grown up

They fear
Injustice for themselves
    and others
Being made fun of by the
    opposite sex
Being left out

Lack of codified rules
Helplessness in the face of
    world problems
Physical inadequacy

They may
Join gangs
Have girlfriends or boyfriends
    in the romantic sense
Be struggling with sexual
    identification
Worry about sexual feelings
    and development
Be self-righteous
Be very shy and withdrawn

They need
Opportunities for social action
    activities
Adults to give them correct
    information about their
    developing bodies
Chances to feel needed
Adults who are loyal to them
Adults who take their ideas
    and opinions seriously
Love and understanding from
    adults and peers

Please complete the following sentence:

After reviewing the list of characteristics of eleven and twelve year olds, I think
I would enjoy helping them to learn self-discipline because...

_____

_____

_____

_____

The most important thing to remember about this section is that schoolagers have developmental phases. When we work with them we need to modify our strategies, programs, and expectations to prevent unnecessary discipline problems and to encourage their ability to learn how to guide their own behaviors.

This chapter contains lots of information. I hope it helped you to get a better understanding of children's development. There is strength in understanding development and magic in discovering your role in helping kids become their best selves.

You have worked hard in this chapter. You deserve a break! Get up, stretch, get a soft drink or a cup of tea. Let your new knowledge roll around in your head. I'll meet you at the next chapter!

Chapter 6

Looking At and Looking In

by Carly

Here's looking at you, kid.

≈ Casablanca

After learning a little about child development, we can learn more about schoolagers by *observing* them (noting children's behaviors, attitudes, and emotions), and by *reflecting* on what it was like to be children ourselves.

Observation

Observation is a key to learning about school-age children. How do you think the experts got to be experts? Observing children in various settings and trying to understand what is happening with them is often the starting place for putting together child development theories. Often the settings that researchers use are controlled to reduce the number of variables that affect children's behavior. The resulting information is interesting and valuable.

Each day you work with schoolagers, you step into a child development laboratory of a different kind. The information you can gather there is also valuable. You have an enviable opportunity to learn more about children in school-age care.

You see the kids in their day-to-day setting—variables and all. Your role with the kids is multi-faceted. You are an administrator, a teacher, a friend, a cook, a cleaner, a nurse, a parent figure, an attendance keeper, a friend, a crisis intervention specialist, a parent counselor. It is amazing what you learn about kids from each of these perspectives. You already carry knowledge of children from being with them. You could probably tell the experts a thing or two that they don't know.

In the following exercise you will list some of the characteristics of the kids you meet every day. For this exercise don't worry about what the experts say or what anyone else might think about your opinions.

Quickly, as honestly as you can, list words that describe schoolagers.
Write a collage of words any way you want. It doesn't have to be neat.
Ready? Set? Go!

Schoolagers are...

When you have finished, set that exercise aside in your mind.

You made quite a list even though with all your duties and the fast pace of school-age care, it is easy to forget to look at the kids.

There are many observation tools available in books. I encourage you to seek them out and study them. Decide which method will be the most useful and the most practical for you.

A few basics about observation might be helpful here. When you are observing children for the purpose of learning about them so that you can interact with and guide them in appropriate ways, you will want to remember some principles.

Get the Facts

It can be difficult to remain objective. Often when you are involved with children in a work setting, you are judging their behaviors. You are deciding if their actions are "good" or "bad." You may develop this habit because you believe that you are responsible for changing children's behavior instantly. You expect that at any moment you will have to intervene.

When you're observing, you can put that often uncomfortable policing role aside. Instead, you can assume the role of an outside observer. You are, for a while anyway, someone who is simply interested in children's behavior in order to report it, as a journalist might. When you make observations, you simply record what happened. Some things you will want to record include:

- What day was it?
- What time of day?
- How long did you observe?
- What did the child do?
- Who else was there?
- What else was going on?

Ask "What?" Not "Why?"

While you are watching children closely in order to learn about them, you are not trying to figure out why they are doing what they are doing. Trying to come up with motives or explanations is another common habit of school-age care staff. Because you are intelligent and caring, you often play the role of psychologist or social worker. This time you don't have to. You can be a recorder rather than a therapist. Enjoy the simplicity of the task and write down as much of *what* happens as you can.

Keep It Short and Detailed

An observation can be as short as three to five minutes. The notes you take can be brief. If the notes get long you may find that you are not adhering to the first two principles of being factual and objective. Factual details are important. For one thing, attending to them keeps you focused on the actions, not on judging the actions. Noting that a child had a dirty face or spoke in hushed tones or was shivering might give you information when you put all the facts together.

Here is an example of a brief observation.

Child's name: Greg Warner.

Age: Third grader—8 years old.

Date: July 3, 1999.

Time: 12:45 p.m.

Length of observation: 5 minutes.

Place: Field trip at zoo.

What happened before the event: Greg rode with his group to the zoo on a school bus for two hours. Greg sat by himself in the back of the bus. The teacher told another child, a sixth grader, sit next to Greg. Most of the children sang songs. Greg did not. He looked out the window.

Actions: Greg got off the bus quickly. He wore a sweatshirt and sweatpants. The temperature was 95 degrees. He bumped into a teacher, Sally, getting off the bus. He asked her, "Why were you standing right in my way?"

Greg ran ahead of the group. A teacher, Steve, called him back. He stood in place waiting for the group to catch up to him instead. The teacher told him, "Wait until the end of the line, seeing that you can't listen."

Greg pushed his way into the middle of the line. He was sweating. He pushed a kindergartner to the ground with his hand.

Steve asked, "What's the matter with you anyway?"

Greg swore at Steve. Then he went to the end of the line, hitting kids with his bag lunch on the way.

Greg followed along in line. Sally walked next to him. Greg took off his shirt. The other kids laughed. Greg put his shirt back on and called the other kids names.

Those are the facts, simply the facts. It would be easy to imagine all the guesses and judgments a staff member might add. Notice that there are no words such as "defiantly" or "sadly" or "cruelly" or "as usual."

How are such written observations helpful? Put together three to five of them and patterns may begin to emerge. You may discover that Greg usually acts out around lunch time, or around a certain teacher, or when he is near younger kids, or when he has to interact with older kids. He may react in negative ways consistently when he is confronted but not when he is simply reminded. Who knows what you will discover, especially if you have the opportunity to compare your observations with other staff's notes.

These kinds of notes are useful for talking about kids at staff meetings and parent conferences. The absence of judgment keeps everyone calmer and less defensive. It feels different to you and to the person you're talking to when you say, "Greg got off the bus quickly," instead of, "As usual, he came storming off the bus. Not caring about anybody else. He's just like his dad that way."

The recording above could probably be done in five minutes. I know you don't always have those five minutes. But you might get into the habit of carrying something to write on so you can jot down the basics and fill in details later.

Another kind of observation is watching one child for a week, without judgment. At the end of each day with that child, write down some of her actions in a non-judgmental way. You will discover that you get to know the child in a different way by tuning in to her at different times and in different situations.

You can also just write, as much as you can, as fast as you can, about a particular child's behavior as if you had a story due to your editor in five minutes. This kind of writing often reveals interesting patterns.

If you really feel that you can't do any writing, at least stay tuned in to the kids, one at a time. Notice what each child does. Not what you think he does, but what he really does. You may be surprised by what you learn.

Whatever you do, remember to pay attention, real attention, to the children you are with. By developing an interest in individuals you will grow to understand them, to want to figure out how to guide them towards a happier and healthier life. And guess what? Your attending to the individual in this way will reduce behavior problems, not only with that child but with other children as well.

Make yourself a promise right now that you will remember each day to carefully observe one of the children in your care. You may want to choose a child whose behaviors are especially challenging for you.

Take a minute now to make the resolution:

I, _____, do promise that each day for a week, beginning on _____, I will carefully, objectively, observe the behavior of one child. I will try to write a few notes about the child. The notes will record facts, not make judgments. If I don't have time one day to write, I will take mental notes and write them down later. I will use my knowledge of that child to relate to her effectively and respectfully.

At the end of the week, summarize your observations. Give the highlights of the child's behaviors that week. (You can feel free to write with some feeling in this exercise—not judgmentally, but with your impressions of events.)

_____

_____

_____

_____

_____

_____

_____

_____

_____

_____

In the space below, write down what you learned in general about the child by observing.

_____

_____

_____

_____

_____

_____

Did your attitudes towards the child change? If so, how?

_____

_____

_____

Did you modify your behavior towards the child in any way?

_____

_____

_____

Can you think of any ways you could interact more effectively with the child as a result of what you learned?

_____

_____

_____

What did you learn about schoolagers in general as a result of your observations?

_____

_____

_____

Which child will you observe next, and on what date will you begin?

_____

The Child Inside

Another way you know about children is that you were one.

If you are a woman, you would be able to work in programs that help men. You could read research on how men function. You could observe men. You would learn about what makes men tick through both of these methods. You would be able to learn enough to do good work.

You would not have the advantage, however, of knowing experientially what it is like to be a man, because you probably haven't been one. But you have been a child. That experience is part of you forever. It is a treasure for you to uncover. Whether or not your childhood was happy, it is a valuable resource from which to draw when you are working with children.

The work you will do in this chapter is different from that which you did in chapter 4 when you remembered your dreams about growing up. Those memories were important in order to see if you are on the track in your life that you want to be on. You remembered wishes that you had for yourself.

The journey in this chapter is different. It is deeper. It is a reflection that will bring up for you what it truly is to be a child, at least in your experience. As we get older we tend to forget what it meant to be six or eight or ten. Many of us trivialize childhood as innocent and carefree. Some of us believe that children today are just worse than children in our day. Most of us probably don't give the nature of being a child much thought at all.

The child we were is still there. She or he is a part of who we are today. She or he sometimes still needs our attention. Old wounds may not be healed. The joy of playing may be forgotten. Whatever the case, the child we were is a teacher for us. She or he can teach us in a way that no one else can about the children in our care, if we listen.

Listen to your child by doing the following exercise that will help you to reach back and learn from your childhood. It is best if you can turn down the lights, put on some soft music and have someone read this exercise to you. If that isn't possible, then just read quietly. You don't want to analyze your thoughts. Just let the memories be a conscious part of you again.

If this kind of exercise seems weird or scary to you, please try to do it in a serious manner anyway. Working with kids is risky business. This is a good place to start taking some risks. If the thoughts become more than you think you want to deal with right now, you can, of course, stop the exercise. But, please, in what you consider to be a safe setting, explore those issues. Unresolved childhood issues can affect your healthy, effective work with children. If this exercise is being done as part of a workshop or class, **no participant should ever be asked to share, in any way, more than they wish to about this exercise.**

Now, begin. Sit in a comfortable position. Take a few deep breaths. Let all the thoughts and worries of the day leave your mind.

Let your thoughts go back to remember yourself at the age of the children in your care. If you can't remember that far back, remember the earliest age you can.

Remember...
What did you look like?
What did you wear?
How did you walk? Run? Skip? Move through a room? Move outside?
Write down what you remember, beginning with the phrase, "I was..."

_____

_____

_____

_____

Remember...
What did you do before school? What could you hear in the mornings? See? Smell? Who else was there?
How did you get to school? How did you feel on the way to school?
Write down what you remember. "Before school I..."

_____

_____

_____

_____

Exercise continued on next page

Remember …

When the school day was over, where did you go? How did you get there?

Who was with you? How did you feel on your way? How did you feel when
you got there?

What did you see? Hear? Smell? Taste?

What did you like to do? Outdoors? Indoors?

Who was your best friend? What did you like to do together?

Write down what you remember. "After school I…"

_____

_____

_____

_____

Remember…

Who was an adult that you liked? Trusted? Wanted to be with? Why?

Who was an adult that you didn't like? Didn't trust? Didn't want to be with? Why?

Write down what you remember. "An adult I had strong feelings about was…"

_____

_____

_____

_____

_____

Remember and then complete the next two statements.

An adult describing you at this age would have said, "She is…"

_____

_____

If you had described yourself at this age you would have said, "I'm…"

_____

_____

Remember and then answer the next two questions.

What happened to you that made you say, "I will never do that to kids"?

_____

_____

What's the one memory from your childhood that you wish all children could have?

_____

_____

Now, make a collage of the words that describe you as a child. Put the words in any order you wish.

As a child I was...

Now compare the word collage you made on page 78, about the children in your care, with the collage about your childhood. How are they different? How are they the same?

Beginning with the first time I did the exercise with a group, and probably a hundred times since, a very interesting thing has happened. The two lists always look something like this:

Schoolagers are...	As a child I was...
loud	scared
obnoxious	shy
aggressive	polite
mean	active
hungry	pleaser
pushy	responsible
ADD (have attention deficit disorder)	lonely
	energetic
self-centered	loved
withdrawn	abused
angry	happy
disrespectful	secure
goofy	helpful
greedy	mischievous
abusive	curious
helpful (about this time someone in the group notices that there are too many negative words and feels guilty)	happy to play outside
	a reader
	a good friend
	sad
	creative
spoiled	a dreamer
lazy	funny
crude	serious
rude	sincere
complainers	worried
destructive	cuddly
swearers	
tattlers	
hyperactive	

As you compare the two lists it is obvious that the first one, "School-agers are," is much more negative. The second list, "As a child I was," is not only more positive, but also more feelings-oriented. Even the not so positive words on list two, for example, "mischievous," are more endearing than a corresponding word on list one such as "troublemaker."

I don't believe the lists are so different because school-age care staff are just negative, don't like kids, or something else sinister. I know school-age care staff too well to reach such conclusions. School-age care staff like kids and want to help them. After much thought and listening to staff, I have concluded that the difference was that because staff see kids in such large groups, and because of poor working conditions (not enough staff, space, equipment, support), and lack of training for the job in front of them, staff forgot. They forgot what it's like to be a kid.

Which group of kids would you rather take care of—the kids described in the first list or the kids described in the second one?

You probably answered list two. Most people do.

Have the children on list two disappeared? Are they gone because their mothers work? Because of violence? Poverty? Drugs? Materialism? Because their parents don't have enough time for them?

No, they're not gone. They are hiding out. They are disguised in the characteristics of the kids on the first list.

A friend of mine had an experience that illustrates this point.

Jim worked at a residential home *for boys ages 8–12 who had stolen, committed violent crimes, and used drugs. Boys who the courts decided needed treatment away from the rest of society. The home was out in the country. Occasionally, a boy would think he could escape and would take off down the rural road.*

One day a ten year old, Austen, did just that. Jim got into his car and headed out to find the boy. He found him hitchhiking, with his shirt half open, jewelry around his neck, and a cocky look on his face.

Jim pulled over. "Get in," he said.

Knowing it was hopeless, Austen got in. Jim noticed a bulge, which he thought might be a weapon, under the right side of Austen's denim shirt.

"What do you have under there?"

"Nothin'."

"Come on. Hand it over," said Jim.

"It's nothing!"

"You know you're going to give it to me sooner or later. Let's get it over with."
Austen turned his head towards the car window. With his left hand he yanked the object from under his shirt and passed it to Jim.

It was Austen's worn-out, one-eyed teddy bear. Of all of the things he could have left with, that was the one thing he took.

◉ ◉

Whenever I see a child who looks tough, who I might judge incorrigible, I picture her with a teddy bear under her arm.

It may be true that there are more kids suffering from their mother's drug abuse or their parents' unrealistic expectations or the trauma around them. I don't know if it is true or not. But I believe that, as family life educator Barbara Oehlberg says, "Children haven't changed. Childhood has" (*Making It Better* [St. Paul: Redleaf, 1996]).

Your job the next time you're with the children is to let them know, any way you can, that you know who they are. That you aren't fooled by their disguise. That you know they are children with the same needs, feelings, and hopes you had as a kid. That you have their number. That the game is over. And that you are there to support them.

And guess what? Doing that one thing, bringing that one attitude change to work with you, will eliminate more discipline problems than you can imagine.

Even if negative behaviors are more prevalent than they used to be, or more mysterious, children are still children. We may have to develop new skills to deal with them. We may need the lessons from new diagnostic tools or medical or developmental research. We may have to design programs and use strategies that are relevant to today's kids. But we must remember that they are kids, and give them all the love and guidance we can. Not only will they get what they need and deserve, but our jobs will be easier too. Understanding and meeting needs are two of the most effective behavior guidance tools available. I know you will use them well.

To conclude your work on this chapter, please read the following poem in a quiet place and reflect on it and on what you have learned:

Don't be fooled by me. Don't be fooled by the face I wear.
For I wear a thousand masks and none of them are me.
I give the impression that I'm secure, that all is unruffled within me,
That confidence is my name and coolness my game.
That the water's calm and I'm in command.
But don't believe me. Please.
Beneath dwells the real me, confused, afraid, and lonely.
I hide. I don't want anybody to know.
I panic at the thought of my weakness, and I fear being exposed.
I don't tell you this. I don't dare. I'm afraid.
I'm afraid your glance will lack acceptance and love.

So begins the parade of masks. And my life becomes a front.
I chatter to you idly, suavely.
I tell you everything that is really nothing and nothing of what is everything.
When I'm going through my routine, don't be fooled.
Please listen carefully and hear what I'm not saying.
I dislike hiding. Really, I do.
Please hold out your hand, even when that's the last thing I seem to want.
Because, each time you're kind, gentle, and encouraging
I get braver,
closer to leaving
the masks
behind
one
by
one.

≈ Anonymous

Chapter 7

Resilient Kids

by Mallory

Persistence of the destructive myth that 'children are resilient' will prevent millions of children, and our society, from meeting their true potential.

≈ Bruce D. Perry, M.D., Ph.D.

How many times have you heard people say things like, "Kids are tough. They bounce right back," or "Don't worry about them. Kids get over things long before adults do"?

Current brain research by Dr. Perry and Dr. James Garbarino and others find that the opposite is true. Children exposed to stress, fear, violence, or maltreatment can actually have arrested brain development. Such stress can lead to a greater concentration of brain cell growth in the midbrain. As a result, the cortex area doesn't develop properly. The child's ability to solve problems may be limited. A predisposition to aggressive, impulsive behaviors and an underdeveloped capacity for empathy may also result (Bruce D. Perry et al., "Childhood Trauma, the Neurobiology of Adaptation, and 'Use-dependent' Development of the Brain: How 'States' Become 'Traits,'" *Infant Mental Health Journal* Winter 1995).

Resiliency in children is a popular subject of workshops, conferences, and writing these days. Some speakers come up with simplistic formulas for resiliency that are akin to the old "pull yourself up by your bootstraps" mentality. Obviously, if there is brain damage, it is going to be more complicated than that. Even if there aren't brain changes, the ability of children to heal from persistent stressors in their lives is a complex issue.

Exactly because children are more softly molded both physically and emotionally than adults, they are not like rubber bands or balls that bounce back at impact. The imprint that trauma leaves on a child's brain, emotions, and sense of self is real and sometimes indelible.

There are often more stressors in the lives of children in poverty because survival is an issue. That doesn't mean, however, that children with more financial resources do not experience trauma or neglect. Trauma can result from frequent moves with an affluent family, or lack of attention in a middle-class family, or overexposure to violence in movies and video games, or death and sickness in any family. It can result from unstable child care arrangements or settings in which children are mistreated or ignored.

"That's all really interesting," you may say. "But what does this information mean to me, reading this book about discipline?"

It means that we have to know what we are doing. We must learn how to avoid causing children any more distress and how to help children compensate for previous damage.

It means that we need to understand that children's negative behavior comes from many sources. Blaming the child is not humane or effective. Negative behavior is hardly ever "just obstinacy" or "defiance" or "a kid deliberately making trouble for no good reason," and knowing that will change how we deal with discipline issues. We would not expect a child with an intelligence quotient of 55 to read Shakespeare. We cannot expect a child with a brain that increases aggression and diminishes empathy to figure out how to get her own needs met in appropriate ways, or to learn easily how to solve interpersonal problems. Not all children who behave inappropriately are lacking in normal brain development, of course. But first of all, we don't have any way of knowing which children are being affected in this way by constant stress. And second, all children depend on us to guide them to improve their abilities to connect with others in healthy ways. Kids can't just shake things off. And they often appeal to adults to help them with their needs, large or small, through misbehavior. All children need our understanding and competent interaction.

The good news is that children with this kind of brain damage can heal. The way we treat them and the skills we teach them can actually cause curative changes in the brain. Children can also learn ways to heal themselves in the future. One way to facilitate the healing process in children is by using the activities in *Making It Better: Activities for Children Living in a Stressful World,* by Barbara Oehlberg (St. Paul: Redleaf, 1996). Children who are healing and learning can develop tools and processes that will allow them to become resilient people.

Resiliency isn't magic. It is, rather, a set of skills and a strong sense of self that allows a person to deal with difficulties while remaining healthy. Characteristics of resilient people include empathy; the capacity to reason and solve problems; and the ability to take constructive nonviolent action, to nurture oneself, to respect others, and to put things into perspective.

This information on brain development and resiliency can affect the way you solve discipline problems. The same teaching-relationship model of behavior guidance we talked about in the first chapter leads us to act appropriately and competently with all children. The old punishment-control approach doesn't.

The following true story illustrates this point.

Korrine is a substitute for school-age programs. *She sees a lot of different settings. She is happy for the chance to learn more about the field on her own schedule while she is getting her degree in child development. She has good skills with children. Her intuition and knowledge serve her well in a job that moves her from place to place almost daily.*

The first time she works with a group, the supervisor or another staff member gives her the scoop on the children, usually highlighting behavior difficulties.

Today is no different. Korrine goes out on the playground with Gemma, the overworked director of a small child care site that has just added schoolagers to its program.

"This is your bunch today," Gemma says, picking up the leg of a broken plastic chair. "They are the kindergartners. We've had most of them since they were little. Over there by the fence is Bobby. He's brain damaged. He cries a lot for no reason. Like if another child takes something of his, he goes on and on. You'll see what I mean."

Gemma walks towards the other end of the playground, telling children that Korrine is their teacher for the day. Korrine follows. Almost on cue, Bobby starts crying. Korrine does see what Gemma meant. The cry is the kind that involves the child's whole body. His upper body bends over to one side. He begins to fall into Korrine. The crying is more of a wail. Syllables mix with sobs. "They...my...want...hurt," he cries. The adults can guess that someone did something to him. They also know that the guttural crying is out of proportion to the specific event. Gemma props his body up away from Korrine's.

"You don't have to cry," Gemma tells him. "Just ignore him," she tells Korrine. She keeps walking. Bobby lands in a heap on the sand. Korrine follows Gemma as she points out other children who may give Korrine problems and gives her a brief outline of the afternoon's schedule. "Good luck," Gemma says as she turns around to go into the building. "You're on your own," she says and waves good-bye with the broken chair leg.

Korrine assesses the situation. All the children except Bobby seem to be playing okay. Bobby is now lying on a bench, curled up and still sobbing. Korrine sits next to him. He throws his head on her lap, continuing his unintelligible protests.

"I'm so sorry you are hurt," Korrine says. The crying gets louder. "I am so very sorry," she says again.

"I want to go home," Bobby moans. "I want my Mom."

"I know you do. I'm sorry she can't be here. Where is your mom?"

"She's at work."

"Then you can't go home. I'm sorry. I know you want to," Korrine says rubbing his head and shoulders. He gets louder and more insistent that he should be able to go home. Korrine continues to sit by him. Suddenly, he gets up and runs over to another part of the playground.

He plays with some sand toys for a while. In about ten minutes, he comes again, sobbing, holding his head, "They…sand…no fair…hurt." Another staff member says, "You're not hurt. You just like to cry. There's nothing wrong."

He shouts and kicks sand. "Hurt, hurt, hurt," he screams.

Korrine begins to talk to him as she did before.

"If you were here every day," the staff person says to Korrine, "you would know that he's just trying to get attention. He needs to learn how to control himself. Stop it now. Listen to my words, Bobby. Stop it now! I have to go in with my group. You'll learn. Babying him doesn't help."

After the other group leaves, Korrine continues to flood Bobby with understanding. He recovers once again and darts off.

The same behavior happens several times. Korrine handles it the same way. During a calm spell, Korrine begins to encourage children who are making their way along the hanging bars. "Way to go!" she says. She holds kids up who feel unsafe. With equal amounts of enthusiasm, she cheers the learning kids and the kids who can go across hanging by one arm. Bobby pushes his way in front of a couple of other kids and tries the bars. He is amazingly strong. "Look at you," Korrine says. "Look what you can do, Bobby. Stretch that arm way out to the next bar. Swing your body."

The other kids look at Bobby. They are surprised to hear him being spoken about in a positive manner. He makes it all the way across the bars. The kids cheer. Bobby, startled, gives a two thumbs up sign and goes to the back of the line. He does this three times. The fourth time his exuberance overcomes him and he pushes his way into the front of the line. The other staff person is out again and sees him pushing. She pulls him out and says, "You have to wait in line like everyone else."

"Do not. Do not. Do not," he screams.

"Yes, you do."

"Do not. Do not."

"Yes, you do. Now you sit over there till you agree."

Bobby begins kicking at her. "I told you how he is," the staff person says to Korrine.

"We hate Bobby. We hate Bobby," a couple of kids chant.

Korrine goes to Bobby. "You can come with me. Find your place at the end of the line like you did before. Then you can do your super bar crossing again."

"We're fine," she says to the staff person who shoots her a "who do you think you are" look.

Bobby waits in line and then does his thing on the bars. "Look at how strong he is," Korrine says.

"It doesn't surprise me," the staffer says. "I feel his strength when he hits and kicks me."

"But he's not doing that now."

The children go in for a rest time. Bobby takes a long nap—something that Gemma told her earlier that he never does. He gets up, gives Korrine a hug. "I like you," he says.

"I like you, too."

He goes to the snack table. He waits for Korrine to pour his juice. "You can pour that juice yourself," she says.

Bobby pours the juice.

"I wish you could stay here."

"So do I," Korrine answers. "But, you can still be strong—like you were today—even when I'm not here. Do you think you can?"

Bobby chomps on a bagel. "Yeah," he says.

◉ ◉

Did Korrine change Bobby's behavior in one day? No.

Did she start to make a difference? Yes.

The staff who were with Bobby every day were tired and frustrated. They also were probably not sufficiently trained. Do you have to have a degree to work competently with children? No. But you do need to be willing to assess your beliefs and techniques. This staff was still using punishment and control to try to change Bobby's behavior. Was their model working? No. Bobby was getting worse. He had been there since he was little and things were not better.

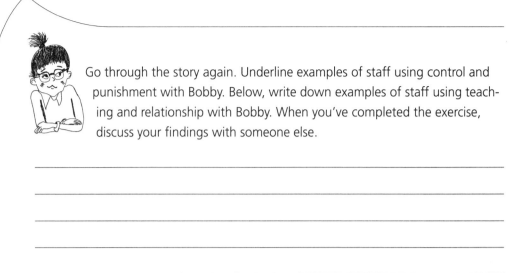

Go through the story again. Underline examples of staff using control and punishment with Bobby. Below, write down examples of staff using teaching and relationship with Bobby. When you've completed the exercise, discuss your findings with someone else.

_____

_____

_____

_____

_____

The staff members in the story, by punishing or attempting to control Bobby, did not permit real change to take place. The staff and the other children had decided who Bobby was. And so had Bobby, almost. The fact that he could respond to Korrine means that he still had the capacity to let people in, that he had somewhere in his life built some resiliency skills.

What are some influences in Bobby's life that may have encouraged the limited resiliency he displays? At least one caring adult and probably several have provided stability and invested time, energy, and love in him. How did these adults support Bobby's resiliency?

1. **Someone helped Bobby become able to tell his story.** Even through the tears, Bobby was able to tell people that he was hurt. He could express his pain. If Korrine had had more time with him, she probably would have learned more about him, from him. Children who are able to express themselves in some way are more likely to be resilient. Communication skills require language. Bobby and children like him need to learn words through storytelling, listening, dramatic play, puppets, writing, and group discussions. The more language skills they develop, the more they are able to free themselves from the isolation of their trauma and stress.

2. **Someone helped Bobby develop a sense of self-worth and competence.** His belief that he was worthwhile allowed him to ask for help. If he had no resiliency skills at all, he would either be mired in depression or continually acting out his rage. Children without

resiliency skills often come from families that believe they are at the mercy of fate—that things are bad for them and they have no control over changing the circumstances. It is then almost impossible to believe in your own self-worth. If you cannot control what happens to you, then you feel powerless, worthless. If that is the way the people around a child feel about themselves, that is how they will probably tell the child to feel about himself.

3. **Someone formed relationships with Bobby.** He learned how to be in a relationship and how to trust others, even if minimally. Therefore, he is able to risk developing other relationships even if he doesn't always do it appropriately.

   Having conversations with children is one of the most important ways to build relationships. You can have conversations while you do activities or wait for a bus or walk down the hall together. At the same time you are building the relationship, you are helping the child tell his story and, just by your attention and interest, are encouraging him to build his self-esteem. This relationship building is at the heart of your work. When relationship building is going slowly or I am reluctant to try one more conversation with a seemingly defiant or reclusive child, I keep this thought in mind:

   "I believe there is a brief magical moment in every relationship when the right statement will change a life. On some level, everything we do with a child is preliminary to that one moment. With each child…one moment" (L. Tobin, *What Do You Do With a Child Like This?* [Duluth: Whole Person Assoc., 1998]).

   Each child you work with deserves that magical moment. So do you.

4. **Someone taught Bobby how to adapt under changing circumstances.** Bobby seems to really be struggling with that issue. If things change —if Mom goes to work, or children are mean to him—he falls apart. Adults working with him need to be adaptable and guide him to learn how to be adaptable too.

5. **Someone taught Bobby that there are alternatives.** He probably learned that through example and guidance. Again, he is not choosing the best ones and is often choosing the same one, loud crying. However, he is not only lashing out. He is still seeking relationships that will help him find alternatives to his hurt.

6. **Finally, someone gave Bobby achievable responsibilities so that he could experience success.** These successes were not necessarily academic. He could cross the bars, pour his juice, take a nap as he did in the story. Or he could kick a ball or play an instrument or set a table. It is important that children not feel unsuccessful because adults give them responsibilities in areas in which they cannot achieve. Many people have successful lives without having been academic or athletic stars.

Children move towards resiliency when adults

- help them tell their stories.

- help them develop self-worth and competence.

- teach them how to connect with others by forming relationships with them.

- teach them how to adapt to changing circumstances.

- help them learn to find alternatives.

- give them achievable responsibilities so they can experience success.

Unfortunately, Bobby also had many adults in his life who didn't provide relationships that supported his resiliency. Or perhaps he encountered traumas that were out of the adults' control—death, illness, poverty—and the adults didn't know how to support him. His behaviors are regressing. Also, what might have worked marginally for him at three and four is becoming less effective as he gets older. People will expect him to become more mature. The crying behaviors will receive more disapproval.

Those who are in Bobby's life now must build on the minimal skills that others have helped him obtain. Otherwise, he will certainly be an unhappy, and perhaps dangerous, adult, and a behavior problem wherever he goes.

Let's leave Bobby now. We wish him well. We hope that the caregivers at his school-age care site, and elsewhere, discover the teaching-relationship model of behavior guidance soon.

Meanwhile, we know that we have the power to provide that "magical moment" in a child's life.

I attended the Children's Defense Fund's national conference a couple of years ago. One event at the conference was a posh dinner attended by community leaders and celebrities. The dinner honored high school seniors who had overcome serious difficulties and traumas. They were responsible people, active in their communities, good students. The Children's Defense Fund presented them with college scholarships. Each recipient gave a short acceptance speech.

I remember one of the young people in particular.

Margarita spoke last. She grew up with a single mother who suffered from schizophrenia. Margarita experienced physical and emotional abuse from other family members. She now runs the household for herself and her mother, who is subject to violent rages. She works with the homeless and edits the school newspaper.

When she received her scholarship, she said, "I want to thank everyone who smiled at me. Everyone who said hello. I want to thank everyone who was ever kind."

In the name of the children who you might not ever know you helped, I want to thank you for getting really good at your work and for smiling, saying hello, and being kind.

Please write your notes, thoughts, or stories here:

Section 11
Do's and Don'ts of Behavior Guidance

Introduction to the Do's and Don'ts

The most effective way to do it, is to do it.

≈ Toni Cade Bambara

It all comes down to this, doesn't it? Doing it. In the first section you looked at various factors that have an impact on behavior guidance: the history of school-age care, your personal history, and children's development. They are all important factors to be aware of and learn more about as you explore all aspects of discipline in school-age care.

But eventually, it does come down to what you do and what you don't do with the kids, every day. What works and what doesn't? What actions will support your new ways of thinking about kids? How can you meet your two objectives: (1) teaching discipline rather than punishing and (2) changing kids' behaviors so that your program runs smoothly and safely?

The do's and don'ts in this section will help you figure out some of that. You already know that this part won't be especially easy, either. But that is one of the reasons your job is so fascinating. You are able to use all parts of your brain. The work helps you perfect skills that are essential in all parts of your life and in any work that you do. You really are lucky, aren't you?

The do's and don'ts will require analytical and creative thinking, an open mind, and a sense of humor. Please remember that this book is designed as an interactive workbook because the best way to learn is through a multi-faceted approach. Reading the text, stories, and exercises is just the beginning of making the ideas your own, ready to put into practice. First, you read the information and/or hear it (or both). You interact with it, you play with it, test it, discuss it, question it in your mind, in your heart, and in your work.

You certainly don't have to agree with everything in this section. But I would ask that you consider the ideas, try to figure out why you do or don't agree. To help you do this, I suggest two rules for this section.

First, no *Yes, but…s*. Give each idea an honest, whole-hearted try, even if you have already tried something like it. Do not dismiss ideas before you internalize them. Give concepts a chance to take hold before you decide that they won't work for you.

Second, enjoy the process. Although it's not always easy, there is much enjoyment in accepting new insights, in practicing skills, in affirming your beliefs.

So, here we go! On with the do's and don'ts!

The Do's and Don'ts

1. **Setting Limits**

   Do: Set limits.

   Don't: Allow children to take over everyone's space and time.

   Don't: Say no very often.

2. **Consequences**

   Do: Use natural, logical, and needs-meeting consequences.

   Don't: Tell children they are inadequate.

   Don't: Rescue children unnecessarily.

   Don't: Use tragic consequences.

3. **Actions Speak Louder Than Words**

   Do: Use actions rather than words.

   Don't: Lecture.

   Don't: Use threats.

4. **Encourage Independence**

   Do: Give children decision-making power.

   Do: Teach responsibility by being responsible.

   Don't: Use bribes.

   Don't: Praise excessively.

   Don't: Belittle.

   Don't: Expect perfection.

5. **It's All About Power**

   Do: Stay out of power struggles.

   Do: Be flexible.

   Don't: Argue with or ignore children.

6. **Cools** *(See chapter 18 for an explanation of this term.)*

   Do: Help children use cools.

   Do: Use reverse cools.

   Don't: Use time-outs.

   Don't: Use corporal punishment.

7. **Feeling Groovy**

   Do: Allow children to express their feelings.

   Do: Notice children's positive behaviors.

   Don't: Always correct children's behaviors.

8. **Who's in the Picture**

   Do: Reframe children's behaviors.

   Do: Use conflict resolution.

Chapter 8

Setting Limits: Do's

by Zahkyia

Children need and want adults to set limits and rules.

≈ David Elkind

Do Set Limits

Children need boundaries. They need and want the security of knowing what is expected of them and of others. Just as we appreciate the stop signs at a busy intersection, they appreciate the rules that help them feel safe.

No doubt your program has rules. You probably have even more than you are aware of. Some of them may not work as automatically as a stop sign generally does, however.

Stop signs work because they are big red octagons that everyone recognizes and understands. If they are hidden behind a bush or a snow bank, they are not effective. If people come from a place where there are no stop signs, they will not understand the limit that the sign represents. Or, if instead of "Stop," the sign said, "Please respect the rights of others to use this intersection," people would not understand what action was expected of them. It wouldn't matter if there were a million stop signs; they still would not be understood.

If a stop sign stood, randomly placed, along a state highway in the middle of the North Dakota plains, with no intersection in sight, it would lose its meaning. The reason people bought into the necessity of a stop sign was that it helped guide them at intersections, and that reason would no longer exist. So, the sign either would get ignored or would cause great confusion.

The limits in your program are a lot like stop signs. If they are not understood or clear or necessary, they lose their meaning and effectiveness. You get into unnecessary debates with children, or they may challenge you to "catch me if you can."

Following a few guidelines will prevent a scenario similar to the stop sign episode from occurring in your program. Effective limits in school-age care meet these three standards:

1. Everyone knows there is a limit.
2. Everyone understands what the limit means.
3. The majority of those affected by the limit buy into it.

Let's examine each standard more closely:

1. Everyone knows there is a limit.

There are many ways to sabotage this standard unknowingly. Remember those bushes and snow banks that covered up the stop signs? The rules in a program can also be hidden. Often they are hidden because they are not defined clearly. In your school-age care program there may be too many rules that are unspoken. You may know the rules because you believe they are "just common sense." But you have not told the children about them. The rules may as well be buried in a snow bank or hidden behind a bush, because the children do not know they exist.

Unspoken rules are dangerous. Sometimes, you believe they are the most important rules because they make so much sense to you. So if your hidden rules are broken, you may be especially disappointed and dismayed, and you may be especially tough with the child who transgressed a rule that is buried in your assumptions about what is common sense. The child probably has a common sense that is different from yours. The child may be genuinely perplexed by the force of your response to his actions. You, being very clear in your mind about the limit's value, may not trust the child's confusion, and a power struggle may ensue. Or, the child may just run as fast as he can from your enforcement of the unspoken rule because it makes no sense to him.

You can often identify hidden rules when you correct a child. The child looks at you and says, "You never told me that," or "How was I supposed to know?" You might respond, "Of course you knew," "Don't get smart," or "Anyone with an ounce of brains would know that," or "It's just the way things are done."

Or you can ask yourself if maybe the rule isn't clearly stated. Is it possible that the child is indeed not aware of the rule?

The child might have suspected that there was a boundary. But think back to the chapters of this book about the developmental stages of schoolagers. Remember that we talked about how kids feel restricted by rules and boundaries, about how they take things literally, and about their great concern for fairness? If there is no understandable boundary, it cannot be fairly enforced, whether or not children guessed that it might be there. Under those circumstances, children can legitimately use the, "Gee, officer, I didn't see the corner of the sign sticking out of the snow bank" excuse. Each person can interpret an unspoken rule in his own way.

For example, let's say you have an unspoken rule about cleanup procedures in the art room. When a child leaves a mess, you might express the rule by saying something like this: "You don't leave a room looking like a tornado hit it." To the child that could mean he should scoop everything into the nearest wastebasket on his way to the gym. To you it could mean that supplies go back in the carefully marked containers that you spent two weeks making after attending a workshop called "Environments Are Essential."

Look at what is happening. The rule is not spoken. A spoken rule would say, "When you are finished with a project, you are expected to put materials away in the labeled containers." Because it is not spoken, you cannot refer to it. So, out of your mouth, perhaps loudly, may come the ineffective and blaming statement about the tornado. You are resentful. You didn't want to go to that environments workshop. After all, they didn't have to schedule it for the same night as the final episode of your favorite TV show. But you went and you learned some things. You tried to put them into practice. You spent hours you couldn't really spare getting the containers ready. And what good did it all do? The kids don't care. You feel like giving up.

Meanwhile, the child is puzzled by your outburst about the ribbons, feathers, and construction paper being left on the table. "That's what we did in this room last year. What's the big deal?" he wonders. "Well, whatever," he decides. "It must be a big deal. I'll keep her happy and put all the stuff in the wastebasket. On my way to the gym."

Of course, his decision just irritates you more. Who knows how long the child with the puzzled look will have to spend picking feathers out of the trash? Or how many tears you will shed that night when your friend asks about your day?

This is not to say that if the rule were known it would be followed all the time. But some of the children would follow it some of the time. Reinforcing it would be a lot easier, and in the child's mind, it would be more fair. In order for a limit to be effective, it has to be known.

Take a few minutes to think about your program or the one you will have some day. Knowing yourself and your expectations, list some of the unspoken rules that might exist in your head.

Example: The kids will put all the materials back in these handy-dandy containers that I spent so much time getting together.

1. _____

_____

2. _____

_____

3. _____

_____

Now use your imagination to think of how you might express those unspoken rules if they are broken:

Example: This place looks like a tornado went through it!

1. _____

_____

2. _____

_____

3. _____

_____

Write a guideline that will make the unspoken rule a spoken rule.

Example: All materials go in the labeled containers when you are done using them.

1. _____

_____

2. _____

_____

3. _____

_____

2. Everyone understands what the limit means.

"Everyone" in this standard includes both children and adults. Often if the children don't understand the limit, neither do the adults. Just because a rule is in some way spoken doesn't mean that it is understood.

Often in school-age care programs you will see the rules posted on the walls. The rules read something like this:

- Be respectful.
- Honor others' possessions.
- Use your inside voice.
- Be polite.
- Listen when spoken to.
- Keep your hands and feet to yourself.
- Be courteous.

Each day the children run into the room saying, "I'm going to read those rules again so I remember them." Right? Of course they don't. Often the rules are read once on the first day of the school year or the summer. After that the sign just hangs there until it is yellow and the corners curl. Or it is moved up higher because it is getting tattered by the children as they pass by.

What does "respect others" mean? What's an "inside voice"? What does "honor" mean? "Sure I'll keep my feet to myself—I'm not going to give them away!"

Most kids don't spend much time discussing the meaning of words. Respect, honor, and courtesy are not concrete words. To children, they are vague.

Abstract words can be confusing even if a child or adult attaches some meaning to them. What is respectful to you might not be respectful to someone else. Where I come from, respect includes looking a person in the eye when you talk to them. To my friend Yoshika, who is from Japan, eye contact would be very disrespectful. It is impossible to enforce misunderstood rules.

Rules that will be understood must be clearly stated in a common language. Involving children in rule making will help. They tell it like it is. What the exact words are will depend on who the kids are, and on what is important to them and to the well-being of their group. In one setting, a rule that says, "No one may bring weapons of any kind to the center," may be essential. In another place, there may not be any need to mention it. If the rule is needed, it certainly is clearer than "Respect others."

Stating limits clearly can also mean breaking a rule that some educators, including school-age care educators, have. That rule states that you never tell a child what NOT to do. There are indeed certain things that we do not want people who live in our communities to do. "No hitting or kicking" is a clear rule. If this sort of limit is needed in any particular setting, it, too, is more specific, and therefore easier to understand than "Respect others." Of course we want children to behave in positive ways. But sometimes very clear announcements of what is unacceptable also have to be made.

Another belief held by some educators is that there should be as few rules as possible. This belief is based on the premise, I think, that having too many rules is confusing. Today's children, given half a chance, can run a computer, program a VCR, know all the statistics of a sports team, know the names of all dinosaurs, and recite the time and the day of the week of hundreds of TV shows. They are not that easily confused. What confuses them is if the rules are not in a language they can understand.

It's the third week of summer *and the school-age program that Rachel supervises is quickly falling apart. As usual, there are new summer staff members, many of them inexperienced. There are 150 kids, many of whom have never seen each other before. Twenty-five percent of the children attend special-needs classes in school. Another twenty percent attend the school-age program only in the summer. Many of those kids are convinced that if they get into enough trouble, their parents will give in and let them stay at home. It is terribly hot. To make matters worse, "Mommy and Me" and other parent education classes meet, calmly and quietly, in the same building every day.*

Parents are complaining. Kids are unhappy. Staff wish they had taken that job at McDonald's. The program's already shaky reputation is going downhill fast. Something has to happen. Rachel gathers the staff and the kids in the common area. The atmosphere is a little tense.

Rachel has never called a large meeting like this before, so the kids know it's important. She begins by saying, "This is the only summer of 1998 that any of us will have. When you are old like me you will want to remember that this was a happy summer. You will want to tell your kids about all the cool things that you did. Look around you. Every person here wants to do the same thing. They want to get up every morning this summer and get that great summer vacation feeling. You all know that 'I don't have to go to school, I'm going to have a fun day' feeling. If you want to have that feeling, if you want to have a great summer, you can cheer now." Everyone cheers to excess, of course. It breaks the tension if nothing else.

The staff and kids divide into small groups. Rachel then tells the whole group that everyone is going to make the rules together. The rules that will guarantee that this will be the greatest summer of 1998 anyone could have. They, staff and children, are to name the rules they think are important. A staff person will write them all down, just as they are said. They can't use bad language. Rachel will put the rules together, and everyone's rules will be included.

The next day she gives each child and each staff person, including herself, a copy of the rules in contract form. In small groups all over the building and outside, staff and kids go over the rules. They ask questions if they don't understand. They speak up if they think a rule they have suggested has been left out. They challenge rules and wording that don't seem fair. Everyone takes it seriously. They understand that everyone, including children, staff, and director, will be expected to sign the contract the next day and abide by it.

Staff meet and make the changes agreed upon in the small groups. Rachel recopies the contracts. They include 86 rules and spaces for the children's, staff members', and parents' signatures. All children and staff sign the rules and recite a short pledge saying that they understand the 1998 summer rules, that they agree to follow them, and that they agree to remind others to follow the rules without being mean about it.

Rachel copies all the contracts and puts them in the kids' and staff's files. She sends copies home for the parents to read, sign, and return. Only about half the contracts come back, but that's okay. Parents have made many positive comments. They begin to ask at the end of the day how the contract thing is going. Rachel distributes copies of the contracts to the other programs in the building to inform them that the school-age care program takes behavior issues seriously. Staff in other programs say they appreciate the efforts and have noticed a difference.

Best of all, the behavior problems diminish dramatically. Staff can remind children about the contract. Children can remind staff about the contract. Children can remind children. Staff can remind staff. Staff can pull the contracts out of the files if anyone needs a visual reminder.

Different age groups make banners and badges that proclaim "1998—The Best Summer Ever" or "Happy Summer Memories—1998." One group takes pictures and tapes them up in the hall under their banner. Another group puts together a yearbook. The small groups meet briefly once a week to discuss how the contract is working. At the end of the summer there is a huge "The Best Summer Yet!" party.

۞ ۞

Could anyone in the program recite all 86 rules? No. But the rules reflected what was important to the kids. They were also written in the kids' words. "Don't peek under the toilet stalls," was not translated by an adult to say, "Provide others with privacy." "No put downs" didn't get translated to "Be courteous." The number of rules didn't matter. The common language and the process did. That is one model of success.

There are many other ways to accomplish the same goal. Some successful programs make, with the kids' input, only one rule. That rule says something like, "We don't hurt people here." Sometimes these programs have each room or group make a list of directions that help people to follow the one big rule. So in that art room we mentioned before, a rule might be "Put away the art supplies when you are done with them. That way no one will be upset when they are looking for what they need. The stuff will last longer so more of us will get to use it. The teacher will have more time to help those who want help. The teacher won't get stuck with all the work." In other words, "We don't hurt people here." In programs with just that one rule, participants discuss its practical application frequently.

The two examples given here took a lot of time for both staff and children. But the kids learned a lot and the programs ran more smoothly than they would have with unclear limits. There are many ways to try to insure that everyone knows what the rules mean.

Write down a limit in your program that you have not formally presented to the children—a limit that you believe they should just know because it is common sense to you.

_____

_____

Give an example of a time when a child did not keep within this limit. What happened? What was your reaction? How did the child respond?

_____

_____

_____

_____

Describe what you will do to make the limit more clear to the children.

_____

_____

_____

_____

3. The majority of those affected by the rule buy into it.

In the previous example, much work went into the buy-in process. If Rachel, as supervisor, had passed out the 86 rules and said, "Sign here," would there have been the same positive response? Not likely.

Why was it successful? For many reasons. Creative, hardworking, sincere staff are at the top of the list. Also, the process met the first two standards. Everyone certainly knew there were rules, and the rules were written in an understandable way.

The process also met the third standard. Buy-in was a key element. A common goal was established for the group: a happy, memorable summer. The goal was based on the self-interest of each participant. Each child or adult wants to have happy days and great memories. Everyone's individual goals can be met if the whole group has and follows guidelines that insure everyone's good time. If the children had been told that they had to do this exercise because there were complaints from other programs in the building, would it have worked? Probably not.

What also made it easy for children to buy into the 86 rules was that each child had a voice in making them. Each individual's suggestions were included and were not translated into a different language. The rules made sense. Each person had an opportunity to review all the rules. Their questions and opinions were taken seriously. Revisions were made based on their comments. Not everyone got exactly what they wanted, but the democratic process allowed the most input possible, and the kids recognized it.

The kids signed the contract. By signing a contract, the children formalized their knowledge of and commitment to the rules. The staff signed the contract. By doing so, they let the children know that the rules were fair and would be followed by everyone. Parents signed, or at least knew about, the contract, so the children knew that their parents knew the rules and that they supported their children and the staff in abiding by them. Buy-in, buy-in, buy-in—children, staff, and parents, being included in the process, invested in it. Their signatures on the contracts were concrete proof that they were all in this together.

Ongoing weekly discussions allowed the children and the staff to continue to refine the rules and how they were enforced and what they meant. Each week, then, the commitment to the contract was renewed. Kids developed projects that were fun, community-building, and age-appropriate to reinforce their commitment. They got positive strokes from parents, staff, and others in the building.

Clearly, the limits were the kids' limits, the ones that were important to them and to their peers. They were also the staff's limits. Staff had equal opportunities to let the kids know what was important to them and why. Both staff and kids were respected during the process, which took time but taught so much.

Getting kids and staff to buy into limits is often difficult. Make up a story about a school-age care program that does everything right around limit setting *except* getting buy-in from the kids and the staff. The story can be as funny or as tragic as you want it to be. Have fun!

_____

_____

_____

_____

_____

_____

_____

_____

_____

_____

Now look at your program and see if any of the behaviors you wrote creatively about in your story are popping up at your site.

If there are no similarities, do you believe that the kids and staff are invested in the success of the limits?

If so, how did you achieve buy-in?

_____

_____

_____

_____

If there are similarities, what are they?

_____

_____

_____

_____

Exercise continued on next page

These behaviors may be the result of kids or staff not buying into the limits. What will you do in your program to increase the level of buy-in?

_____

_____

_____

_____

Keep up the good work of setting limits and making rules with children. You are giving them what they need and want as they begin to internalize guidelines and become self-directed.

Please write your notes, thoughts, or stories here:

Chapter 9

Setting Limits: Don'ts

by Zahkyia

True self respect, being different from false pride, leads inevitably to respecting others.

≈ Virginia Moore

Don't Allow Children to Take Over Everyone's Space and Time

One of the dangers of having children in child care and school-age programs throughout childhood is that they may not learn how to respect other people's time, possessions, and space. In a home setting there are things that belong only to the adults or to other children. There may be knives, computers, sewing machines, or Grandma Maria's mahogany table that cannot be touched by the children. They may not be allowed to use their siblings' toys or clothes without permission. The adults' and siblings' bedrooms may be off limits. Also, in a home, adults have many tasks. They don't spend all their time interacting with the children. They may be busy paying bills, cooking supper, talking on the phone, or doing the laundry.

Most programs do not have those boundaries. In good programs, equipment and supplies are at the children's level and available for all the children to choose. Everyone in a child-centered school-age program is there for the children, and that is the way it should be. Supervisors tell the staff that it is their job to interact with the kids. They are not to have their own conversations or sit by and just watch children.

I certainly don't want to suggest that the children should have fewer materials or that the staff should not spend the majority of their time with the children. However, there is a need to teach children in programs the same principles they might learn at home. Children need to learn that the world doesn't operate just for them. They need to learn how to respect other people's time and space.

Those respectful attitudes can be taught in a variety of ways. Part of learning to respect others' space and time is having one's own space and time respected. For example, children should know that they are free to use materials by themselves. If someone asks to play with them, they may say, "No, I want to play by myself right now." Children can learn to negotiate a plan that will allow the other child to play with the toy at a later time. They can also learn to listen to the other child's request and take a minute to think about whether allowing the other child to join in might be a good idea. Forced "sharing" only teaches a child resentment. There certainly are times when adults don't want to hand over the book they are reading or the quilt they are making, just because someone else wants to use it.

The program can be set up to value each child's space and time. Children should have some space in the program in which to keep their own possessions safe. A hook is not sufficient. We are all too familiar with the coats and hats all in a pile on the floor to think that that might work. The private space may be a locker, a milk crate, a box, a cubby. Enough space is needed for children to put their things from school and to neatly store finished or ongoing projects. A large project that cannot be finished because of time constraints, like a block castle or a model airplane, should be stored in a safe place until the child can complete it.

Programs can also respect children's space by providing spaces in which children can be alone. Children who tend to be introverts can be overwhelmed with the constant need to interact. Children who are always on the go need places where they can stay out of the action for a while and calm down. All children need places and times when they can be by themselves to think, imagine, or just be. Some programs have a small tent that can be used by only one person. Or a bunch of pillows on the floor that can be used only by three or fewer people who want to have a conversation. Some programs have "alone rooms" where children can go to do solitary activities. The rooms are designed by partitions and furniture placement to provide nooks and corners where children can read, listen with headphones, write, draw, or daydream. Conversation is left outside the door. Being with peers from morning until night can be stressful, and kids under stress act out.

In order for children to learn how to respect the space of staff members, staff can have certain areas that are for adults only. Sometimes it is possible to have a staff lounge or office. If that space is at such a distance that it is not easily seen by the children, another space should be designated for staff in the children's area. The old scary teachers' lounge tucked away somewhere in the building , where kids went by on tiptoe, was great for staff, but it didn't do much to teach respect for boundaries in a common space. Perhaps a small section of a large room can be partitioned off to provide a place where staff can have a place to relax or work. A cupboard or two or some shelves could be for staff use only. Staff can have a chair with perhaps a bookshelf next to it with staff books. The chair and the books are used by children only if a child asks and a staff person agrees.

It is important that you not only set up such places for staff and kids but that the reasons for the space are explained and alluded to often. Carefully thought-out ideas sometimes don't get used appropriately by the children because adults forget to teach them why they exist and how to use them.

Montessori programs often introduce classroom materials one at a time. Every few days or so the children learn how to use a new material, what its purpose is, what the limits around its use are, what words they need in order to understand the material. When the children are comfortable using one thing, another is introduced. School-age programs could, perhaps, slow down a little and use similar techniques.

We sometimes flood schoolagers with environments that are full of possibilities without giving them the time, information, or language they need to be competent. Children can learn the meaning of words like *privacy, alone, respect,* and *conversation* if they are put into a meaningful context and used with some frequency. They can understand the limits and opportunities that you are offering them. Children who know that their space is respected learn more easily to respect others' space.

For example, consider what is happening in the following scenario:

Melanie saunters into the staff area. *One staff person is on the phone. Another is on break, reading a book.*
"*So this is what you guys do back here,*" *Melanie says, picking up papers and pencils from the desk and examining them.* "*You gab on the phone and sit around. Pretty easy job, if you ask me.*"

⊚ ⊚

A knee jerk response to this statement could easily be, "No one asked you. If you think it's so easy try it sometime. Put those things down right now. Get out of here. You know kids aren't allowed in here."

Obviously a power struggle is about to take place here. In the course of the struggle the child and the adult will say things that are negative and blaming.

Another response, if the program is respecting kids' space and teaching them to respect others' space, could go something like this:

Staff member Jill responds, "*Melanie. Hi. You know we're crazy about you but this is our space. One of the things that we do around here is let each other have space, right? We don't interrupt you when you are in the alone tent or the conversation pit, do we?*"

"*Oh, yeah you do. You made me leave the tent yesterday.*"

"*Why did I do that?*"

"*I don't know. Why did you?*"

"*Come on, Melanie, you do know that your mom came to pick you up for your dentist appointment. Different situation. Right?*"

Melanie nods her head.

"*Okay, off you go. Catch you later.*"

๑ ๏

This exchange starts on the positive note that the child is liked. It's not about her, it's about the mutually recognized respect that children and adults get in the program. She is taught again about the value of privacy. She is asked to affirm the reality of the situation. Yes, her privacy is respected whenever possible. Yesterday was an unavoidable exception. She is expected to act now in a way that respects the staff's space.

Children's conversations should also be respected. Adults need to ask permission to interject their comments. In case of necessary interruptions, the situation can be explained. "I'm sorry to interrupt your conversation with Jared, but we have to use this table to prepare snack now. You can move to that table if you wish. Thanks."

In turn, children need to respect adults' conversations. They also should interrupt only if necessary. "I'm sorry to interrupt you, Jenny, but my cooking club is meeting in five minutes. Could you put this project on the piano for me so that I can finish it tomorrow? Thanks."

Intentionally teaching children how to respect others' time, possessions, and space not only helps the kids develop attitudes that will be valuable throughout their lives, but also reduces kids' and adults' stress. Children who are developing a sense of self, of their own need to be alone, or to be quiet, or to use something all by themselves, won't have to carve out space in the program in other ways, like fighting over materials, excluding others in a hurtful way, or losing emotional control because they are overwhelmed by constant demands and stimulation. Clearly, the boundaries that protect their space and privacy will eliminate a number of behavior problems.

Visualize the physical space of the program you work in or with which you are familiar. Think of three physical changes or additions that you could make to give children and staff a sense of privacy:

1. _____

_____

2. _____

_____

3. _____

_____

What materials will you need to make the changes?

_____

_____

What words would you teach the children to help them understand how to respect the intent of the physical changes?

1. _____

2. _____

3. _____

4. _____

How and when would you explain the changes to the children?

_____

_____

_____

Don't Say No Very Often

This rule is like a thermometer for how successful you have been at setting, teaching, and getting children to buy into limits. If you find yourself saying "no" all the time, you can think of yourself as having a temperature, indicating that the "no" virus is infecting your program. It is time, then, to evaluate what allowed this virus to spread. Sometimes it means that your resistance is temporarily lowered. You are exhausted or it's the day after Halloween or the day before summer break. In these cases, it is only a twenty-four hour flu.

A second possibility is that you just say "no" too much. You may have a bad habit. This habit allows your "no" temperature to remain elevated for long periods of time. You don't even know it. You just know that you are kind of cranky, slightly angry, and often tired. To determine if habit may be the problem, make a temperature chart and follow the prescription to reduce your temp. Even if you don't think this is your problem, please try this exercise. If you are not in a program, track your negative responses in another part of your life to see how often "no" is your response. You may learn something about yourself.

For the next five days that you work with kids, mark down every time you say "no" or anything that means "no," like "Stop that ruckus!" or "Cut it out!" For these five days you don't have to hold back. When you feel like saying "no," go ahead and say it. At the end of the five days, count the checks on a piece of paper. You really have to develop a system to physically mark down the number of no's or you will under- or overestimate significantly. If you work with someone, the other person could mark them down, quietly, and give you the results at the end of the five days. Or you could carry a piece of paper with you and make a check mark on it every time you catch yourself.

Assuming that you are with the kids about four hours each day, you should have about twenty hours of teaching time tracked after five days. If you spend significantly more or less time with kids every day, just keep track for about twenty hours of teaching time.

After the twenty hours are over, complete this statement:

I tracked the number of times that I said "no" for twenty hours of teaching time. I said "no" about _____ times.

Then, fill in the thermometer and read your temperature:

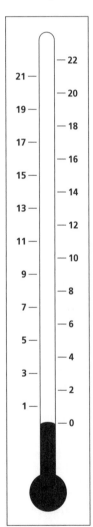

0–3 No's: You forgot to record. Try again.

4–10 No's: Normal temp. You're doing just fine.

10–15 No's: Elevated temp. For the next five days, stop yourself before you say "no" and ask yourself if it's necessary, or if you could just let it go by without anything catastrophic happening.

15–20 No's: Dangerous temperature. You probably need a vacation or to fix something in your personal life. If you can't do either, take the strong medicine of not saying "no" or anything like it for the next five days. See how it feels. Observe what does or doesn't happen. Things should improve.

21+ No's: Re-read this chapter. Take an attitude inventory. Review the standards for setting limits effectively. Take a hot bath and a vacation. Fix your personal life. Do whatever you have to do to break the pattern. It takes too much out of you to be that negative, and it contributes to a highly charged environment for the kids. That atmosphere will, of course, lead to more misbehavior, which will lead to more no's if the virus goes untreated. You can fix it!

Evaluating the Program

Sometimes a high "no" fever indicates that one or more of the three standards of limit setting are not being met. While you plan your vacation, work on fixing your personal life, and break old habits, you can evaluate how you are meeting the three standards in your program.

Remember the three standards?

> **1.** Everyone knows that there is a limit.
>
> **2.** Everyone understands what the limit means.
>
> **3.** The majority of those affected by the limit buy into it.

If you have a high "no" temperature, and especially if other teachers in the program do as well, it's worth a look to make sure that the program in general is meeting kids' needs for limits. There are several ways you can evaluate your program to see how well it is meeting the three standards.

One way is to survey the children. You can send the survey home and ask the parents to help their children complete it. Or you can have older children ask younger ones the questions and write down the answers. The older children can complete the surveys themselves. You can get high school volunteers to help children complete the surveys. Or, you can complete the surveys with individual children over a period of time. The time it takes to complete the survey will be put to good use. Children and parents will know that you take discipline and their input seriously.

Here are some questions you can ask on the survey:

1. What are the five most important limits in our program?

2. Give one example of what each rule means you can or cannot do.

3. Which of the rules do you think is important? Why?

4. Which rules don't you agree with? Why?

Evaluate the surveys to be sure children know what the limits are, understand what they mean, and buy into them. If one or all of these isn't true, you have some work to do in the program before you recover from your "no" fever.

Another way to evaluate your limit-setting process is through informal discussions with kids. Use the same basic survey questions. Put their answers up on flip charts as they give them. Ask other staff members to do the same with other groups of kids.

Another possibility is to track, along with other staff, the limits that are most frequently not met, and how the kids respond when they are told that they are overstepping a limit. Discuss the findings at a staff meeting. If it is not possible to involve the supervisor and the other staff, analyze the findings on your own. If you find that the children consistently violate limits which you know have not formally been explained to them in multiple ways (group announcements, letters to parents, kids' and parents' newsletters, one-on-one conferences, signed contracts, student handbooks, and so on), you have identified part of your problem. It is likely that some children do not know there is a limit.

You may notice that kids are often saying, "I didn't know you wanted me to..." or "I don't get it," or "How was I supposed to know you didn't want me to . . ." You may notice that consistently, as a group, they are not meeting expectations. Either of these situations are signs that the children may not understand what the limits mean; your program is not meeting the second standard. You may have to check the language of the limits. You can reword the limits into simpler, more direct words and see if that helps.

You may not be meeting the third standard, which requires that children buy into the limits. You can watch and listen to see if children are accepting the limits as important. If you hear a lot of "I don't care" or "It doesn't matter to me" or "So?" you may have to work on getting the kids to see the value of the limits through contracts, discussions, or some other means.

You can probably think of other ways to assess your program in this area. Whatever means you decide to use, remember that behavior guidance takes time and that it's worth it. Even if you feel things are going well in your program and you aren't saying "no" too often, ongoing evaluation is helpful.

The following exercise will help keep you on track. If you are not currently working in a program, decide which way you would proceed with evaluation and decide how you would solve the problems.

Please complete these sentences:

I evaluated the three standards by…

_____

_____

I determined that these standards were not being met or could be met more fully:

_____

_____

The actions I plan to take to meet the standards are…

_____

_____

_____

Two weeks after the actions are implemented, evaluate again. (Please remember to do this. Put it on your calendar.) Track the number of times you say "no" for another twenty teaching hours to see if the number has changed.

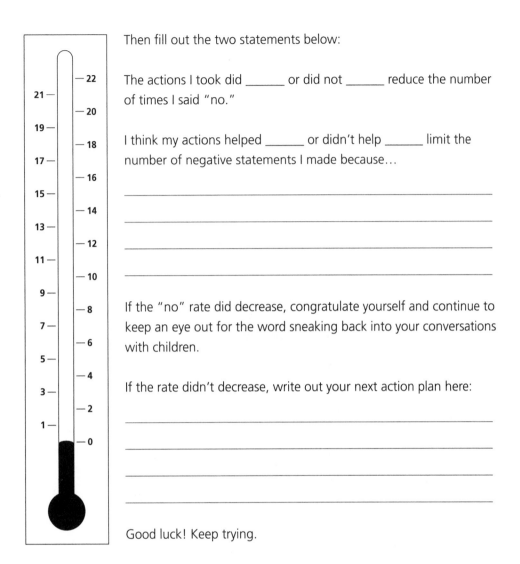

Then fill out the two statements below:

The actions I took did _____ or did not _____ reduce the number of times I said "no."

I think my actions helped _____ or didn't help _____ limit the number of negative statements I made because…

_____

_____

_____

_____

If the "no" rate did decrease, congratulate yourself and continue to keep an eye out for the word sneaking back into your conversations with children.

If the rate didn't decrease, write out your next action plan here:

_____

_____

_____

_____

Good luck! Keep trying.

There you have them, the first Do's and Don'ts. Right now, DO give yourself a little break. DON'T get discouraged or forget to come back. You are well on the way to being even more competent in the work you do and reducing the stress that it takes to do it. Congratulations!

Chapter 10

Consequences: Do's

by LaNaya

A person ultimately decides for himself! And in the end education must be education toward the ability to decide.

≈ Viktor Frankl

Do Use Natural, Logical, and Needs-Meeting Consequences

Consequences. A huge problem in school-age care. What do you do if a rule is broken? If a limit is exceeded? If a child does something inappropriate? There are many answers to those questions. The goal of behavior guidance is that the child will learn how to judge for herself what the consequence of her actions will be, and then learn to handle those consequences. Perhaps, she will learn that she doesn't want to deal with those consequences again, and then try to avoid the behavior that produced it. But, be wary! The learning has to flow from the event. If consequences are imposed in a punitive, demeaning, shaming way, children will learn anger and self-hatred. Those lessons will perpetuate the misbehavior.

When thinking of consequences, please remember the discussion about punishment from section I. (See page 4.) You did not get into school-age care to punish kids. It is around the issue of consequences that we often get caught in the punishment trap. The dilemma is that children don't know all the consequences of their actions. They don't always think ahead. They make mistakes. They may have learned to function in ways that are harmful to themselves and others. Until they learn to make their own decisions in a competent way, you have to deal with their behaviors. You don't want to punish. You can't ignore the behaviors. How do you teach children in a way that keeps your program safe and secure for all of them? You may choose natural, logical, or needs-meeting consequences as teaching tools.

If behavior guidance is about teaching, then consequences should help children learn. In their book *Children the Challenge* (New York: Duell, 1964), Rudolph Dreikurs and Vicki Soltz developed the concepts of *natural* and *logical* consequences. These consequence have some connection to the child's action. There is a natural or logical link between the action and the consequences of the action. In most cases, the logical nature of the consequence will help the child learn how to decide for herself how to react to the results of her behavior. Or, to stop the behavior if the consequences are undesirable.

For example, if you are driving to work today and get into a fender-bender accident, the police are not likely to tell you to go sit on the curb until your mother gets there and write, "I will not get into any more accidents," a thousand times. But you will have to call the insurance company, get three estimates on the damages, and take the bus while your car is in the shop. You will have to deal with the consequences. And in the future, you will probably leave a little more distance between yourself and the driver in front of you. It is very important that the children who are in school-age care programs learn how to clean up their messes. It is also very important that the consequences that teach them how to deal with their behavior are sensible and logical. The kids may not like them, as you may not like doing what you have to do after a car accident, but as long as the consequences have something to do with repairing the damage done by the child's behavior, they will help the child learn.

*Ill*ogical consequences are often simply punitive. They deprive children of the power to learn from a situation, to truly learn the consequences of their actions, to decide how to deal with the consequences, and to move on with their lives.

I remember a conference I had with the parent of a seventh grader. He was one of those kids who is always in trouble. His mother was baffled. "I've tried everything," she said. "I've taken away his stereo. He can't go out of the house after five o'clock. He can't talk on the phone. He can't ride his bike. He can watch TV only on the weekends."

"How does he get his stereo back?" I asked. I was really just curious. Parents have the toughest job in the world; I try to be supportive.

"Why, when he gets to be responsible."

"When will he be able to go out after five o'clock?"

"Same thing, when he shapes up."

It turned out that she couldn't remember why she decided on any of the individual restrictions, and she had not told him what he had to do to lift them. The boy was stuck. He had no way out. The restrictions had nothing to do with his actions. He wasn't given the information that would allow him to handle the consequences of his actions. Discouraged, he had given up.

The consequences in that story were illogical—they were not specifically related to the boy's behavior, and they didn't help him repair the damage done by his behavior. *Logical* and *natural* consequences make more sense and are less discouraging.

In the chapter opening illustration, the girl spills a carton of milk. It happens. What will the consequence be? The staff person in the example suggests a *logical consequence.* "It looks like you have some cleaning up to do." Nicely put, assuming it is not said in an angry voice. The staff person gives the girl the information she needs to find a mop and a bucket. After the girl cleans up the puddle, the staff person might say, "I see you finished cleaning up. Do you want some more milk?"

That is a *logical consequence.* It makes sense. It is not punishment. It is what the staff person would do if she spilled her milk. The girl learned that she needs to clean up her own spills. She even learned where the mop is. She may or may not have been able to prevent the milk from spilling. That doesn't really matter. It had to be cleaned up and she did it.

A *natural consequence* for this situation might be that the girl doesn't get any more milk. In this case, the natural consequence feels punitive.

When I imagine how the girl would feel if she received that consequence, I remember the time I knocked over the display of cereal boxes in the grocery store. I was embarrassed. Everyone stopped and looked at me. We all wondered what my consequence would be.

In that moment, the moment between the action and the reaction, what a child or even an adult feels is fear. Fear of humiliation and blame. Do you remember moments like that in your life? How your stomach felt? How your fear lay in waiting as the consequences loomed? "If you get blamed or shamed," your fear may say to you, "you can get angry, kick a cereal box, and leave the store in a huff." Or, your fear might say, "If you get blamed or shamed, you can cry and feel even worse about yourself. You deserve it."

But imagine that instead of humiliating you by banning you from the cereal section, the manager says, "Accidents happen." You heave a sigh of relief. Fear goes away, along with its familiar script. Your self-esteem says, "She's right. I just brushed the cereal stack with my coat. It could happen to anyone." You help pick up the boxes and go on with your life.

In the case of the girl who spilled the milk, there was probably that moment of fear. If she had to follow the natural consequence and sit with her friends, eating dry cereal, she would feel humiliated. She might react by pushing the cereal aside and leaving in a huff. Or she might internalize the shame and cry her way through her corn flakes. The natural consequence would have taught guilt. And the child would not have the nutrients, both vitamin D and self-esteem, that she needed for the day.

L. Tobin named two other kinds of consequences in *What Do You Do With a Child Like This?: Inside the Lives of Troubled Children* (Duluth: Whole Person Assoc., 1991). Tobin describes these consequences as *needs-meeting* and *tragic*.

A *needs-meeting consequence* could be added to the logical consequence in the example. Perhaps the staff person noticed that the girl opened the milk carton incorrectly. Because of that, when she tried to pour the milk, it spilled. The staff could help the girl learn how to open the next carton.

A *tragic consequence* might occur if the staff person said something like this: "I can't believe you spilled your milk again. What a mess! The custodian is going to be really angry. That's it, no more milk on cereal for the rest of the year. You can just eat it dry. Now get out of here. You're done eating." The tragedy is clear. The child would be humiliated, wouldn't get her breakfast, and would have learned nothing. The staff person would be tired from her angry outburst and would be left with the mess to clean up. The room would be tense for everyone. The child might cover the shamed feelings by saying, "Who cares if I eat that junk anyway!" The staff person might respond angrily and a long, senseless scene could ensue.

Natural, logical, and needs-meeting consequences are the most appropriate tools from which to choose. Be sure to think through the effects of each type of consequence. In the example above of the spilled milk, the natural consequence was not a good choice, because it felt punitive. With practice, you will be able to assess a situation quickly and decide which consequence teaches the most. Be careful not to use these consequences as a way to disguise punishment. A tragic consequence can be the result of hidden punishment.

Because it is possible to twist the consequences into another battle over power, control, and punishment, some educators do not advocate the use of natural, logical, or needs-based consequences. However, if you use them thoughtfully as ways to help children learn from their mistakes, find a way to fix what was broken, and move on, these tools can be respectful and effective. They can help kids find their own solutions.

The very next time a child does something that makes you want to punish, talk loudly (maybe even yell), lecture, or give a time-out: STOP! THINK! "Does my reaction have anything to do with the child's action?"

If you come up with something that is

- more logical

- more naturally linked to the action

- not punitive

- not shaming, and

- will help the child learn how to clean up after himself in the future,

you are on your way.

Later, you will want to think about what other options you had. You can then ask yourself if the consequence could or should have been needs-based rather than natural, or logical rather than needs-based, or if a consequence was necessary at all. Eventually, practice will make perfect—well, almost perfect.

Practice Scenarios for Giving Consequences

Let's practice giving consequences with a few scenarios. I hope you are in a situation in which you can discuss the scenarios with others. If you are taking a class or working through the book with other staff, let the instructor or supervisor know that you need time for discussion. One way to integrate these consequence options into your setting is to think out loud with others. Their challenges, encouragement, and differing viewpoints will help you.

If you are working with this book on your own, you are first of all to be commended. The children you are with are fortunate to have you in their lives. Secondly, find other people who are interested enough to talk with you. These people don't have to be in the field. You could talk to your spouse, friends, siblings, roommates, whoever will debate the ins and outs of consequences with you.

If you are a parent, discussing these issues with other adults who are involved in your children's lives would be great! Often, after a workshop, a participant will tell me that she gained insight into her parenting role as well as into her professional one.

Scenario 1:

The setting: It's late afternoon in the school-age care program where you work. Children are mostly engaged in self-directed activity and some parents are coming to pick up their children. You are the only staff person in the room. One child, Brad, is building contentedly by himself in the block corner.

The incident: Jones kicks down the block tower that Brad just completed.

Natural consequence: Jones has to deal with Brad and his reactions to the situation.

Logical consequence: You tell Jones to help pick up the blocks. You ask Brad if he wants Jones to help him rebuild or if he wants to do it alone. If Brad wants to rebuild by himself or doesn't want to rebuild at all, Jones is to leave Brad alone.

Needs-meeting consequence: You help Jones and Brad pick up the blocks. You engage them in a conversation about what happened and how it made each of them feel. Together you come up with the next step.

Tragic consequence: Jones is put on a time-out. He is forced to apologize to Brad. He is told he cannot be in the block area for the rest of the week.

Which consequence do you think is the most effective? Why?

_____

_____

_____

_____

You probably found that you had questions about the kids involved that you couldn't answer with the information I gave you. Your answer depends on what you know about the children. As you will see throughout the Do's and Don'ts, your relationship with the kids with whom you work is the biggest single factor in effective behavior guidance. A relationship allows you to tailor your actions to the children's needs. It lays a foundation of trust so the children are more likely to respond to you in a positive way.

Let's say that Jones is a loner without many friends. You have been talking to him about how that must feel. He hasn't been very responsive, but he has seemed to listen. You have told him that when he is feeling left out, he can come to you. Together you can try to find a way to solve his problem. Brad is pretty easygoing and thoughtful. He's popular with his peers. It's even unusual that he would be working on a project alone. You and he have an ongoing joke-of-the-day contest.

Given who the children are, and their relationships with you, the natural consequence might be a good choice. You stay out of it. Keeping an eye on what happens, you let Brad tell Jones how he feels and if he wants Jones to do anything about it. It may work out fine. Later, you might talk to Jones about what happened and try to get him to recognize what he was feeling. He may conclude that he was feeling left out. You can figure out with him why he didn't come to you for help. If he feels that asking for help wouldn't work for him, you can help him devise other strategies, such as watching the goldfish or playing with clay when he feels angry about feeling excluded.

The logical consequence is probably not a good choice in this situation. Jones probably feels inferior to Brad. He may get angry about picking up the blocks. He may act out or refuse to pick them up. Brad will probably respond gallantly, feeding Jones' sense of inadequacy.

The needs-meeting consequence appears to be another good choice. You have already had some conversations with Jones about his feelings, so talking that way wouldn't be brand new. You have a comfortable relationship with Brad. He will probably cooperate. It might be interesting to find out why Brad was working alone. Some positive things about being alone might emerge.

If Jones isn't just the bad guy but can contribute ideas that are helpful to the solution, he may become more aware of his friendship skills. Brad might also recognize those skills. Brad and Jones will have the opportunity to begin building a relationship in the process of solving the problem.

The tragic consequence is just that, tragic. Jones is further isolated from the group and left alone to dwell on his inadequacies. He is thrust into the role of the bad guy. Brad is seen as the really good guy. Jones can easily conclude that he can never be that good. His banishment from peers in the block area is proof, for a week, that he is a rotten kid.

Consequences for Swearing The next scenario concerns swearing, a problem common to many school-age care programs. Like many school-age care teachers, I have spent time trying to eradicate it.

I was the teacher for the fifth and sixth graders in a school-age care program. I was at my wit's end about the problem of swearing. The site had children from home situations that differed greatly. In some homes swearing was common and more or less accepted. Swearing in some homes was offensive; in others it was sinful. I was under pressure to eliminate it from the program. I tried to give the kids some time to change, because some of them were going to have difficulty breaking the habit. Usually I didn't make pronouncements and list universal consequences. But I felt I had to make it obvious that I was doing something about the problem.

I worked long into one night coming up with what I thought was a solution. I invented a system that I put on a chart and explained to the children. It seemed reasonably logical and fair to me.

No Swearing Policy

1. The first time you swear, in a week, you will be verbally reminded to stop.

2. The second time you swear you will get your name on the board with a check.

3. The third time you swear you get another check and stay out of the gym (where most of the swearing occurred) for the day.

4. The fourth time you swear you get another check and I call your parents at work.

5. The fifth time you swear you are suspended for a week.

6. At the end of the week, all checks are erased.

The kids listened. There was a moment of silence when I finished explaining. They were figuring out what it meant to them.

"I get one free swear a week!" called out one of the main culprits.

That inspired more comments. "I'm going right to suspension," said another.

"My parents don't care if I swear, so I get four free swears!"

"You just try to keep me out of the gym!"

And so forth and so on. I pulled rank and told them this was going to happen whether they liked it or not and that we'd see if their parents cared. That brought on a barrage of swearing from those who had to test the system. I kept the swearers in the room. The rest I sent to the gym.

By this time, I had figured out that I had blown it. I think I got such a boisterous response because I was acting in a way that I didn't usually act. The kids were used to being treated fairly and having some input. They couldn't verbalize those things, but they knew that in some sense they were being treated unfairly. And they reacted to it.

Partially because I didn't have a clue how to undo what I had done, I told the kids we wouldn't discuss the plan anymore that day. They could choose to do activities in the room; I would work on cleaning out the closet. After about half an hour, my head began to clear. I told them that we would meet the next day, and that I wanted some serious help with solutions to the swearing problem.

They came the next day with many ideas. One child walked beside me as we moved from the bus to the room. "I stayed up all night thinking about this," he confided, very quietly.

I announced that the group that had gone to the gym the previous day would go again, and that the other group had decided to have a meeting. Some of the gym kids wanted to attend the meeting. "Not this time," I said.

The meeting began. No one questioned whether or not swearing should be prohibited. They all knew it had to be. The kids started sharing their ideas. They would remind each other to stop. Because they knew that swearing was a signal that they were losing control, they said they would walk away and think for a second after they swore the first time. They thought that staff could just touch them on the shoulder when they forgot and a bad word came out.

They talked about not wanting to be looked upon by the other kids as the bad kids. Why couldn't people tell them once in a while what they did that was good, in front of those other kids? Could they be given a leadership role like hall monitor sometimes? If they swore, maybe someone else would get to do the job for a while. They would keep other words in their heads that they could use instead of swear words. They would try to think of one or two of those words as they walked into the school-age care room each morning and afternoon. They suggested putting up a sign that said "Swear Free Zone." A few said that if their parents were called at work they would get punished and that would just make them madder. And so on and so on.

We discussed over three days. On the fourth day we brought all the kids together and shared the ideas. We asked for other suggestions. The "meeting kids" (as they were now known) got positive feedback on their ideas. The other kids offered to help. Some admitted that they had some bad habits, too.

We all wrote a letter to send home to parents that said we were working to be a "Swear Free Zone." Swearing diminished greatly. Not completely— some kids didn't buy in and had to be worked with individually. But the program became a more pleasant place. At the end of each week we evaluated our progress. After four weeks, things were going so well that we decided to improve other aspects of the program. By the end of the school year, we had proudly posted signs outside of the room that said:

"You are entering a swear free zone."

"You are entering a put-down free zone."

"You are entering a violence free zone."

The kids learned self-discipline and community-building skills and taught me lessons I will never forget.

This exact solution won't work for every group. It does illustrate what helped one group. Try to identify logical, natural, and needs-meeting consequences the kids came up with. Amazingly enough, they figured them out without ever having heard of any of the terms.

Scenario 2:

The setting: The children in your school-age care program understand that swearing is not acceptable. You have a rule that says "No one swears here." You speak to the children often about the fact that swearing produces negative feelings, and that swearing invites fights and anger. You tell them that their school-age care program is a place where everyone is learning to resolve problems in a way that hurts no one.

You do not have an automatic consequence for swearing, like doing 50 pushups or writing a nice word 500 times, or suspension. You believe that those consequences are only punitive and don't model behavior resolution skills.

The children are third through fifth graders. Swearing is accepted by some families but not by others. The program is in a YWCA that serves pretty conservative downtown workers who come to work out and take classes. Some of the spaces used by your program are visible, and audible, to the Y clients. You have been asked to do something to eliminate swearing. You don't like swearing, either, and are working on it.

The incident: One day, the group gets to use the pool. On their way to the locker rooms to get their swimming suits on, the kids walk through the main lobby. Kelly, a fifth grader, teases Corie, a third grader who is small for his age. A YWCA client sees the incident. She rushes to Corie's aid. "I heard that. I'll tell your teacher what happened, little guy," she says. Corie looks right past her. He focuses on Kelly and calls her some very inappropriate names. Kelly responds in kind. The client leaves, muttering something about "kids these days."

What you know about the kids: Kelly is going through one of those growth spurts that girls sometimes have when they get sort of round. She is embarrassed by her growth but is otherwise pretty sure of herself. She's usually a pretty good kid. You and she sometimes are the last ones left at the end of the day. You have established a comfortable relationship. You have noticed lately that she has been experimenting with using swear words, a new behavior for her. You have not dealt with it yet.

Corie is very small for his age. He looks somewhat undernourished and has circles under his eyes. His hair sticks up straight. His movements are often random. He swears a lot. You've been working on a behavior modification reward program with him. It hasn't been successful. No reward seems big enough to eliminate the swearing. He fails to meet his goals almost daily.

What would be a *natural consequence* for both or each of the children?

_____

_____

_____

_____

What would be a *logical consequence* for both or each of the children?

_____

_____

_____

_____

Exercise continued on next page

What would be a *needs-meeting consequence* for both or each of the children?

_____

_____

_____

_____

What would be a *tragic consequence* for both or each of the children?

_____

_____

_____

_____

Which consequence or consequences would you choose to use in this situation? Why?

_____

_____

_____

_____

Which consequence or consequences wouldn't you use in this situation? Why not?

_____

_____

_____

_____

Scenario 3:

You get to do the next scenario. You can use something that has really happened in your program or one you think could happen. Use the space below to describe your program, what happened, and what you know about the kids. Then try to figure out what the possible consequences are for the behavior, which one you might use, and why.

The setting:

_____

_____

_____

_____

The incident:

_____

_____

_____

_____

What you know about the kids:

_____

_____

_____

_____

What would be a *natural consequence*?

_____

_____

_____

_____

Exercise continued on next page

What would be a *logical consequence*?

_____

_____

_____

_____

What would be a *needs-meeting consequence*?

_____

_____

_____

_____

Which consequence or consequences would you choose to use in this situation? Why?

_____

_____

_____

_____

Which consequence or consequences wouldn't you use in this situation? Why not?

_____

_____

_____

_____

It is probably getting easier and easier for you to think in terms of non-punitive, instructive consequences. Keep up the effort! It's paying off.

Please write your notes, thoughts, or stories here:

Chapter 11

Consequences: Don'ts

by LaNaya

Guilt: the gift that keeps on giving.

≈ Erma Bombeck

Don't Tell Children They Are Inadequate

When children handle their own consequences it is important that adults do not make them feel incompetent. The chapter opening illustration shows the same girl who, in the last chapter, cleaned up her puddle of milk, got some more for her cereal, and went happily on with her day— but here she's getting a different message. The adult may have shown her to the mop but couldn't accept the clean-up job that the child had done.

One of two things could be going on here. The child may be too young to complete the job (although most schoolagers should be up to the task). Or the adult's standards are too high. It is likely that the cafeteria will get cleaned again that day. What is necessary is that the extensive milk spill get cleaned up, and that the child learn to clean up after herself. The adult should first determine whether the consequence is within the child's ability, and then accept the child's level of competency.

Certainly there will be times when a child whizzes through a task that you are sure they can do better. The child may be in a rush, may be unhappy about doing the task, or may not be as skilled as you think. In any case, the adult can handle the situation so that the child continues to learn.

If the child is in a hurry, the adult can simply say, "I know that you want to finish your breakfast, but there's still a lot of milk on the floor. It'll only take another minute to make it disappear."

If you think the child is purposefully not doing a good job, you can stand by her and say, "There's still quite a pond on the floor. I know you can fix that."

The case of a child lacking skills can be tricky. Here's a story about a friend of mine who experienced that with her own child.

Seven-year-old Lizzy is very bright. *Lizzy has been having some difficulties at school academically and socially. Knowing that her abilities are high, her mom is puzzled. So she has her tested. The results come back saying that yes, Lizzy has a very high intelligence quotient. However, she has learning problems that make it difficult for her to assimilate processes involving multiple steps. These processes include small and large muscle activities, social skills, and following complex directions. Lizzy's self-esteem suffers because she and others recognize that she can't always do what seems like a simple task to others. The psychologist tells Sherry, Lizzy's mother, to give Lizzy many opportunities to be successful and to recognize her accomplishments. She tells Sherry that it is important for Lizzy to know that she is competent.*

When Lizzy and her mom get home from the conference, they decide to mix up some punch. Remembering the tester's advice, Sherry decides to let Lizzy make it. She figures Lizzy will succeed. Sherry will be able to tell Lizzy how much she enjoys the punch and appreciates the help. Lizzy has watched her mother make punch from powdered mix a hundred times. She has probably stirred it dozens of times.

"Why don't you make the punch while I open this mail," Sherry says, and watches her daughter out of the corner of her eye while she opens the first envelope.

It's a winter day in Michigan. Lizzy leaves on her coat, hat, and mittens, and goes straight to work on her task. The pitcher is on a shelf at Lizzy's eye level, where it always sits, but Lizzy fumbles among the pots and pans in a cupboard. She takes out a large soup pot and pours the powder in it. She struggles to push it across the counter towards the sink. She pushes it too hard and it lands upside down, purple powder flying. Lizzy turns the pot over and tries to scoop up the melting granules from the sink.

When she sees Lizzy getting the pot, Sherry thinks that Lizzy is joking. But as she watches, she realizes that Lizzy's tight-faced efforts are sincere. Blinking back tears, she says, "Hey, Lizzy. Looks like that pot isn't cooperating. Why don't we hang up our winter clothes and then finish making punch. We can use the grape pitcher. It may be in a better mood than the pot." And so they do. Lizzy learns how to make punch.

"I learned a lesson the hard way," Sherry tells a friend through her tears that night. "Not to take things for granted. I know Greg [her four year old] would have known how to make the punch. How many times has Lizzy been through struggles like that? How many times has she been ridiculed or felt stupid? I should have known." Sherry has a master's degree in early childhood development.

☙ ❧

The child learning how to deal with a consequence is in a vulnerable position. Most likely, she has done something that she isn't too proud of, and others have noticed. Now she's trying to fix it. You know how you feel when you spill your water at a friend's dinner party. Imagine how you would feel if the hostess said, as you try to mop it up with your napkin, "Why would you think that would help? You're only making it worse!"

Children in vulnerable spots often become more of what they are. If they are very active, they get more hurried. If they are clumsy, they get more clumsy. If they have poor skills, they become even less skilled. Even if you are certain that it is not your standards or your mood that makes meeting the consequences unacceptable, please remember the child's vulnerability and the lasting imprint your judgment can make.

When I was about eight years old, *my favorite aunt came over for Sunday dinner. One reason that she was my favorite aunt was that I thought she was rich. She had a tiled bathroom and a fireplace in her house, after all. I wanted to impress her. I knew that we would, because we were using my mother's dishes with the pink roses on them. I set the table for dinner, and then I stood back to admire my work. Cloth napkins, candles, and the pink dishes. I had seen my aunt watching me. I felt certain she was pleased. As I headed for the living room, I heard my aunt talking to my mother.*

"Why do you let Mary set the table with all your pretty things? She always does it wrong," my aunt said. Unknowingly, I had put the knives where the forks belonged and vice versa.

"I think she does just fine," my mother responded.

⊚ ⊚

What my mother said mattered some but didn't take away the sting from what my aunt said. Somewhere I stored the message that she sent me. On the day of her funeral, thirty years later, I remembered it. I didn't want to. I had had lots of good times with my aunt since then. But there it was, a part of me, a part of what I believed about myself: "She always does it wrong." That one statement certainly didn't ruin my life. But it lived in me—it was there to attract and validate other negative messages about myself, because an adult who was important to me had said it.

Most adults in kids' lives are important to them, whether the kids and the adults want to believe it or not. You are important to the children you work with. As you teach them discipline, as you guide their behaviors, give them words that will live in them and make them feel competent. Not only is it important to their healthy development, but (yes, you guessed it) children who feel competent have fewer behavior problems.

Remember a story from your childhood when an adult said or did something that made you feel good about yourself.

Write the story emphasizing exactly what the adult did or said and why it had such a positive effect on you.

_____

_____

_____

_____

_____

_____

_____

Now write a story about a time when you gave a consequence to a child in a way that you think had a positive effect on the child's self-image. What do you think the child learned about self-discipline as a result?

_____

_____

_____

_____

_____

_____

_____

Don't Rescue Children Unnecessarily

On the road to helping children build their independence, there is a large pothole that adults often drive right into: rescuing children.

As adults we are concerned that children be successful now and in the future. We fear that if a child takes on too much or doesn't have us to intervene, the child will fail. So, we tend to rescue children. In fact, they need to practice small failures and learn how to recover from them, or they will not be able to function on their own in the future.

There were probably times in your childhood when you got yourself into scrapes and had to figure your way out of them. Today's children need to do that also. We impede children from becoming independent if we don't allow them to experiment, fail, and succeed on their own. So the next time you want to find the right puzzle piece for a child, or wipe up a spill, or intervene with a heated discussion among friends, or put the last block on the block structure so that it won't tumble—stop yourself for a moment. Ask yourself if this is a risk that the child can manage. If it is, back off. Let the learning and the capability building continue.

Sometimes when I am consulting at a school-age care program, I ask the staff to do the following exercise with a child. A staff person and a child sit together. Each pair has some blocks, some self-stick notes (or paper and tape), markers and pens, small cars, and toy people. The child is to build a town with roads for the cars and places for the people to live and work. When the child is finished, she is to tell the adult about the town. The adult's role is simply to watch and talk with the child. Adults often have a very difficult time allowing the children to do the project on their own. I remember one time when a child built a road and put a person on it. The adult snatched up the person and said, "The person is going to get run over standing on the road. You can't let that happen." Other times adults have told children that the roads didn't lead anywhere, or that the store should be closer to the houses, or that there should be a bridge here or a hospital there.

The lesson is that even when the risk doesn't involve anything real, the adults have a hard time allowing the child to make mistakes or take chances. The adult becomes overly protective. The child feels overly controlled, inadequate, frustrated, not taken seriously. We know that these feelings can result in acting-out behaviors.

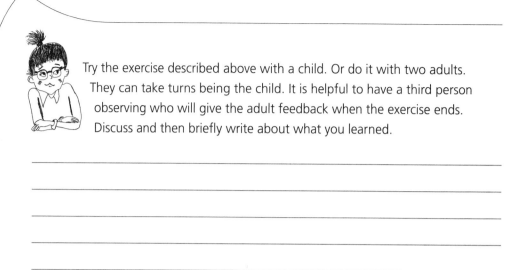

Try the exercise described above with a child. Or do it with two adults. They can take turns being the child. It is helpful to have a third person observing who will give the adult feedback when the exercise ends. Discuss and then briefly write about what you learned.

_____

_____

_____

_____

_____

Children need to learn how to care for themselves. They need to know how to dress and feed themselves, how to brush their teeth and comb their hair. They need to know how to keep themselves clean and how to tie their shoes. Just as they need to learn those self-help skills, they also need to learn how to face the consequences of their actions.

Just as you would step back to allow children to learn how to dress themselves and complete their own puzzles, I recommend that you rarely do anything for children in the realm of social skills that they can do for themselves. While learning self-help skills, children sometimes need help. They need patience when they forget. But just as you need to let them button their sweaters crookedly, you also need to let them fumble a bit when facing reality.

Child care has been around long enough now that there are long-term studies regarding the effects of being in child care. There is a generation of people, now in their twenties and thirties, who spent much of their childhoods in professional child care settings. Many of the results of their experiences are positive. In general, they feel secure in attempting new things. They are less limited by stereotypical male and female roles. They have good social skills.

The negative effects are most apparent when things don't go smoothly. They move, change jobs, and divorce more frequently than adults who were not in child care. I believe one of the reasons is that in child care, there was always an adult there with a solution. When children stayed at home, there wasn't always an adult around when they fell off their bike, had a fight with a friend, moved the wrong chess piece, stole a candy bar and got caught, lied to a friend. Kids had to learn to get themselves out of some scrapes by themselves—how to accept the consequences.

In child care, adults watch the children at all times. For many reasons, that is a good idea. What is not helpful, however, is having the adults rescue children from the consequences of their actions. Even when the adult's solution is to punish, an adult is deciding how to resolve the child's dilemma. When the going gets tough, someone else fixes it. Although it may be difficult, children need to learn to clean up their own messes. They need to figure out how to make amends, to negotiate, to change the behaviors that cause them and others distress. If they are needlessly rescued, they will not learn.

Sometimes staff feel sorry for certain kids. For boys and girls who come from homes with challenging situations. (Girls evoke this sympathy more often than boys.) Staff may know that the kids are neglected. That Dad drinks and Mom is gone. That the children share a room with four siblings or don't get the clothes they need. Or Grandma hits them. Or maybe staff feel sorry for the child who is blind, or has a learning disability, or uses a wheelchair, or the child who is always left out by others. These kids, like all kids, do deserve your loving care.

But all children need to know that they can handle their lives. That they can behave in acceptable ways.

All children need to be introduced to the tools they will need. They need help practicing, or when they forget. But they can, and must, learn that they can handle their lives. If they don't learn that, they may act out with rage and frustration, or live caged in helplessness. In either case, not only will the child not learn self-reliance, but he will cause more discipline problems.

Read the following scenario. Underline or circle the sentences that show children being rescued unnecessarily.

Naomi and Jeremiah are best friends. They sometimes play with Gordy.

Gordy is a computer whiz who comes to school with dirty, smelly clothes and hair. They also play with Heather, a petite redhead whom everyone likes. Jeremiah uses hearing aids. Naomi is from the Cherokee nation.

One day Jeremiah and Naomi are doing a project in the science corner. They are adding food coloring to water and putting celery in it to see what will happen.

Naomi reads from the project card, "Add blue coloring to one glass of water and red to the other."

"Let's goof it up and put red in both glasses," says Jeremiah.

"I don't think we should," Naomi says. "The experiment might not work."

She goes over to the science shelf to get the celery. While her back is turned, Jeremiah puts red in both glasses.

When Naomi returns, she gets angry. "What did you do that for? Why won't you follow the directions?"

Willy, the staff person, comes over. "Naomi," he says softly, "Didn't I see you reading the directions to Jeremiah?"

"Yeah, so what?"

"He probably couldn't hear you. Let's just start over and pretend this didn't happen."

Jeremiah who is an excellent lip reader, says, "I'm sorry I get stuff mixed up so much, Willy."

"That's okay, it's not your fault. We'll leave it the way it is. It's not a big deal. Jeremiah, it looks like Gordy could use some company over at the computer. I know you try to be nice to him. Naomi, you go read books until that temper of yours cools off."

Naomi makes a face at Jeremiah as she heads for the book corner. Heather is already there, flipping quickly through books. In her haste, she tears a page out. The book happens to be the story of a boy who lives on a reservation. "What's wrong with everybody today? First Jeremiah. Now you! Look what you did to this book, little Miss Perfect. You are so stupid!"

Fran, the director, walks by the room as Naomi's voice explodes.

"What's going on here?" Fran asks, taking the book and sitting between the two girls. "It was an accident. She called me stupid!" Heather cries.

Fran looks at the book and says, "Do you know how sad it makes Naomi feel when she sees you rip up books about her people? How would you feel if she tore up your family's pictures? You apologize to her."

In the meantime, Jeremiah has gone over to the computers.

Gordy really does smell today, he thinks.

"Hi," says Gordy. He's moving the computer mouse with one hand and holding a carton of juice in the other. "Want to play?" he asks, spinning in his chair.

The juice flies all over the computer area. "Hey, you'd better clean that up!" one of the kids says.

"How would he know how to clean anything up?" another kid says. "Take a whiff."

Willy, the staff person, comes across the room wondering to himself if 6 o'clock will ever come. "Yo, smart guy, out of here," he says to the taunter. "Gordy, you find something else to do with Jeremiah. He likes you. I can clean this stuff up."

Count the number of times children were rescued unnecessarily in the scenario. Write that number here: _____

Choose one of the situations you noticed. Describe what happened.

_____

_____

_____

What do you think the child(ren) learned in this situation?

_____

_____

How would you have handled the situation?

_____

_____

What would the child(ren) have learned from the way you dealt with the situation?

_____

_____

Don't Use Tragic Consequences

Tragic consequences leave children feeling shamed, angry, and confused. Children who feel those ways act inappropriately more, not less, often. So neither of the two goals of behavior guidance are met:

1. The children do not learn skills to manage their own behavior.

2. Discipline problems do not decrease.

How can you tell if you are using tragic consequences? One way is to pay attention to how the consequence affected you. If you felt pulled and stretched, tight and angry, or overwhelmed and stressed, you probably were reacting in a way that was not helpful to the children. Your feelings are clues that remind you to reexamine the consequence. If it was tragic, change it.

When you are engaged in teaching children behavior guidance, rather than punishing them with tragic consequences, you feel in control of yourself. The feeling is similar to how you feel when you are solving a difficult crossword puzzle, watching a serious and well-produced movie, quilting, climbing a mountain, woodworking, writing an essay, making pottery, or playing a difficult piece of music. You are working, concentrating on the task in front of you, perfecting your skills, thinking, creating.

You may be tired, even exhausted, when you finish. But you are not panicked or tensed up. Your shoulders aren't up by your ears and your face doesn't hurt. If you feel more stressed and angry after you give children a consequence, you have probably lost sight of your role as a guide to children. It is very likely that you gave a tragic consequence, that you punished or put down, rather than taught or related to, kids.

Be aware of how *you* are reacting to what you do with the kids. Reassess and change inappropriate consequences right away, and learn for the next time. As you reflect on your actions and change your responses, behavior guidance becomes your craft, your profession, your art. You will continually gain satisfaction and confidence from doing it. Even though halfway through you might not feel up to the task, you will naturally continue to move forward. You can trust that your knowledge, intuition, and openness will guide you. That your actions will be helpful. That the effective words will come out of your mouth. And that you will get better and better at it.

Here are some other clues to help you evaluate the consequences you give to children. They may be tragic consequences if at least one of the following is true:

- **The effect of the consequence was punitive.** It did not naturally occur because of what the child did. It was not logical—something that could have occurred because of what the child did and helped her learn from her actions. It did not meet the child's needs so that the inappropriate action on the child's part was no longer necessary.

- **The child reacted to the consequence defiantly.** Sometimes children react this way even if a consequence is not tragic. However, a defiant reaction can be a signal.

- **You get into a power struggle with the child because of the consequence.**

- **You feel guilty or physically stressed.**

- **The child continues similar behaviors after she pays the consequence, or the behavior accelerates.**

Each of these clues is a sign for you to consider the kind of reactions you are having to misbehavior. You may be giving consequences that leave the child feeling shamed and angry and leave you feeling frustrated, wanting to give up. Use these signals to help you understand how you approach problems, and to learn how to approach them in more effective and less harmful ways in the future.

Don't get too discouraged if you discover that your knee-jerk reactions are punitive more often than you wish. Eventually, tragic consequences won't be part of your repertoire. A new potter might make a vase that is thick and misshapen. But it is a vase. The potter will perfect his skills. Eventually, his vases will be thin and graceful and glazed with interesting colors. If he gives up, he will have only a lump of dry clay. Learning to give consequences that help children learn also takes thought, time, and lots of practice. Please do the following exercise:

Remember the last time you had the opportunity to practice behavior guidance and you gave a tragic consequence. (Don't be embarrassed. It happens to all of us.)

Describe the situation and what you did about it:

_____

_____

_____

How do you think the child(ren) felt when it was over?

_____

_____

How did you feel when it was over? Physically? Emotionally?

_____

_____

If you could do it over again what would you do differently?

_____

_____

How will you stop yourself the next time you start to give a tragic consequence?

_____

_____

Write yourself a positive affirmation about learning the craft of behavior guidance.

For example: "I am practicing and learning every day how to be more effective in guiding kids."

Your affirmation:

_____

_____

You help children become self-reliant people who can face the consequences of their behaviors in healthy, competent, and empowering ways. Your job requires developing and implementing a complex set of skills. The more you learn and practice, the easier it will become. It will be second nature to react in ways that enhance children's abilities to cope constructively with their world. The kids, and the world, benefit from your serious commitment to your work.

Chapter 12

Actions Speak Louder Than Words: Do's

by Holly

Keep it simple.

Do Use Actions Rather Than Words

In the illustration, an eight-year-old child, Mabel, is drawing on a table with a marker. The adult, Ralph, walks by the table and gently removes the marker from Mabel's hand.

The next illustrations might show Mabel standing up. Walking over to the sink. Getting the cleaning supplies. Washing off the table. Going back to the sink. Putting the cleaning supplies away. Giving Ralph a shrug of the shoulders that can be interpreted to mean, "I don't have a clue why I did such a thing as write on a table." She then might go outside and join the basketball game.

If you're surprised by the ease with which Ralph was able to deal with this situation, consider this: Mabel is the same girl who spilled her milk in the illustration in chapter 10. She was six years old then. She has learned how to clean up her messes, although she still doesn't always remember not to make them.

Another possible follow-up illustration might show Mabel continuing to sit at the table. She shrugs her shoulders at Ralph in a way that can be interpreted to mean, "What? What did I do?" Ralph points at the sink. The rest of the illustration is a repeat of the scene above.

This second possibility shows the same girl, who's had years of learning how to deal with the natural consequences of her behavior. She's just in a bad mood. So Ralph gives her another clue. She picks up on it and they both go on with their days.

If the story had gone another way, the illustration might show Mabel scribbling on the table, and Ralph seeing her from across the room. "What do you think you're doing, Mabel?" he calls across the now interested sea of children's faces. Mabel doesn't answer him. She keeps scribbling. Ralph thunders over to the table. Standing over Mabel he says, "I can't believe how irresponsible you kids are. We go through thousands of markers. And just look at this table. How much do you think that cost?"

"About five hundred dollars, I bet," says one of the other kids who's trying to earn teacher points.

"Listen to him, Mabel. He's right! And where do you think the money comes from? Answer me."

"How'd I know?" Mabel snarls, still writing on the table.

"I know," chimes in another kid, having witnessed the points that his peer earned earlier. "From our parents."

"Right. You should listen to your friends. Are you still marking up that table? Give me that marker. Hand it over now!"

Mabel tosses the marker on the floor, gives the table a shove, and leaves the room.

Ralph picks up the marker. As he heads for the cleaning supplies, he says, "I'm really tired of this. I'm just going to put all the markers far away until I think you guys know how to take care of things."

This whole scene took a lot more time. Mabel learned nothing about consequences. She did hear that she is irresponsible. Often we become what we are told we are. The teacher looks like the loser to the kids. The table isn't cleaned up and all the kids have a consequence that they did nothing to deserve. Ralph will witness their resentment for the unfair treatment.

All because of what? All because the writing on the table needed to be stopped. Did Mabel know that writing on the table was not a good thing to do? Of course. In the first two examples, simply taking the marker and using past learnings about the cleaning-up consequence did the job. Nothing else needed to be said.

Ralph's simple actions worked because there was a relationship between him and Mabel. Also because the limits were clear and the consequences understood. Ralph and Mabel both knew that writing on tables with markers was unacceptable. They both knew, through experience, that the consequence was to clean up your own mess. The relationship was strong enough that the nonverbal cues worked. Ralph understood that Mabel was making a mistake. Mabel knew that Ralph didn't judge her to be evil but did want the behavior to stop. Mabel knew it was her job to clean up. They each left with the relationship intact and the undesirable behavior stopped, a win-win situation.

The moral of the story is, when you see inappropriate behavior, or even sense that it is about to happen, move your body over to the scene of the action!

The next time you find yourself about to try to stop misbehavior by talking at children about it, stop. Close your mouth. Move your body closer to the problem. On the way over, think of the simplest *action* that you can take to get your message across. Remember, your simple message is, "The behavior has to stop and any mess that was made because of it needs to be cleaned up."

How many times have you seen a staff person, maybe even yourself, stand on one end of the playground and say things like, "Knock it off you two!" You may shout out six similar messages. But nothing stops happening until the you get over to the scene. The more time you spend trying to talk or shout the message, the more the problem accelerates.

If what you see is a shove, there really is no time to waste. It could be that the problem will stop with the shove. Maybe one child overstepped his bounds with another child, and the offended child shoved. The other figured he had it coming and left. It's not the solution that you might advocate, but the misbehavior has stopped and everyone is okay. That's fine. Ask the kids what and how they are doing and if they would like you to help them make the sand fort.

Or it could be that the shove was going to be returned, but out of the corner of his eye one child saw you coming and decided to quit. Again the misbehavior stopped. If no one was hurt physically or emotionally, let it go.

Perhaps by the time you get there, the children have pushed each other around several times. Think of how much worse it would be if you were still on the other side of the playground.

Sometimes it is downright inconvenient to get to the action. You're bandaging someone's knee, or a parent is talking to you. It is still worth making the move. A couple of things happen if the adults in a program consistently take the action of moving themselves physically to the location of the trouble.

The children who frequently misbehave start to believe that someone is going to do something about it. Children who are often in trouble have heard all the words that adults use to try to make them understand how bad their behavior is. They also know how many times adults will yell before they do anything. They can read body language and voice pitch. If they know they have only three more yells before the staff person gets on her feet, they throw those punches as fast as they can. They figure they're already in trouble, so they may as well make it worth their while. Once they know the way things are done around here is changing, they will reduce the number of misbehaviors.

I remember walking into a room *of a school-age care pro-gram I was supervising. I had only been on the job for a month. Across the room, I could see three boys. They consistently got themselves in trouble for bothering girls.*

This time, they were ready to invade a group of girls practicing for a play. I could see the boys' plans in their eyes. You know that look! I started walking calmly towards them. The boys saw me and knew that I knew. One of them headed for the girls anyway. Another boy said to him, "I wouldn't do that. This one means it."

I took the warning as a compliment. I didn't punish kids. I wasn't cruel. But I did "mean it." We all knew they had decided to act inappropriately. It was my job as an adult to do something about that. And just yelling or lecturing wasn't going to be it. They would have to look at their actions and make some decisions about the consequences. The boys casually wandered over to the Lego plastic building blocks and started playing. I walked over to them. "Are these Legos interesting enough to keep you busy for a while?" I asked.

"Yeah, sure."

"That's good to hear. I really hope you have fun."

"Thanks."

"You're welcome."

❧ ❧

I didn't intimidate the kids. My moving toward them didn't signal cruel and unusual punishment. What it said, in this case, was, "Things have changed. This person will not just talk. She will act." That meant that the boys had to think about their behavior. They had to decide if they wanted to continue to do things that they knew were clearly not acceptable there, even though they may not yet have known why.

In this case, I wasn't sure the boys understood the reasons for the limit. Their repeated harassment of girls indicated that they might not. I also believe that boys need to start thinking at an early age about how they treat girls. I decided to talk to them about the issues some other time, when the conversation would be less likely to be heard as a punishment lecture.

When I saw the boys in the hall *the next day, I stopped them.*
"Come over here for a minute, please." We sat on a bench.
"I was wondering something. Why were you going to mess
up that play practice yesterday?"

They shook their heads. "I don't know," said one.

"I bet you have some idea."

"It was just going to be fun."

"Had those kids ever done anything to you?"

"They weren't kids. They were girls."

(At a moment like this it is okay for you as an adult to raise your eyes to the heavens and say "Thank you," in your heart. Having done that, I continued.)

"Oh. I see. You do it because they are girls."

"Yeah, right." At this point the boys looked hopeful. They thought I got it, that I would accept this as a logical answer.

"Why would you do something to them just because they're girls?"

"Because it's fun."

"More fun than it would be to do it to boys?"

"Yeah."

"Why?"

"Because they're pretty, so it's fun."

"Oh. Why is it fun because they're pretty?"

"It's something guys do. Like whistling at girls and shouting stuff at them. Like my dad and his buddies do. All guys do it."

"Maybe you kind of like the girls because they're pretty."

"Yeah, maaaaybe."

"But it's not cool to say you like girls, huh?"

"No."

"You guys try hard to be fair, I know. And I know you want people to treat you fairly. Right?"

Three heads nodded up and down.

"Do you think it's fair to ruin the girls' play because you don't want to tell people that you like them?"

"Nooooo."

"Is there anything else that you do to girls that isn't fair?"

"Yeah."

"What?"

"We chase them and pull up their dresses and stuff."

"Why do you do that?"

"You know. Because it's fun. Because they're girls. Because they're pretty," said one boy.

Hearing the statement voiced by their friend turned on the light in the other two boys' eyes.

"That's not fair, is it?" asked one boy.

"Nope," said the others.

"So it's making sense to you guys that being mean to girls just because they're girls isn't the right thing to do."

"For sure," exclaimed one boy. "I so get it. I'm never even going to look at a girl again."

"Never?" I asked.

"Well, never like that, I mean."

The other two boys, eyes sparkling with their new-found insights, nodded their heads in agreement.

§ ©

We went on to figure out how the boys would let the girls know that they would not treat them unfairly in the future. This is, I think, of all of the conversations that I've had with kids, my favorite. These boys, who came from families with multiple challenges, were good thinkers. Watching them understand the underlying concept and supporting each others' changed belief system was a joy. By the way, their relationships with the girls did improve a hundred percent.

There were many words spoken in this example. But not at the time that the limit needed to be set. Then, the behavior need to be changed. The verbal teaching part of behavior guidance, in this case, came later, when emotions were stable and learning could go on. Actions rather than words. Stop the behavior. If necessary, explore it at a teachable moment.

Describe the action you might take in each of these situations to stop the inappropriate behavior.

1. Two children are leaving a room. They meet in the doorway. They are shouldering and elbowing each other in an attempt to be the first one out of the door. While using the fewest words possible you could:

_____

_____

_____

2. A child is plugging the faucet in the room's clean-up sink with his finger. Water is spraying all over. While using as few words as possible you could:

_____

_____

_____

3. You are reading a book to a group of children. Each time you turn a page, a child in the back makes a gross noise. You could:

_____

_____

_____

4. A. The special ed class walks past your room's open door. Two kids make mean comments about the special needs kids' appearance. You could:

_____

_____

_____

Exercise continued on next page

B. You stopped the name-calling misbehavior in the example above. However, you still doubt that the children understand the need to behave differently in the future. So, later, in a private place, you have a conversation with the children about their actions. Describe what the conversation might be:

_____

_____

_____

_____

_____

_____

C. Read the conversation you just described, to someone else. Ask them if any of the conversation sounds like punishment. If it sounds like a lecture. If the children might feel belittled or shamed by the conversation (shamed kids continue to misbehave). If they think the kids understand. Record any feedback:

_____

_____

_____

Please write your notes, thoughts, or stories here:

Chapter 13

Actions Speak Louder Than Words: Don'ts

If I've told you once, I've told you a hundred times... Tell me you'll never do it again or you'll never play outside again in your life. How selfish!

by Holly

The bus to take the kids to the roller-skating rink was late. Confined indoors by a rainstorm, the ten year olds got restless. David decided to pelt eraser bits at the girls. Linda, the supervisor, heard the commotion.

"Get into my office right now, young man."

David slouched his way into a chair and stared at Linda.

Linda didn't usually go on like this, but it had been a long week. She peppered her five-minute conversation with words like "responsibility," "effort," and "cooperation." She ended by asking, "Do you have anything to say?"

David looked at her quizzically and said, "How did you get those wrinkles?"

≈ Jean Steiner and Mary Steiner Whelan

Don't Lecture

Lectures

All the while that Linda was talking excessively, inducing guilt, and hoping for an apology, David was examining her face. He had heard the lecture a dozen times before from a variety of people. So, he kept himself busy trying to figure out how a face gets those wrinkles and hoping it would never happen to him.

Linda (who is a real person and a great teacher) didn't teach David anything that day, but David did teach her something: The methods she was using were another version of the punishment-control model of behavior guidance. They were just disguised in a discussion. She pulled out her power to lecture at him and tried to control him with it. It didn't work.

There is a difference between lecturing a child and having a conversation with a child. Lectures usually happen at the time the misbehavior occurs or the adult first learns about it. The lecturing adult believes that if she says enough, if she "drums it into his head," the child will understand the seriousness of the grievance and will therefore never do it again.

However, the child's lack of understanding is rarely the problem. Even if it is, as illustrated in the last chapter, the offending behavior still needs to be stopped immediately. Later, when a real conversation can happen, the child and the adult can learn about the roots of the behavior.

Lecturing rarely gives the child new information. Nor does excessive talk give the adult any insights into the child's behavior. In a lecture, the adult decides what the child's motivation is; may name the child as bad or irresponsible; and gives the child no opportunity to make amends or correct the situation. The only way the child can stop the excessive talk is to agree with the adult's foregone conclusions about her behavior, bow her head, and say, "I'm sorry." That usually brings on another but shorter lecture from the adult. Something about, "I hope you get it this time. I've heard you say you're sorry before. But I haven't seen you change one bit." If the child can refrain from getting angry and accept the implication that she will probably never improve, she is off the hook for a while. She hasn't received any new information. And she hasn't had to face her misbehavior except to survive a lecture that she has heard many times before.

You have probably been on both sides of a lecture. The lecture seems so valuable, so logical, if you are the one giving it. It seems like such a waste of time if you are the one receiving it.

I am the oldest of three children. *My brother, John, is two years younger than I. I took my role as the firstborn very seriously. I often felt that it was my job to make sure that John was perfect. I would sometimes dash home from school ahead of John, to fill my mother in on all of John's transgressions. "I saw him run in the halls today," I would report. Stories about authorities noticing his evilness always got an especially good reaction. "I heard Sister Alphonsis yell at John for not doing his work. In front of the whole class! I, uhmm, just happened to be walking by his room."*

John would barge in, his muddy blue and red school bag dragging on the floor. The slamming door shook the kitchen. He would look at me and say, "Shut up!" (That was another punishable act in our family, so I had already gotten him in trouble.) He would then stand slumped in front of my mother, with an angry look on his face that didn't win him any more points, and listen to the lecture. Being the teasing older sister that I was, I would stand behind my mother mouthing her words along with her. John, of course, dared not point out my evilness because it would get him in more trouble. Had he and I heard all the words before? Of course! Did my mother think that she was doing what she needed to do to raise responsible kids? Of course!

※ ※

It took my brother a few years to forgive me. I did eventually outgrow the need to be seen as the good one. He gave up the role of the bad one. I'm happy to say we are good friends now. (For those of you who have children who fight with each other, there is hope!)

When I had my own children, did I repeat my mother's behavior? More often than I would like to admit. My kids gave my lectures titles. "Uh-oh," they would say to each other. "You stayed out past curfew? Now you're going to get the lecture called, 'I Trust You. It's the Things that Can Happen to You I Worry About.'" Hearing their comments reminded me to keep my promise to "never do that to my kids when I grow up."

Forcing Children to Apologize

Forcing children to apologize and to promise better behavior are two other ways that we adults sometimes use words as guilt-inducing weapons.

How many times as children were we told to "March right over there now mister and apologize"? What did we think as we marched across the classroom, or playground, or street? Did we think, "I really am sorry. I'm so glad that adult reminded me that I am so sorry"? Or did we think things like, "Next time I'll make it worth my while. I'm glad I did this evil deed. It was worth it"?

Have you ever participated in a scenario like this one? Jasmine punches Francie in the stomach. Jasmine often reacts first with her fists. You come across the room and say, "Jasmine stop!" Without even looking up, Jasmine says, "Sorry! Sorry!"

The reflex is built into the child who consistently is in trouble. She has been told to apologize so often that it is meaningless. A response to her automatic "Sorry!" might be to put your hand on her shoulder and say, "Let's walk away from this problem for a minute." You have just used an action. You have stopped the inappropriate action. Now is not time for a lecture but for a lesson.

Assuming that your touch and the distancing from the scene has been enough to calm Jasmine down you might say, "Jasmine, you just hurt Francie."

"Yeah, so?"

"That's not okay. I feel bad when people are hurt. I think you do too. The trust that people can feel safe here is broken. I know you and Francie can think of a way to start repairing that trust. Are you ready to go over to Francie with me and figure out how to do it?"

Now you have begun to teach Jasmine how to be accountable for what she did. You are leaving the solution up to the kids but you will be there to guide and consult. You have not used excessive talk. You have not told the child that she is hopeless. You have not demanded an apology. You are in the process of acting with the children and empowering them to act in responsible ways.

Another common scene in school-age care is a child with eyes dutifully cast to the floor and an adult standing over her saying, "Tell me that you will never, ever, do that again. Do you hear me?" Usually this demand comes at the end of a lecture. The child has probably tuned out by this time. That is why the sentences, "Tell me you won't do it again. Do you hear me?" often have to be repeated. The child may agree, perhaps saying under her breath that she will never get caught again.

If the child says, "Cross my heart and hope to die it will never happen again," she can go on with her day, but she hasn't learned anything. She hasn't been made accountable. She has only made a promise that she and the adult both know she probably won't keep. How discouraging for all concerned.

Another ending to the scene can be, of course, that the child refuses to say that she will never repeat the behavior again. In this case, a battle of wills between the child and the adult often takes place. When the fight is over there are no winners. Because the child has not learned and the relationship has been damaged, the same behaviors will occur, or even similar but more belligerent ones.

When we feel like talking *at* a child, instead of *to* a child, when we feel like inducing *guilt* instead of building *competency,* when we feel like *making* her say what we think she should say, instead of *encouraging* her to find a solution, we need to remind ourselves once again that we are in the business of *teaching* and *relating,* not *punishing* and *controlling.*

Our words and our body language can be signals to us that we may be using words as weapons by talking excessively, moralizing, or forcing apologies or promises. Here are some examples of words that we use frequently when we are in that mode:

You	Don't
Never	Can't
Should	Always
Right now	Because I said so!

Often the body language that we use with these kinds of words adds to the punishing and controlling nature of our actions. When we are overpowering rather than empowering, we are likely to do some of the following things:

Point our finger at the child	Talk across a room or other space at the child
Talk at the child in a loud voice or yell	Fold our arms across our chest
Stand over the child	Grab the child by the arm
Lean towards the child in a threatening way	Get red in the face

We use different words when we are in relationship mode. Here are some of the words we use then:

I	Might
Feel	Believe
Can	Sometimes
Do	What do you think?

Our body language usually is different when we use these kinds of teaching and relationship words. We will probably notice ourselves doing some of the following:

Speaking in a matter of fact, calm, or quiet voice

Touching the child easily on the shoulder

Sitting or kneeling at the child's level

Stretching out our arms

Putting our hands on the table or on our laps or holding the child's hands if this is appropriate and acceptable to the child

Talking to the child from no farther than two to four feet away

Allowing silence to happen so that the child can think and talk

Relaxing facial muscles

Compare the following sentences:

1. *"You never act responsibly."*

2. *"Do you have any ideas that might help you remember to sign out when you leave?"*

Read the sentences a second time. Imagine what the speaker's body language is like.

Now put yourself in the receiver's position for each of these sentences.

If you hear, "You never act responsibly," you might feel hopeless. What can you possibly do about never being responsible? Either you could shrug your shoulders and wait for the rest of the lecture, which is almost certain to come. Or, you can argue about the last time you were responsible or call the person talking to you a liar or some such thing. The other person would fight back and there would be a barrage of words that would leave you both feeling angry. The immediate problem would not get solved.

On the other hand, if you hear, "Do you have any ideas that might help you to remember to sign out when you leave?" you feel differently, don't you? You might even feel valued as a problem solver. The problem is specific enough that it can be dealt with. Your entire reputation as a person is not being threatened. You are part of the solution rather than the object of judgments. You can come up with some ideas, choose the one that seems most helpful, agree to give it a try, and go on. You feel competent and the person talking with you feels helpful. The immediate problem has at least a chance to be solved.

Now try the following exercise. I know you can figure out from the sentences what kind of familiar scenarios preceded the responses.

1. The staff person says, **"I've tried everything with you. Now you can just sit here and listen to me again. I've had it with this constant meanness of yours."**

Now think of another way that the staff person could deal with the issue. Remember to be specific, respectful, and guiding. Use the list of teaching words on page 179 if you want some help.

Complete this sentence: "The staff person could say,

_____

_____

_____

Discuss both of the sentences with someone else. Ask him how he feels when he hears each one, and how he might respond.

2. The staff person says, **"Get over here right now! What do you have to say for yourself about all of this swearing that you've been doing. I have a mind to make you tell your Mom what you said. What do you think would happen then? You never speak anything but potty talk."**

How could this staff person use teaching language? Complete this sentence: "The staff person could say,

_____

_____

_____

Ask someone for feedback as you did in number 1.

Exercise continued on next page

3. The staff person says, **"You should apologize to the whole school for this behavior. You are an embarrassment to Kid's Club. Who do you think you are to always be causing a commotion?"**

Draw a picture of the adult and the child that illustrates the staff person's remarks. Exaggerate body language that might help express each person's feelings.

How might you feel and react if you were the child in this drawing?

_____

_____

_____

Think about what response might help solve the problem, and then complete this sentence: "The staff person could say,

_____

_____

Draw a picture of the adult and the child that illustrates your response. Exaggerate body language that might help express each person's feelings.

How might you feel and react if you were the child in this drawing?

_____

_____

_____

Don't Use Threats

According to the dictionary, a threat is "the expression of the intention to inflict evil, injury, or damage." (Webster's Collegiate, 10th ed.). This is what we are doing to children when we threaten them with dire consequences if they don't stop what they're doing right now—telling them that we intend to do them evil, injury, or damage. Is it any wonder that threats, tied to punishment and control as they are, simply don't work?

What is the purpose of a threat, really? Is it an announcement of a consequence before the next transgression that the child makes? So that she is informed about what will happen? So that, in order to be fair to her, there are no surprises if she repeats a behavior? Maybe. But let's look at some of the flaws in that way of thinking. One, we are telling the child that we expect her to repeat the behavior. Let's say that the child lies to us. We might say, "The next time I catch you lying, you will have to write, 'I will tell the truth' a thousand times." "The next time" assumes there will be a next time. We are letting the girl know that we expect her to repeat her behavior. Children often live up, or down, to our expectations.

Another problem with this stance is the "I catch you" part. Even if we don't state it that clearly, it is implied. We cannot carry out the threat, after all, if we don't know about the unacceptable behavior. This stance turns misbehavior into a game. *If I don't get caught*, the child might think, *I won't have to do that terrible thing you said I would have to do. So, I won't get caught.* The child will learn how to get better at hiding inappropriate behavior. In this case, she will get better at lying.

If we do "catch" the child again we will impose the consequence that we predetermined will "teach her a lesson." The problem with this approach is that we don't take circumstances into account. We are being totally subjective, we are not including the child in finding different ways of dealing with the world that will lead to a healthier life, and we are probably not stopping the behavior, just postponing it and driving it underground. We are punishing and controlling.

If we are honest with ourselves, the logic behind threats is to scare children. As the definition acknowledges, we want to make them afraid of what we can do to them in an attempt to get them to straighten out. Relationships that are built on fear are not teaching, nurturing relationships in which we let someone know that we want the best for them and those around them. They don't usually work in the short run, and they never work in the long run. Scaring children does not help them become competent in dealing with the world in healthy ways. When we try to motivate children through fear, we are more likely to hear ourselves saying things like, "It doesn't matter what I do to her. She just keeps on lying." This is because we are working from the old, ineffective punishment-control model.

Another problem with threats is that they don't usually deal with the problem at hand. They talk about what will happen "next time" or "if." But what about now? Children operate in the "now." The behavior that is inappropriate is inappropriate now. The time they can learn from their action, and from your response, is at the time at which the action happens. It is much more effective to deal with their behavior by acting immediately and moving on.

Is it a problem right now for this child or others that she just told a lie? If so, we need to deal with it now. In the case of lying, the solution might be as simple as letting the child know that she is not telling the truth and holding her accountable for that.

A conversation around the issue might go something like this:

"Deb, I saw you tear up the papers on my desk. I really needed them for a report that I am writing."

"I didn't tear them up."

"I saw you do it, so I know you did. I'll tell you what, I have another set of those papers in my computer that I can run off in a few minutes. So this time that isn't the main part of the problem."

"I didn't tear them up."

"The problem is that I want to be able to believe you. I don't lie to you and I don't expect you to lie to me. Also, I know that when people lie they carry around a heavy thing inside of them that makes them feel icky about themselves. I think you are a neat kid and I feel sad when I know that you have to carry that ugly feeling in you. So, all you have to do is tell me that you tore up the papers and you can leave. I won't do anything to you. I just don't want you to have to feel bad about yourself."

"I didn't tear them up."

"I'm going to run off a new set of papers on the computer right now. Why don't you sit here while I do that, and decide how you want to feel about yourself. (A few minutes go by while you busy yourself with printing out the file again, or other work, focusing your attention on the work and not on the child.) Okay, I'm done. What do you think?"

"I did tear them up."

"Good for you for telling the truth. I'm happy for you. See you later."

"Bye."

It is over. This example is what William Glasser calls reality therapy (*Reality Therapy: A New Approach to Psychiatry* [New York: Harper, 1965]). Just admitting what happened is often the most important step in deciding that you don't want it to happen again.

What if Deb doesn't admit to the lie, you ask?

The conversation might go like this:

"I'm done now. What do you think?"

"I didn't tear them up."

"I'm sorry for you that you decided to carry that lie in you. I saw you so I know that you did tear them up. If you change your mind and want to tell me some other time, I'll listen or read a note that you write me. See you later."

The child chose the consequence here. She has chosen to live with the lie. You wish she hadn't but she did. Did she get off without being accountable? No, she is accountable to herself. You have made her aware of the cost of lying to herself. She will notice it now and may not want to feel that way again. It's hard to tell what she will choose in the future, but you did solve the problem about the papers. The rest is up to her. If you had threatened her, she would be at war with you. You would be the enemy and her role would be not getting caught. Now she knows that you care about her and her role is living with herself. You also gave her the option of telling you in some way later, so that she is not left stranded.

Group Threats

Another common threatening technique is the group threat. We sometimes find ourselves using this technique when we are tired and overwhelmed.

"If I see one more hand waving out this bus window, we will never go on another field trip again!"

Have you or any staff you know ever said something like that? I have. So have staff I've worked with. When I was a director I got a call from a parent of a quiet little child who was on a bus similar to the one in the example. He said, "Sandy is afraid that he isn't going to be able to go to the zoo next week because a child put his arm out the window on the bus today. He has really been looking forward to that trip. I tried to assure him that you wouldn't punish the whole group for what a few children did. But he is pretty sure the teacher really meant it."

I didn't get a similar call from the parents of kids whose hands were out the window. Those kids were probably saying to themselves, "Threaten me if you wish, but it only matters what you really DO, and this will blow over and you won't do anything."

Here are some of the problems with threatening a group of children:

1. The children who are not misbehaving may be anxious that the adult's threats are to be taken seriously.

2. The children who are misbehaving probably don't believe that the adult's threats are to be taken seriously.

3. The children who are misbehaving may be uncertain about whether or not the adult will or can follow through. This uncertainty will promote behaviors such as avoiding the adult, a defiant, defensive "I don't care" attitude, or a fearful withdrawal.

4. The adult usually can't or won't follow through because the adult is not thinking clearly. Therefore, the threats are often unrealistic and cannot be enforced. Or, after the adult has a chance to calm down, she realizes that the threat was a bit much and decides not to go through with it. This makes the adult seem wishy-washy and look foolish. It is difficult to have respectful relationships with people whom we consider wishy-washy and foolish. So children will tend to respect the adult less and to learn less from them.

In the end, the point is that threats are not effective. They are manipulative and come from a punishment-control model. Here's an exercise to help us remember what it feels like to be threatened:

Describe the most recent incident you can remember in which someone threatened you to try to change your behavior.

_____

_____

_____

_____

_____

How did you feel?

_____

What did you do? Did you change your behavior? In the short and long terms?

_____

_____

_____

How do you feel about the person who threatened you? What did you learn about that person?

_____

_____

What did you learn about yourself in the situation?

_____

_____

How do you think your experience is similar to or different from those of the children you work with?

_____

_____

_____

Instead of talking excessively, let's close this chapter with an action. Please stand up. Please say, "I will act thoughtfully, gently, firmly, quickly. I will not subject children to harm with my words. I will use my words to teach, relate, and encourage."

Now please sit down. And breathe. In and out. In and out. In and out.

Chapter 14

Encourage Independence: Do's

by Lindsey

Someone spilled apple juice in the refrigerator and didn't clean it up. I discovered it when it was sticky brown slime on the bottom shelf.

"I know who's to blame for this," I said to myself. "Those schoolagers. Gary lets them come in here, use the fridge, get things out of the cupboard. I'm sick of it."

Then I went into the storeroom to get my preschoolers' snack. I heard the schoolagers lumbering in. Gary chatted with kids about their day at school.

One child said, "Can I get anybody a glass of juice? How about some crackers and cheese?"

"Count me in," said another child and added with a sigh, "Whew! It's great to be home."

"There's no place like it," I mused. "But we can try. We can try."

You feed the souls of kids when you allow them to become independent, confident people, even if it means things get a little messy.

≈ Jean Steiner and Mary Steiner Whelan

Do Give Children Decision-Making Power

When I was supervising a large school-age program, I often tried to go out for a walk around the neighborhood before the children arrived from school. The walk helped me with the transition from paperwork to kid work. One day, my walk lasted a bit longer than usual. The school buses dropped children off at the end of each block. I watched as a group of children jumped off the bus. Dragging their backpacks along the ground, they kicked a few stones back and forth along the curb. They went to one kid's garage, got a basketball, and shot a few baskets in the driveway. Then they moved, running sometimes, shouting at each other in fun, until they got to another house. They emerged with juice boxes in one hand and sandwiches in the other. They sat on the grass munching and laughing. Then they separated into groups of two and three, talking, some in earnest, some in jest.

I thought about what was probably going on in parts of the site that I supervised. In some rooms, no doubt, kids arrived and heard things like, "Pick up that backpack. Put it on the hook. Your coat, too. Your parents pay good money for those things. They don't expect you to wreck them. Sit down. Keep those hands to yourselves and close those mouths. Eat the snack at your table. Hurry up. You don't have time to be dawdling. The next bus is arriving soon and we need you to be out of here and on the playground. Line up by the door when you're finished."

Now every child didn't hear all of this every day. But put it all together and those were too often the messages. Because of the numbers, the setting, and the schedules, we ran a pretty tight ship. I suddenly felt sorry for our kids. We certainly had a good program. But without realizing it we were programming kids to fit the situation rather than programming the situation to fit the kids' needs.

After a structured day at school, after being told what and how to learn, after the scary tests and the peer pressure, the kids needed some slack. They needed to regain some control. They needed to make a transition—just as I did on my walks.

Those kids coming home on their own had created a pretty good balance for themselves. Some group time, some food, some fun, some physical activity, some talk: transition time that they made choices about. I understood better why so many kids, especially the older ones, thought they wanted to go home on their own rather than be in school-age care programs. They knew they could really meet most of their needs on their own. They wanted some independence. Of course, they didn't know that they would also get lonely, be scared sometimes, miss great activities, or wish they had an understanding adult to talk to. But they did recognize the need to meet their developmental task of becoming independent.

School-age care programs promote children's well-being by meeting their developmental needs in various ways. The program's structure, its activities, the interaction between children and adults, and the types of materials available can all contribute to the goal of promoting positive growth in kids. When kids' needs are not met, there is almost always an increase in behavior problems. If the need to be independent is not recognized and encouraged, the children will feel hemmed in, discounted, not respected. They may respond by refusing to participate, by consistently resisting limits, and by "talking back." You will hear statements such as, "You treat us like babies. This is bogus. BORING!"

You will, of course, hear some talk like that even if your program is doing a good job supporting independence. The statements themselves are another expression of independence. However, such talk can be a clue that it is time to assess the independence factor. Talk to the kids about why they think the behaviors are happening. (That is one of the things that I love about schoolagers. You can talk to them!)

Back to my walk and insights: I shared my observations at the next staff meeting. We decided to look at the program and see how we could keep the structure required by the kids, the administration, and physical setting, and at the same time allow more independence. At that meeting, we focused on arrival time in the afternoons. We asked ourselves, "What are we doing for the kids that they can do for themselves?" We came up with a pretty good list. They can pour their own juice, make their own snacks, decide when they want to eat them (within a certain period of time), and decide if they want to be inside or outside.

For the next few days we asked the kids what they thought. They came up with everything that the staff had listed, and they added: signing themselves in, deciding on snack menus, getting the snack stuff from the kitchen, deciding what the main outside game would be for the following day and writing it on the white board, monitoring the storage lockers, writing up reminder tickets when children left something on the floor around their locker space, and monitoring the numbers in any given area with a system involving colored sticks.

Implementing the changes took planning and time. We had to redo staff assignments. We had to change systems. Everything didn't work the first time. We had to let go of fears and trust the kids to follow through (and check to see if they did). The results were well worth the trouble. Instead of experiencing that daily thud, that unspoken, almost depressed, resistance we had been feeling from the kids, we began to see kids arriving with an air of anticipation. They talked more freely and provoked arguments less. They interacted more informally with each other and with staff. They weren't coming home, exactly. But they were coming to a place where they felt respected and included. The harsh remarks that staff had found themselves making during this time of day almost disappeared.

One afternoon about a month after we changed the system, one of the kids who usually greeted us with a swear word or a rude gesture tossed his jacket in his locker and said sideways to two staff members, "Good to be here, man. Gotta go get snack." As soon as he was out of sight, the awe-struck staff members gave each other a hearty high five.

Allowing children to make decisions is an important part of building independence. Decision makers are not usually troublemakers. Children who feel that they have some power in their lives are less likely to try to obtain power in inappropriate ways.

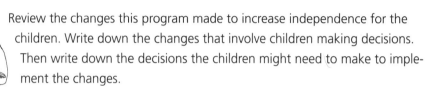
Review the changes this program made to increase independence for the children. Write down the changes that involve children making decisions. Then write down the decisions the children might need to make to implement the changes.

Here's an example:

Change: Children monitor locker space and give tickets to those who need reminders about leaving materials on the floor outside of their own space.

Decisions: Who will get a ticket? What will be the guidelines for getting a ticket? Will it matter if it is a friend's locker? Who will be the monitors? What will the tickets say? What will happen if a ticket is ignored and there are repeated incidents?

Change:

_____

_____

Decisions:

_____

_____

_____

Change:

_____

_____

Decisions:

_____

_____

_____

Change:

_____

_____

Decisions:

_____

_____

_____

Change:

_____

_____

Decisions:

_____

_____

_____

The power to make decisions, to feel more and more independent as they get older, is a basic need for school-age children. In the example, structuring the program in a way that met this need achieved a significant change in behavior patterns and attitudes. Children are not, of course, going to make perfect decisions. They are in the process of learning. They need adults to be part of the process, not to criticize them at the end. For example, if the kids decide that the locker reminder ticket should say, "We ain't going to put up with this mess anymore. You're busted!" the time for the adult to guide is not after the children have printed up the tickets and are distributing them. The adult should be an active observer and consultant during the process. Once children come to a decision, we need to respect it unless it violates someone's rights.

In the beginning of the process, when the children decide they want to issue tickets, the adult might say, "Remember that we don't punish people here. We try to help each other learn. How can you use your ticket idea to help people learn?" If this sort of guideline is established, the inappropriate wording might not be suggested.

On the other hand, maybe someone *would* still suggest that wording. If that happened, the adult might try some role playing. She could have one of the children pretend that he has left something outside his locker storage area where someone could trip over it. She could have another child issue the ticket and read it out loud. Then the adult could ask questions like, "How did you feel when you heard the ticket? Did the ticket teach you anything? How did you feel about the person giving you the ticket?"

Then, the adult could talk about how to change the language and redo the role play until the child receiving the ticket and the other children thought that the ticket was a good reminder and helped them want to cooperate. The ticket might end up saying something like, "Please remember that we all share this place. When you keep your stuff in your own space, we can all enjoy this place more. Thank you for cooperating."

It is essential to the success of these behavior guidance techniques that the children be involved in the entire process. Imagine how much less effective and how much less the children would learn if the adults came up with the idea, or even if they took the children's idea, came up with the wording, and announced that this was how it was going to be.

The group that you work with might be too large to have the whole group involved in every aspect of every change. A small group might choose (notice the word "choose") to work on the locker issue. They could then be responsible for informing the larger group about the procedures and the reasons for them.

Is all of this time consuming? Yes!

Is it worth it? Yes!

As a matter of fact, what better use of time could there be? Remember, these are lessons that make a difference for life. Be proud of the fact that you are teaching kids the most valuable skills of all, and at the same time eliminating discipline problems.

In the example, the staff and children worked on building more opportunities for independence into the after-school arrival time. Use the following exercise to look at your program. Focus, perhaps, on a time during which discipline becomes a problem.

Describe the time of day and how it is currently structured. What is happening? What are the adults doing? What are the children doing? Where are the children? What happens before and after this part of the program? (If you are not currently working in a program, talk about an imaginary program).

_____

_____

_____

_____

_____

_____

_____

_____

Ask yourself, "What are we staff members doing for children that they can do for themselves?" List those things here:

_____

_____

_____

_____

_____

Exercise continued on next page

Ask the children in your program (if this is an imaginary program, you can use imaginary kids for this part, too) how they think they could be more self-sufficient during this time of day. The question might sound some thing like this, "I know that you kids are old enough to be on your own a lot. I was wondering what things happen during club time that you could be in charge of. What are the adults in charge of during club time that you think you could handle?" List the kids' ideas:

_____

_____

_____

_____

_____

_____

Make a list of program changes you and the kids will have to make to implement these ideas.

_____

_____

_____

_____

_____

Make a plan for how you will include kids in figuring out one of these changes.

_____

_____

_____

_____

_____

A month after this change is made (put a reminder on your calendar), write a description of the results of the change. What worked and what didn't? Did you notice any changes in the kids' behavior? If so, what were they?

_____

_____

_____

_____

_____

_____

If you are working with kids now, don't wait for this whole process to be completed to make any changes. Right now think of one small thing that you now do for the children that they will start to do for themselves, tomorrow.

Complete this sentence: Tomorrow the children in my program can…

_____

_____

Tell the children what you decided and ask them what they think about it. And then watch what happens.

Will all kids respond to this approach? It might take more guidance for some children to learn than for others, but most children respond very positively to the opportunities to be in charge of parts of their lives, to brainstorm and discuss issues with other kids, to come to mutually acceptable decisions, and to be able to teach other children about their decisions. It is often the children for whom we think this way of operating will be the most difficult, who respond the most enthusiastically.

The staff calls them the "Gang of Three." *Although they are only second graders, Joshua, Lonnie, and Markus pretty much run the playground. Their guerrilla tactics scare, annoy, and hurt other children. From name-calling to rock-throwing, they make life miserable for other kids and for the staff. Almost daily someone sends them to the supervisor's office. Natalie usually just lets them cool off, tells them to stay away from each other for the rest of the day, and carries on with her paperwork. Mind you, in the past she has tried lots of other things: behavior charts, parent conferences, lectures, threats, and so on. Nothing has worked. She has decided not to waste her energy anymore. Instead, she prays that one or two of the boys will move to another state—soon.*

One day, bored with her reports, Natalie chats with the boys, who sit sprawled over a table in her office. The table doesn't serve much purpose other than being the place angry staff can plunk the ornery threesome.

Natalie does find the boys rather charming. Joshua wears his brother's hand-me-down shirts and jackets. The arms are so long that no one knows for sure if he has hands. He uses the long sleeves to wipe his perpetually running nose.

Lonnie rarely speaks. He kicks at things. His shock of dirty brown hair, to which he adds grease each day in an attempt to look cool, sticks to his forehead. His squinty eyes don't let anybody look in. They do occasionally show twinkle wrinkles around the edges.

Markus can swear a blue streak. He can also look you in the eye, bat his long black curling eyelashes, and say the kindest thing you've heard all week.

That's what happens on this day. He lifts his head from the table when he notices Natalie's eyes straying from her work. Looking directly at her with his soft brown eyes, he asks, "Do you really love kids so much? Is that why you're always working like that?"

"I guess so, yeah," she answers. "I love you guys, you know. I just don't know what to do about you anymore. What if we make a deal? You stay out of trouble on the playground from Monday to Thursday, and on Friday I'll let you do something special. Think about a special responsibility that you would like to have. Something you're in charge of for the other kids. What do you think?"

The boys look at each other. They bob their heads and say, "Sure. Why not?"

"Okay, come in on Monday with your idea and we'll try to work this out. Now scram. And behave for the rest of the day."

Monday comes. Natalie has actually almost forgotten about her idea. Joshua, Lonnie, and Markus haven't. The threesome appear in her doorway the minute she comes back from a meeting. Markus is the spokesman (the kids know, as most kids do, what their strengths are).

"We thought of something we want to do," he says, tilting his head slightly to give the full effect of his long lashes. "We think you'll like it. It'll make your job easier."

"Lots easier," sniffles Joshua.

"So, what's the plan?" Natalie asks, somewhat fearfully.

"We want to be playground emergency people."

"How would you do that?"

"We would wear badges and have medical kits. Then we could walk around the playground making sure that no one was getting hurt. We want everyone to be safe here, as you always say," Markus says, keeping a businesslike, yet charming, attitude.

"I think you can make that work," Natalie says.

The corners of Lonnie's eyes wrinkle.

Soon three shoe boxes appear on the table in Natalie's office, each labeled "First Aid." Staff members help write slogans all around the boxes. The kids meet with the school nurse to get ideas and a mini-course in hygiene, boundaries, and when to get adult help. The kids bring things from home. Natalie and the staff contribute bandages, magnifying glasses, a stethoscope, clean rags, small splints, and other useful things. The deal is that if the kids don't end up sitting at the table from Monday to Thursday because they have acted inappropriately, they can get the boxes on Friday and do their chosen work.

They show up in Natalie's office every Friday, and only on Fridays, for the next four weeks. "Who would have thought," Natalie asks herself that fourth Friday, "that this tough bunch would think being the first aid patrol was so great?" She watches them as they walk down the hall, noting how they keep their shoulders back and hold their heads high. Joshua's shirt sleeves are rolled up. His clean hands are wrapped tightly around the shoe box. Printed in black marker letters on the side of his box is "We're All Safe Here."

Kids who chronically act out lose more and more control over their lives. Perhaps they have never learned that it is even possible to have any control. They are excited and more than willing to be involved when offered the chance. They will need coaching throughout. They will make mistakes. They may test the system. But if they are encouraged, they often will learn and thrive.

Here's a follow-up *to Joshua, Markus, and Lonnie's story.
After the boys' emergency club became successful, a second
grade girl, Heidi, approached Natalie. "How come the bad
kids always get to do the fun stuff?" she asked referring to the*
first aid patrol.

*Natalie explained that the boys found it challenging to act appropriately. It
was very hard for them. When they worked hard and overcame their difficulties,
they got to choose a new responsibility. Heidi agreed that the boys' behavior had
changed. Natalie said, "We could make a deal like that, too, if you want. Is there
anything that's hard for you to do? That you don't particularly enjoy?"*

"I HATE to clean stuff."

*"Well, you're in Pat's room. She likes it to be super clean, as you know. We
could set something up with her. And then you can let me know what special
responsibility you would enjoy. Think about it."*

*A couple of weeks later, Natalie saw Heidi in the hall. "Have you come up
with an idea of what you might like as a special responsibility if you do more
cleaning?"*

"Nah," Heidi said, "I decided it wasn't worth it."

☞ ☟

Often you worry that if you spend extra time with the kids who have
trouble staying in line, the other children won't get the attention they
deserve. That is a legitimate and caring concern. It helps to remember,
though, that the children for whom appropriate behavior is the norm benefit every day from the activities, environments, materials, and special
events that you plan for them. They can easily engage in conversation with
children and adults and are often affirmed for being who they are, for acting appropriately. Because it isn't so difficult for you or for those children,
you don't realize that they are getting their needs met daily. You provide
a great atmosphere for kids who can readily take advantage of it and you
reach out to those who can't. Behavior guidance is all of that.

Do Teach Responsibility by Being Responsible

Teaching responsibility is also an important element in the new behavior guidance model. There are at least two ways to teach responsibility. One, already discussed in this chapter, is to give children as much responsibility for their own lives as they can handle. You are there to help them assess, to guide and encourage, and at times to hold them accountable. As they assume responsibility, they will experience the personal power that comes from being capable. They will also learn their limits and when to ask for help.

An equally important way to teach responsibility is to act responsibly. The old adage, "Do as I say, not as I do" never made much sense, and is not effective in guiding children's behavior. Children learn more by watching what we do than by listening to what we tell them to do.

There used to be a public service commercial on television that showed an adolescent boy standing in a telephone booth. It is night and a storm rages. Clad in a black leather jacket, hair spiked, rings in his nose and ear, the boy picks up the phone and puts it back several times. The narrator says, "He ran away. He's scared—scared to call home and scared not to."

The camera tightens on the boy's face. We hear the voices he is remembering. A woman's slurred, drunken voice says, "I just don't know why you can't be responsible. Please, just for me. I need you to help me. Be good, won't you?"

Next, a man's voice angrily shouts, "Stop babying him! He's a bum. I'll knock him around. A good beating—that'll shape him up. It always has."

The boy's tears drip down his face, and the rain pours down the glass booth. A clap of thunder crashes as his fist slams the telephone. We'll never know what the boy decides. A runaway youth hotline number rolls across the TV screen.

In this example, what the teenager's parents said and how they punished him didn't teach him responsibility. Instead, people would say he acted irresponsibly. He ran away from home, probably dropped out of school, maybe did drugs or some stealing. "Caused his parents so much heartache," people would say. Actually, he acted as he saw them act. Numbing the pain, running from reality, being angry, not doing his job responsibly.

Of course, not all kids act out because their parents don't fulfill their responsibilities as parents. All discipline issues are not the result of irresponsible staff behavior. But modeling responsible behavior is one way to promote responsible actions.

How can you model responsibility for schoolagers?

First of all, you need to love your work. You show up every day ready to do the job. You let the kids know by your actions, and your words, that you are enthused and ready to be the adult that they need in their lives. You can say things like,

> "I'm really glad to be here today."

> "Let me know how I can help."

> "I've got the dye and fabric for tie-dye that I promised."

> "Let's review that conflict resolution plan at group check-in today. A couple of you said that you needed some clarification."

> "I'm sorry I didn't talk to your parents last night, to tell them how well you're doing. I tried four times but the line was busy. Find me when they come to pick you up today. I'll give them the whole great report then."

What's happening in these examples? What are you doing to set up responsible behaviors in kids? You accepted a job and have a good attitude about it. You speak respectfully to the children. You made a promise and you kept it. You are acting responsibly as an adult by being there to guide and solve problems. When you couldn't fulfill another promise, you let the children know why and told them what you would do about it. Your actions and attitudes clearly demonstrate responsible behavior.

You do not let the children hear you saying things like these:

"I can't believe what I have to do around here. I get paid less than a burger flipper. Why should I have to work so hard?"

"These kids are hopeless. I might as well sit here and let them go wild."

"That supervisor is totally unreasonable. I have no intention of coming up with a new activity every day. I've got more important things to do with my life than getting tie-dye stuff together."

"It doesn't matter what we do. With the parents these kids have it doesn't matter. Their parents just don't care."

"I don't owe you respect, kid. You earn it."

Not only are words like these not teaching kids anything, they are also destroying kids' respect for you and their view of you as a responsible person.

On the other hand, when you do your job well, keep your promises, speak respectfully, and work in partnership with parents, you are building a trusting relationship. The relationship will be strong enough to support you when you hold the children responsible. You will be able to have conversations like this one:

"Tanya, you lied to me today when I asked if you were one of the people who shot spit balls all over the restroom ceiling. I'm confused. I thought we respected each other. Do I ever lie to you?"

"I don't think so."

"Well, you have my word that I don't. I think you know that I make mistakes sometimes. But I let you know why and tell you that I'm sorry and how I'm going to try to fix it if I can. You know that, don't you?"

"Yeah."

"Well, then, I don't understand why when you made a mistake today and got involved in that restroom ruckus, why you lied to me. I don't think that's fair. Do you?"

"No."

"Thanks for saying that. Can we make our deal again that we will tell each other the truth, even when we make mistakes?"

"Okay."

"Shake on it?"

"Shake on it."

"Now about today…"

"I know, what am I going to do about all of those spitballs?"

"And the janitor's time."

"And the janitor's time."

If the adult in this conversation hadn't been a responsible role model, Tanya could have reasonably argued with her. As a matter of fact, the adult probably wouldn't have used this track of mutual responsibility at all. Instead, she would probably have relied on the old model of control and punishment and would have handed down a sentence for the wrongdoing. A power struggle may very well have ensued, and the vicious cycle for control between the child and the adult would continue. The child wouldn't become responsible—just controlled. And there would be many more episodes of inappropriate, irresponsible behavior as a result.

Adults do not have to be perfect, but they do have to have integrity, to be reliable and trustworthy, and to be role models for responsibility. I am going to tell you a true story that is difficult for me to share. I do so because I hope that it will illustrate the cost of acting irresponsibly with children.

I taught third grade in a large inner-city school. The kids were very poor and moved frequently. Many of their parents struggled with addictions and violence and were illiterate. Children arrived at school malnourished, tired, belligerent, or withdrawn. Classes were way too large, supplies were limited, and the district supervisors rated teachers on the appearance of their rooms and the quietness of their students. Working under these difficult conditions, most teachers had given up on the kids. They kept order with severe punishments and put-downs. I tried not to do as they did. There were times when I doubted my beliefs. The kids tested and re-tested me and my changes from the status quo. But together the kids and I moved forward. I did see the light starting to shine again in some kids' eyes at the same time that the kids improved academically.

When I learned that the district supervisor was coming to observe me, I had a chat with the class. "She's coming to see if I am a good teacher. She's not coming to judge you. But, if you could help me out by being your most cooperative selves, I would appreciate it. We do some different things in Room 308, don't we?"

Most of the heads nodded and the kids said, "Yes, teacher."

"I want her to see that what we are doing helps you to learn your school lessons and how to get along with each other. I'm proud of you and you're proud of yourselves. So be yourselves, okay?"

"Okay," they said.

One boy, Billy, sat without answering, although the narrowing of his washed-out brown eyes told me that he was listening. Thin, tense, and smart, Billy had attended 12 schools the previous year. His mother wanted the best for him but knew that she couldn't provide it. So, shortly before the school year started she had dropped him off at his grandmother's house and left. Billy hadn't seen her since. Living in crack houses, watching his mother being abused, being left alone for long periods of time, had left Billy silent except for a few swear words, and unable to read and write. His grandmother and I worked well together trying to help him restore his trust and develop a sense of self. Billy came to reading group but would never read out loud. I didn't know if he was learning or not.

The supervisor arrived just as Billy's group gathered for reading. When I asked if anyone wanted to read there were the usual two volunteers. I asked again and Billy raised his hand. He read a paragraph. Haltingly, mispronouncing a few words, he read in a new voice, soft but not scared. I thanked him for reading and moved on. As my eyes filled with tears, Billy and I exchanged a look. In the look, I said, "Thank you. Thank you," and he said, "You are welcome." Simply, lovingly, filling my heart.

About three weeks later, on a hot, sticky day, the children were surly and I was exhausted. The custodian, James, sauntered into the room to work on the windowshade roller that would occasionally release the shade and send it flop, flop, flopping up the window. Billy, upset because the toothpick tower he built had fallen apart, stood up and called me a swear word. The custodian looked at me and looked at Billy. Billy kept swearing.

"You gonna let him get away with that?" James asked. "No kid would talk to me that way. What the heck are you running in here, a circus? Let me have him outside with this roller. He won't swear at nobody again."

The silence, a quarter of a second long, melted the heat and froze everything in the room in place. Only my mouth moved. I blurted out, in an angry voice, "Sit down, Billy, I'm tired of your outbursts. I'm tired of dealing with you. Just sit down and be quiet. Don't you dare say anything until I tell you you can. Do it now. Right now!"

The room began to move again. Kids looked at each other. Yelling and traffic from the street pushed through the open windows. The custodian stepped up onto his ladder, roller in hand. Billy stood still, thin and tense. He looked me in the eye. "I knew you'd turn out to be just like the rest of 'em," he said, in a voice that I hadn't heard before, soft, tough, and sad.

I'm not sure what I did. The look on Billy's face, his words, branded my being.

I made my apologies to Billy the next day. He sat silently through them and wouldn't respond. The year went on. Billy didn't quit trying altogether, but he didn't try as hard or as often in his work. He didn't try to connect with others as he had before. He swore at me more often. I didn't let my guilt get in the way of dealing with those incidents, but it was clear that he felt very little responsibility towards me or himself. Billy and I never mended our relationship.

☉ ☉

I had done many things well with the children, including Billy, that year. And I don't believe we can expect ourselves to be perfect, even in the areas of responsibility and trustworthiness. Usually we can go to the child and make amends, and the child learns something from that, too. With a child just a little less fragile, the results of the mistake probably wouldn't have been as dramatic. The relationship might have been stronger, the child more sure of himself. But Billy didn't come with much resiliency. I was probably his start. I hope that he carried a little of that start with him and that others nourished it. I don't beat myself up for the mistake, but I believe that this story dramatically reminds us of the influence we have around children. Children watch who we are and what they do, and they follow our examples. If we want them to become responsible, we need to help them take on responsibility, and believe in them, and remember that they are watching.

I did learn from my mistake, not always and everywhere, but many times. Billy's voice and face are still with me and are still teaching me. Often when I feel the urge to shirk responsibility because I am tired, or pressured, or whatever, I take a breath and say, "This one's for you, Billy, wherever you are." I pull myself together and put my skills and soul back to work trying to be trustworthy and responsible.

I hope that you never have seen a look like Billy's on a child's face. I hope that you have never heard those words. If you have, I hope that you learned from it.

The following story happened later in my life. It shows what can happen when we do act as responsible adults in children's lives. This one's for you, Billy.

Trent's mother died. *She died at home, hooked up to tubes and holding her son's hand. His father didn't know how to shield Trent from the pain and couldn't deal with the scars it left, so he yelled or remained silent.*

Trent carried a wild look in his eyes and raging loneliness in his heart. I had worked for two years to try to establish a relationship with him. One day when he built a block structure, I asked, "What are you building?"

With a swift kick, he toppled the tower, shouting at me, "Go away stupid."

"Trent," I said gently, "I am here for you no matter what."

"Not if I call you bad names," he said.

"I don't want you to do that, but I will still love you."

"Not if I spit at you."

"I'll still love you."

He invented more gruesome possibilities. I kept reassuring him.

Finally he asked, "Can I go now?"

"Are you okay to play safely?" I asked.

"Yeah," he answered and tore out.

A second later, he popped his head back into the doorway. "I believe you," he said and darted away again.

≈ Jean Steiner and Mary Steiner Whelan

Trent's swearing decreased dramatically after this incident. He was less reclusive and more able to interact peacefully with others. Things weren't perfect, of course, but hanging in there with him did make a difference.

To close this chapter, write yourself a letter. Tell yourself what you want to accomplish when you work with children. Talk about what kind of person you want to be with them. What do you hope they will learn about independence, decision making, and responsibility? How will you use behavior guidance to help them learn those things? What will you use, as I use the story about Billy, to keep you on track when times get tough?

Take your time. Think things through. Remember what your strengths are. Enjoy talking things over with the person who knows you best—you!

Dear Me,

_____

_____

_____

_____

_____

_____

_____

_____

_____

_____

_____

_____

_____

_____

exercise continued on next page

Please write your notes, thoughts, or stories here:

Chapter 15

Encourage Independence: Don'ts

Anonymous

Imagine the joy of day by day growing into a fuller understanding of who you are—who you are, really, the power you really have.

≈ Tae Yun Kim

Don't Use Bribes

A bribe is, in the context of this book, an offer of something that an adult thinks a child wants in order to get the child to behave the way that an adult wants. All of us probably remember being bribed as kids.

For example:

"Eat your vegetables and you'll get dessert."

Read that sentence again. How easy would it be to turn the bribe into a threat?

"If you don't eat your vegetables, you won't get dessert."

It would be that easy.

In chapter 13, we discussed why threats aren't effective. They are controlling and punitive, and they scare kids into doing things rather than helping them learn in this case, about nutrition and how to take care of their health. It is easier for us to understand that a threat is controlling and harsh than it is to understand that the same thing is true of a bribe. Children quickly see the similarities between threats and bribes because both are contests between the adult and the child. The adult has what the child wants. The child has to figure out how to get it. One way would be to do what the adult wants. In many cases, including the example above, what the adult wants is subjective. Does "eat your vegetables" mean a piece of the corn and a bean? This is how we end up in conversations that begin, "What do you mean, all of the vegetables, that's not fair. What about two more beans?" and so on and so forth.

What is the child learning? Is he learning how to make decisions about his health? Is he learning that finishing everything on his plate is always a good thing? (Do you eat everything every day, or are there days when you just don't want any beans?) Is he being respected as someone who might care about himself enough to make good decisions?

There seem to be more and more ads in the media that operate from the premise that if children knew what was good for them, they wouldn't have anything to do with it. If it's food, you don't tell them it has vitamins. If it's an educational toy, you don't tell them they'll learn anything. All of these forms of manipulation keep children from learning how to be responsible. Children are more concerned about their own well-being and more intelligent than adults often believe.

For example, I recently overheard a six-year-old girl tell another child about the dangers of secondhand smoke. The girl smelled smoke on the other child's clothing. She told her friend, matter-of-factly, that if you are around smoke, a lot of the smoke goes up your nose and into your body. She said it turns inside parts of your body black and makes them sick. She also said that it made her nose itch and her mouth taste funny. "I hate that. I leave the room if somebody is smoking," she said.

Her friend listened attentively, and they went on with what they were doing. The girl did not say, "I'll be your best friend if you don't go by smoke." Rather, she presented the facts and assumed that her friend was smart enough to understand her.

We adults can learn from that girl. She didn't bribe her friend. She believed that he would want to know that the smoke could hurt him. She didn't try to trick him into doing what was good for him. And she remained his friend.

Children want their bodies to be healthy, and they like to learn. We as adults don't want to teach them that we are the enemy forcing what is good on them or that they themselves are "cute" at best, stupid at worst.

Bribery assumes that children aren't interested in doing the thing that is best for themselves or for others. It assumes that children can be motivated only by extrinsic rewards. By assuming that, adults teach children that rewards are the reason for doing things. What might seem like a nice gesture on an adult's part, like offering a piece of candy for cleaning the room, ends up teaching the child that we do things to get stuff for ourselves. It implies that the child is not caring or smart enough to help because it would be good for everyone to know where the toys are, for example.

A bribe can also lead to more monitoring. It turns the adult into a police officer and a judge. Let's say the bribe is a trip to the gym when homework is completed. You have to check to make sure the homework is done before the child can go to the gym. You are likely to end up debating, "What does 'done' mean? What's 'homework'?" The standards are subjective, and the decision is in the hands of the adults. The child is doing her homework to get the reward, not because it needs to be done, will save her time later, or will teach her something valuable.

If she wants to get to the gym in a hurry, she can lie to you. If you make her complete it, you are taking away the chance for her to learn what will happen if she doesn't. Maybe she will get in trouble with her teacher or parents. Maybe she won't learn what she needs to know on the next test. Rather than bribing, you can help her think rationally about options and possible outcomes. And you can respect that she wants what is good for her. If she doesn't, she will have to face the results. Bribery won't teach her about options, outcomes, or respect.

Another problem with bribery is that it often doesn't work. What if you offer a child stickers for getting into line to leave the gym? You may hear, "I don't want those stupid stickers, anyway." What then? You have to do something else to make the child comply. You may very well get into an argument. You could be setting up power struggles as well as missing the opportunity to teach children the value of internal motivation and doing things for the community's benefit.

Here is an example of some of the results of relying on bribery:

I worked with a teacher *who gave kids gum for everything they did. She was friendly and creative and liked kids, but she didn't have a clue what to do with them. One day I substituted in her room. I asked a child to empty the wastebasket.*
"How much gum do I get?" she asked.

"None," I said.

"Then why should I do it?"

"Well, it is full. Kids are working on art projects that are going to make more scraps. The room will get messy if it isn't emptied. We all deserve a nice place to hang out without garbage around. You're a strong kid who knows where the dumpster is. That's five reasons. Can you think of more?"

The child entered into the reasons game, as I thought she might because I knew that she was a cool kid with a good sense of humor. (Remember that part? Get to know the kids.) We ended up giving each other reasons like "because the chances of Superman coming in and doing it are zero." We laughed. She emptied the basket.

The second thing that happened, of course, was that the teacher and I had a conversation about building a group dynamic that taught kids to do things for the good of the group and because it was a good thing to do, instead of because they would get gum. The next day she told the kids about the no-more-gum policy and began the complicated task of teaching kids how to internalize responsible behavior.

☙ ☙

Another danger in bribery is the group bribe. "When you are all quiet, we will watch a movie." All but two kids get quiet. What then? Do you punish the whole group? Do you wait for the kids to turn on each other with loud comments like, "Will you shut up?" Do you show the movie although it's not really quiet, because in your judgment it's quiet enough, this time?

What can you do instead, if you are ready to show a movie and the room is too noisy? First of all, decide if the room is really too noisy. Does it have to be completely silent for you to turn on the video? Probably not. Next, you could ask how many kids want to watch a movie. Those who do will probably watch. Those who don't could have other choices. Perhaps having everyone do the same thing at the same time is the problem. Watch yourself to see if your expectations are just habits. Perhaps they are based on what you learned from your teachers.

Bribery is sometimes disguised in behavior modification techniques. There may be some children for whom behavior modification is a helpful tool. In this case, the program should be set up by an expert who is familiar with the child's particular challenges and with behavior modification systems. What often happens when school-age care staff attempt to set up a reward system is that we tell the child that if he can control his behaviors for a specified amount of time, a week, for example, he will get a reward. We often use this method for children who have ADD or ADHD or who we think have similar impulse control issues.

Staff spend a lot of time designing a system, buying the reward, setting up charts, and talking to the child. We tell the child that at the end of the week he will get that new toy he wants. The child is excited and we have hope that the plan will work. What often happens is that in a short time, sometimes in the first hour, the child acts inappropriately. He fails once again. The system becomes worthless. The child has nothing to lose any more. Actually he has lost everything, including his sense of competency and self-esteem. He may as well do what discouraged children do: act out. We want to throw up our hands and say that nothing we try works and go back to punishment for specific incidents of inappropriate behavior.

Or, we can revise the system, give him a few more chances, a smaller reward, a shorter time frame, or some other modification. We begin a complex series of subjective, adult-controlled decisions about whether or not he will ever be able to get the carrot at the end of the stick. He learns once again that he is not able to control himself but must depend on extrinsic rewards and adult interventions. And, even then, he will probably fail. If the child could control himself, he wouldn't need these rewards. Because he hasn't learned (or for some reason can't learn) intrinsic control, behavior modification will not work for him. Instead, he will get frustrated, angry, and convinced of his own incompetence.

I understand, from personal experience, situations in which rewards offered as bribes or as behavior modification have not been effective.

Years ago *my husband and I moved back to Minnesota from the East Coast to be closer to my widowed father-in-law. Over the next several months, we were in several car accidents, we had a third baby, my father-in-law died, and my grandmother suffered a stroke. One day when I was driving my kids to see Grandma in the nursing home, I suddenly became ill. I thought I was having a heart attack.*

What actually happened was that post-traumatic stress syndrome was entering my life. The series of accidents and stress triggered anxiety about driving. For the next year I tried everything to beat it. I had counseling, took drugs, was attached to biofeedback machines, did acupuncture, learned yoga, and, yes, participated in a behavior modification program. Time after time I failed to be able to drive. The anxieties began to affect other parts of my life. Finally, a sensitive counselor said, "You've earned this phobia. Instead of beating yourself up over it, why don't we figure out how a competent person like you can function without driving."

I still don't drive. I have spoken to thousands of people around the country, run school-age care programs, written books, parasailed, worked as an editor, set up my own business, traveled alone in Africa and Mexico. Nevertheless, in this car-dependent culture, people think there is something very wrong with me because I can't drive.

Although it is different from the problems of a child with self-control issues, my experience with driving is also similar. It wouldn't matter if someone offered me a million dollars if I could drive across the state at the end of the week. No bribe would work. I will probably always deal with the issue, but I am not incompetent or bad. If I had continued to believe that, if others had kept holding out rewards I couldn't obtain, I would have gotten more and more engaged in the cycle of anxiety and failure. I can and have learned how to deal with getting around. Not in the same way that people do who drive, but in my own ways. So it is with children who have behavior difficulties. No amount of bribery or behavior modification programs will work if the children do not experience what they can and can't do for themselves. They can learn to handle their lives in their own ways.

We can help them learn how to deal with who they are. We have to let them know that they are strong, that they have options and abilities. The longer they fail while trying to do things the way we think is normal, the worse they will feel about themselves, and the more they will give in and act out.

It is not always easy for me to wait for a bus in the cold or ask for a ride. Not because the task is necessarily so difficult but because it makes me feel different from others and replays tapes of being a failure. But I have learned from my home, my friends, and my own successes that I am okay. That is what we need to help children learn: that it is not easy, but that they can do it. We need to encourage and sometimes push them a little to find their own courage and to celebrate their successes.

Write about an issue in your life that was or is difficult for you to deal with.

Write what helps you to deal with it, and what doesn't, and why.

_____

_____

_____

_____

Now write about a time you attempted to help a child deal with his issue by using rewards or bribes—and it didn't work.

_____

_____

_____

_____

What are some reasons that it didn't work?

_____

_____

_____

_____

What could you have tried instead?

_____

_____

Why do you think that might have been more effective?

_____

_____

Don't Praise Excessively

A school-age care staff person *stops to watch Gillian, who is painting at the easel. "What a magnificent sunflower you painted. It looks so real!" she says. "You are a great artist! Sweetie, you will have to do something with that talent. Don't just let it go to waste. You should take art lessons. Look, boys and girls, isn't this the most beautiful picture of a flower you've ever seen?"*

                 ⑨   ⑨

At first glance, we might think that the adult is doing a fine job of giving Gillian positive strokes for what she is doing. But let's look again.

What a magnificent sunflower you painted. It looks so real.

"Magnificent" is a strong word and is in the eye of the beholder. The child may not think it is magnificent. She may wish that the leaves were larger or the center more brown. The adult has used her power to judge and label and has taken away the child's right to assess her own work.

Also, it may or may not look real. The child may think, *I've never seen a sunflower that looks like this one.* The teacher's opinion becomes suspect. And, how important is looking real? The child who hears this may keep trying to make things look real rather than experimenting with design and color. Unknowingly, the adult stamped "looking real" as good—as the kind of art that is desirable. Is the teacher even completely sure that the painting represents a sunflower?

You are a great artist!

Again, the words are too strong. She is probably not on the same level as Georgia O'Keeffe or Michelangelo. We are all artists in our own way, but this statement puts things out of balance with reality. The child knows that she is not a great artist. She will learn to mistrust both her own view of what she does, and the adult's view. She doesn't need to be a great artist. She is a kid experimenting with her own creativity.

Sweetie, you will have to do something with that talent. Don't just let it go to waste.

A cute nickname like "Sweetie" can sometimes be an intimate term of endearment between two people who know each other very well. But used casually, it can sometimes make the child feel babied and not respected. Such cutesy words are frequently part of praise and reinforce the child's belief that this is not a realistic evaluation of her work, but rather a sign that the adult doesn't take her seriously.

Then, the adult tells the child that she has to "do something" with the talent that the adult has decided she possesses. The adult tells her not "waste" her talent. The shaming implication is that simply enjoying the art she does in the here and now is not valuable.

These stretches from the here and now into a vague responsibility in the future also often come up in excessive praise. Without knowing it, the adult has taken control of the child's work by judging it and her. It is easy, then, for the adult to play the traditional adult role of projecting control into the child's future.

You should go to art school.

At some level the child responds, probably not out loud, "I was just trying to paint a simple picture here. Give me a break!"

I am remembering a story about a group of kindergartners who went on a field trip to a nature center. One child said to another, "There's a fox running through the woods."

The other child responded, "Cool, but don't tell the teacher. She'll make us write a story and draw a picture about it."

It is important to help the children in the moment. Try not to take over their futures.

Look, boys and girls, isn't this the most beautiful picture of a flower you've ever seen?

Oops, now the adult has really done it. The child's private relationship with the painting has been brought into the public forum without the child's permission. The child may be very embarrassed. She has just been placed before the whole class for judgment. It very likely isn't the most beautiful picture of a flower that the other children have ever seen and some of them might say so, or at least think so. The child's work has also been singled out as the standard for all other children, who may not be able to achieve it. They may retaliate against the painter by making fun of her for being teacher's pet, or they may just feel inadequate.

A child who depends on adult validation and attention will become more dependent. What happens tomorrow when she is painting another picture and the adult just looks at it and keeps walking? Of course, that painting won't be a beautiful one in the child's eyes because she has learned to see things through adults' eyes.

The teacher in this scenario, at first glance, seems to be helping Gillian. But because of the excessive praise, the girl might have

- developed mistrust of the teacher at the same time that she learned to be more dependent on the teacher's opinion.

- become less confident in her own ability to judge things.

- felt shamed.

- been embarrassed in front of other children.

- felt controlled.

Was this what the teacher wanted? Of course not! But by taking control through excessive praise, she robbed the girl of her chance to learn how to be in control of her own thoughts and enjoyment.

Those of us who grew up with this kind of adult control may still experience it. What if you get a new haircut—maybe even one that you spent more on than usual—and no one at work comments on it the next day? Is it a good haircut? For many of us the answer is, "No." If no one said it was great, we reason, it must be unattractive. Do we do a better job at work that day? Do we work better with the people who we believe don't like our haircut? Is there a spring in our step and a stronger sense of our capabilities?

Probably not.

Women may be more able to relate to those kinds of feelings than men—especially about personal appearance. We need to help girls not base their self-worth on their appearance. Boys receive positive feedback, for the most part, on what they do well. Girls receive it for how they look. The next time you want to comment on a girl's appearance or on what she is wearing, try to think of something else to say such as, "You seemed to really be into that game of chess yesterday. Where did you learn to play?"

Excessive praise may seem to have only subtle effects, but its effect in the long run is to reinforce the punishment-control model of behavior guidance. Children who don't learn to rely on their own judgment, who feel fooled, or looked down upon, are more likely to choose inappropriate ways of seeking control and opportunities for independent thought and action. We want children in the new relationship model of behavior guidance to trust themselves and us so that they can take risks and gain independence in ways that further their growth and don't encourage negative behavior.

What do we do instead of praising excessively? Three alternative ways to support children are recognition, encouragement, and coaching.

Recognition

In the above example, recognition might be stated this way: "Gillian, cool sunflower."

No judgment. No taking over her work or her future. Just a statement that says, "It's neat. I like it." You might also say, "Tell me about how you made those petals." The child can then talk about what she did and feel good about it. You let the child keep control of the project and what she thinks about it.

Encouragement

A conversation that included encouragement would sound something like, "It looks like you really enjoy painting."

"Yeah, guess I do."

"Some people who paint sign their work to let people know that they are the person who made the creation. Would you like to know how they do that?"

"Yeah."

You noticed the work. You gave the child the chance to take pride in it and in the fact that she did it. You raised her work to the status of other art by suggesting that she sign her work without patronizing or condescending.

Coaching

Coaching helps a child build on the skills she has and to develop new ones. The conversation might sound like this:

"You mixed those colors in such an interesting way. What colors did you use?"

"I think brown, orange, and yellow."

"Do you like how it looks?"

"Sort of."

"What do you mean?"

"Well, I was hoping it would look sunnier."

"I wonder how you might be able to do that?"

"The sun's yellow, so I guess it would make sense to try more yellow."

"Give it a try. What do you think now?"

"Still not sunny enough."

"Maybe it would help to look out the window. See that bright green leaf?"

"Yes."

"What colors do you see in it?"

"Green, of course. But I guess I see some yellow and some black."

"I see that too. You could experiment on this small piece of paper with some other colors along with the yellow. Maybe some darker ones and some lighter ones. You might find what you want to add to the sunflower."

The child told you what outcome she wanted. You asked her to use her observation skills to come up with a solution. Then, you gave her a tool—the idea about the smaller paper. You used her observation about what she saw and gave it a slightly different name—lighter and darker. You then said that you believed she could find her own solution through her own experimenting.

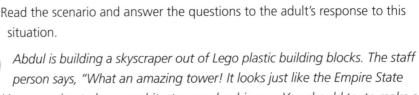

Read the scenario and answer the questions to the adult's response to this situation.

Abdul is building a skyscraper out of Lego plastic building blocks. The staff person says, "What an amazing tower! It looks just like the Empire State Building. You are going to be an architect some day, big guy. You should try to make a new building every day. Practice makes perfect. This building is sure perfect. Wouldn't your mother be proud if you became famous some day? You're a smart thing, you are."

What would a recognition response sound like?

_____

_____

_____

What would an encouragement response sound like?

_____

_____

_____

What would a coaching response sound like?

_____

_____

_____

Share your responses with someone else and ask them to respond to your ideas.

Don't Belittle

It's lunch time on a non-school day at a school-age care program. Gregory unpacks his lunch, a jelly sandwich with potato chips, a candy bar, and a can of soda pop. Kris, the staff person, rolls her eyes at the other staff and says, "Great nutrition, huh? He'll be in a state of hyperactivity in half an hour. His parental units must be real winners." She thinks that using words like "nutrition," "hyperactivity," and "parental units" will keep Gregory from understanding what she's saying. She believes that because his lunch isn't balanced, Gregory (like his parents, she assumes) isn't very bright. He may or may not understand all the words, but he does know that she is talking about him.

The other staff members laugh, and one says, "No wonder we can't control him."

Kris says, "Sure you got enough sugar there, buster? You need to tell your mom that you've got enough problems without getting more goofy from sugar."

Now Gregory has to deal with Kris's sarcasm, her judgment that he is a behavior problem, and her calling his parents inadequate. If he is four feet ten inches tall on the outside, he is feeling about one inch tall inside. What will he do with this belittling experience? Perhaps withdraw. More likely, given the staff's impressions of him, he will cause trouble. He might say, "It's none of your business what I eat." When he leaves his candy wrapper and soda can on the table and Kris tells him to come back and throw them away, he might say, "You do it. Or are you afraid sugar stuff will kill you?"

"He's a real winner," Kris might respond to the other staff. They might chuckle and nod their heads.

If Kris feels the need to correct this disrespectful talk, a discipline crisis then begins. Also, establishing a positive relationship through which Kris could encourage different behaviors becomes impossible.

For the children you work with, belittling statements, sarcasm, jokes that they can't understand, and talking about them to others in front of them in unkind ways are barriers to their developing relationships with the adults who treat them that way. Such treatment also interferes with their sense of confidence in themselves.

Belittling is especially dangerous when we deal with children from cultures different from our own. Negative and disrespectful comments about their clothing, use of language, food, and customs cut to the core of self-esteem. As does mispronouncing their names or giving them nicknames because we find it difficult to pronounce their real names. Like the people in the restaurant, we may find it easy to make fun of what we don't understand.

In the lunch scene above, sarcasm raised its ugly head. Sarcasm has no place in our work with children. Humor certainly does. Many tense situations are diffused by lighthearted, respectful humor. Humor builds relationships and positive feelings about ourselves and others. Sarcasm tears them down. When we use sarcasm we assume that the other person is somehow less valuable than we are and deserves to be mocked. Sarcasm is mean at its roots. It doesn't serve any healthy purpose. Monitor it and drop it from your repertoire.

Some of us are so accustomed to using sarcasm that we don't notice it. There are several ways that you can reflect on whether you are being sarcastic or not.

- Is what you said kind? If it were taken out of context, would it sound kind? For example, a child trips over a chair. You might say, "You are such a klutz," and mean it in an affectionate way. But if you listen to just the words, they are insulting. It would be just as easy to say a kind thing such as, "Are you okay?" or nothing at all.

- What is the tone of your voice? "That's a good idea!" can be said in a positive way or a sarcastic way. I'm sure you know how to say it either way.

- Does what you are saying enhance the relationship? The reason we want to use humor is to lighten up situations, share fun, and communicate with someone. If a child tells you she is going to be an astronaut when she grows up and you say, "I'll send you to the moon—the dark side!" are you enhancing the relationship? Probably not. In this situation the child probably wants to talk about her dream, a little anyway. Your comment ended the discussion and put you in charge in a threatening way.

We all really like to hear positive things—affirmations about the fact that we are important. In our society, for some reason, we are often uncomfortable giving and receiving positive statements. You can start changing that by giving and asking for positives. You'll be surprised what changes you will see in the kids: less defensiveness, more openness, fewer arguments, less swearing. You will even be surprised by how much better you feel.

Another common belittling tactic that comes up in discipline situations is putting a child down for failing to "act your age." Statements like "I know four year olds who have more sense than that," or actions such as putting a fourth grader in with the kindergartners for a day because "you're acting like one, so you may as well be one," shred children's self-esteem and breed belligerent behaviors.

Calling children sarcastic names like Hot Stuff, Tubby, or Dummy, or saying, "You're as weak as a girl," also have a belittling effect.

Structuring a program so that children don't have choices and independence is also belittling.

Warning signs that belittling may be going on in your program include

- Children "talking back."
- Children using sarcasm or talking disrespectfully about adults.
- Children making fun of each other.
- Children refusing to talk to adults.
- Children being afraid to state their own opinions.
- Children acting helpless.

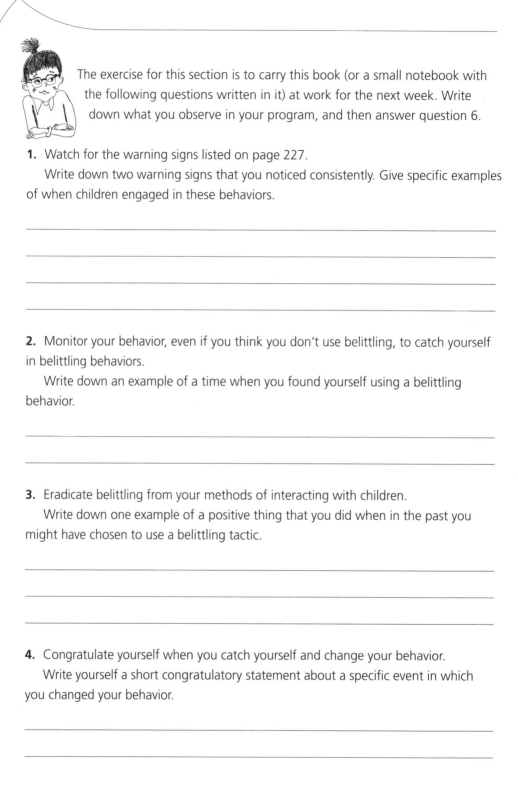

The exercise for this section is to carry this book (or a small notebook with the following questions written in it) at work for the next week. Write down what you observe in your program, and then answer question 6.

1. Watch for the warning signs listed on page 227.

Write down two warning signs that you noticed consistently. Give specific examples of when children engaged in these behaviors.

_____

_____

_____

_____

2. Monitor your behavior, even if you think you don't use belittling, to catch yourself in belittling behaviors.

Write down an example of a time when you found yourself using a belittling behavior.

_____

_____

3. Eradicate belittling from your methods of interacting with children.

Write down one example of a positive thing that you did when in the past you might have chosen to use a belittling tactic.

_____

_____

_____

4. Congratulate yourself when you catch yourself and change your behavior.

Write yourself a short congratulatory statement about a specific event in which you changed your behavior.

_____

_____

5. Observe some behavior problems diminishing because of your change in behavior.

Write down one change you noticed in a child's behavior or in the group's behavior that you believe is due to less belittling going on.

_____

_____

_____

6. Come back to this page in a week (put it on your calendar), and write down your observations of the children and your changes in behavior. If you are not working with children now, write about what you think your difficulties in this area might be and what you can do to overcome them.

Don't Expect Perfection

Often we don't think that we are expecting kids to be perfect. We believe that we just want them to do things the "right way." Often, when we expect children to be perfect, it has less to do with them than it has to do with us. Where did we learn that there was a "right way" to do things? Where did we learn that things have to be right or it's a reflection on us? Probably from our families, teachers, partners, and others. The trouble is, what one person thinks might be the right way may not be what the next person thinks is correct. Another problem is that no one is perfect, including us. Expecting children to "do it right" consistently is unrealistic and leads us to feel frustrated and children to feel incompetent.

We might not recognize that we are perfectionists. However, the need to have everything done right, even when it hurts us and those around us, is a sign that we have those tendencies. A perfectionist can never relax, can't tell the big stuff from the small stuff, controls others, procrastinates, and can get to be very crabby. Sometimes perfectionism can almost be an addiction. It becomes an end in itself. Relationships suffer, and the person suffers, because being perfect becomes the focus, not the good of the other person or our own good.

So watch yourself by doing the following exercise:

Write down some quick answers to these questions:

Name a time recently when you asked a child to do a task and the child did not meet your expectations.

_____

_____

How important was it, in the overall scheme of things, that the task be done perfectly?

_____

_____

_____

_____

When is the last time you made a decision that the child could have made herself about how she should do something? Why did you make the decision for the child? What will you do next time to allow the child to make her own decisions?

_____

_____

_____

_____

What task that you dislike would get done more quickly, or on time, if you didn't have to do it perfectly?

_____

What task could a child get done more easily if you didn't expect perfection? Explain.

_____

_____

How often are you tense or irritable because you feel that all events and all people depend on you to make sure things turn out right?

_____

What effect does that have on the children you work with?

_____

_____

Are there any ways in which you jeopardize a quality relationship with children because you are too picky? Give two specific examples of how relationships have been affected because of your expectations.

_____

_____

_____

_____

What don't children get to do, that they should be able to do, because you expect too much of them? How will you change that situation?

_____

_____

Now think of a project that you are planning to do with the kids. Jot down your thoughts about the following questions:

What is the goal of this interaction or project?

_____

Can it be met without perfection in every detail? What details can you say you will not worry about?

_____

_____

Does there have to be a goal at all? Or could things just flow? What can you do to help make the event more relaxed?

_____

_____

_____

If you are not a perfectionist you may still find yourself asking children to do things perfectly or to meet a standard that they are not capable of meeting. And, you may be doing it for what you think is their own good. Because you want them to be successful people. We have to remember that no one was born writing a symphony, or producing great art, or designing a computer, or mopping a floor until it's spotless. Trial and error are essential teachers, and children are still learning. They are not little adults and even if they were, how many perfect adults do you know?

Here's a story about a teacher who wanted to do things the right way.

Anna is a school-age care teacher. *She works hard and really likes what she does. But often the children don't seem to like her. She grew up in a home where there wasn't much structure, encouragement, or support. She often feels that she could be better at things and know more if her parents had guided and taught her. Her mission, therefore, is to help children do many things well.*

She brings in science experiments, reads them poetry, teaches them keyboarding and cooking. She expects them to do a lot for themselves but is quick to point out their mistakes. "So, they will know, for heaven's sake, the difference between a good job and a sloppy one."

After choice time, the kids have their assigned tasks. Farah's job this week is wiping up the art area floor. Farah finishes and is headed outside to play.

"Come back here and take a look at this floor, please," Anna says, not in an angry way.

Farah puts down her soccer ball and goes to the art area. She looks down at the speckled tile and says, "What's the problem? It looks clean to me."

Anna gets down on her hands and knees. She points at a small circle of brown paint. "If it were clean, would this still be there?" she asks.

"I suppose not," Farah answers and gets a sponge and dutifully cleans it up. She's watched other kids argue with Anna about this kind of stuff and decided it's not worth it.

Later in the day, a few kids are waiting for their parents to pick them up. Farah and her friend Julian are playing a game of checkers at a table. Anna is putting things away.

"I can't believe she made you clean up that tiny spot. She's such a crab,"
Julian says.

*"Yeah, she is. I don't want her to teach me anything. Like that poem I wrote
last week and she told me to do it over because it wasn't my best. How would she
know? I liked the stupid poem. She makes me feel dumb,"* Farah says.

*"Not me. She makes me mad. I wanted to join the cooking club last week, and
she told me to join computers because she thinks I'm better at cooking than I am
at computers. I'm not going to join any club. She makes me sooo mad."*

"Me too." Farah says.

⊚ ⊚

Anna's behavior couldn't achieve her goals with the kids. Her need to
have children achieve at an adult level in an attempt to make them competent blocked her ability to relate to them at all. They didn't care about what
she could do for them because of what she did to them. In her program,
they were not learning to make decisions, accept their own thinking, try
again, or attempt new things. They also didn't cooperate with Anna. Julian
acted out and Farah acted in but neither of them acted the way that Anna
hoped they would.

Here's the next chapter in that story: Farah is a real person. She is a
young adult now. Her mother was a lot like Anna, so she grew up with the
same perfectionistic expectations at home, that she experienced for three
years with Anna in her school-age care program. She has a terrible time
making up her mind about almost everything. She doesn't trust herself or
even feel her own feelings very often. Certainly this didn't all come from
her school-age care experience, but it was reinforced there. Remember earlier in the book we talked about school-age care staff as being the people
who need to offer life-altering experiences in order to help kids look at
themselves and their world in different ways. Anna had a chance to do that.
But unwittingly she reinforced Farah's unhealthy beliefs about herself.

Make one of these two signs:

Don't sweat the small stuff. And lots of it is small.

**I'm not perfect but parts of me are amazing.
Ditto for the kids I work with.**

Put the sign up where you can read it often. Think about it. Act on it.

Dealing with children honestly, respectfully, and realistically is the theme of this chapter. Don't manipulate or bribe, patronize or praise excessively, humiliate or belittle, hover or overprotect, or push or expect perfection. That's lots of don'ts. But they all will disappear if we treat kids the way we want to be treated—with respect, support, encouragement, and trust.

Please write your notes, thoughts, or stories here:

Chapter 16

It's All About Power: Do's

by Aneesa

Never get into a power struggle with a child that you can't win. And you can't win any.

≈ Ray McGee

Do Stay Out of Power Struggles

What is a power struggle? The easiest definition is probably an argument—a fight about who is right. It seems like a fight about who is right and wrong, but it really is a fight about who has the power and who is going to end up with it. The subject matter isn't the issue. The real issue is who will win.

Why does Ray McGee say that the adult can never win? Because the child has already won by engaging the adult. There is no reason for an adult to fight with kids. Adults are adults. They have a certain amount of power because of their position. It is not theirs to give away. Rather, it is their job to help children find their own power and learn how to use it appropriately. As long as adults believe that there is a finite sum of power in the world that is theirs to dole out in small amounts as they see fit, children will challenge them to get some of it.

If adults allow children to begin this struggle, they will always lose because they are allowing children to get the power that does rightfully belong to adults. The adult will lose because she will either give in, saying something like, "Okay, fine. The sky is green. Whatever you say," or she will get into an argument with the child—in which case the adult, not the child, looks foolish. In this case, the child becomes the hero to the other children because the child managed to bring the adult to her knees by entering into a fight with someone who is, at most, a third her age and half her height. A third possibility, once a power struggle has begun, is for the adult to try to hold on to power by becoming more and more punitive. "Sit in the time-out chair until your mother picks you up." "No gym time for a month." "Do as many laps around the gym as it takes for you to believe that the sky is blue." Again, the adult is fully engaged in the old control model of behavior guidance, a model that leaves the child feeling put down and angry and the adult feeling frustrated and incompetent.

This issue, in my experience, is the most common problem in discipline issues in school-age care programs. So if you don't remember anything else from this book, please pay close attention to this chapter's techniques for eliminating power struggles.

The first step in eliminating power struggles with kids is to remember that you are the adult. Stop reading right now and make a sign that says, "I am the adult. They are the children." Now think of the adult in your life who most helped you and guided you. If there was no one like that in your life, imagine what such an adult would be like. That is the adult that you want to be for kids. One who guides and nurtures. One kids can count on to be steady and set boundaries and tell them why. One who knows more than they do and shares that knowledge in a way that helps kids to grow. An adult who the child can look up to as the kind of person he wants to be.

Okay, now that you've made the sign, put it up at work and home. Put it on the visor over the steering wheel of your car and say it out loud before you go into work every day. Or stick it in your wallet and pull it out every day before you get off the bus or finish walking to work. When you read it out loud or in your head, do so in a calm but assured voice. Practice now, softly: "I am the adult. They are the children." There is nothing punitive in your tone. You are simply stating a fact. You are not out to "show them who's boss." You are merely responsibly assuming your role.

This is one of the lessons of this book that I learned the hard way. My first year of teaching was in an inner-city school. I assumed that if I just loved the kids enough there would be no problems. I was wrong. The class was totally out of control. Kids threw spitballs and talked loudly and disrespectfully. They wandered around the room at will. They wouldn't sit down or stand up when I wanted them to. In October, the kids took standardized tests, or were supposed to. There were children literally jumping from the top of one desk to another while others kept their heads down trying to concentrate.

I was a wreck. I didn't want to admit to other staff how bad things were in my room. I had worked hard to get a job at this particular school, where the pay was a little higher. I had many student loans; I didn't want to lose my job.

One day my fiancé came to pick me up while school was still in session. "That was your classroom we just left, wasn't it?" he asked as we got into the car.

"Yes."

"And those are the kids in your class. The ones that you cry about every night, right?"

"Yes," I answered. I started to cry, again. "Did you see how terrible they are?"

"But, Mary," he said as gently as he could, "they're only this tall," and he held his hand above the ground to indicate their short stature.

From what I had said about the kids he had imagined they were ten feet tall.

The conversation stopped me short. It must have come at one of those famous teachable moments, or perhaps it was sent from a teachers' angel through my fiancé's voice.

I assessed my position that night. "I am the adult. They are the children," I said to myself. "I can do this." The next day, I went into the classroom with a new attitude. Without knowing it, I had changed my whole framework for behavior guidance. I shifted from saying to students, "I have all the power to change your lives by understanding you and telling you how great you are and being your friend," to "I have the power a teacher has to help you learn self-discipline, to help you set boundaries, to teach you, to relate to you as an adult to a child."

Even in my well-intended belief that I could love them into cooperation, I had been taking on all the power, and they had been wrestling me for it. In the model I had been using, it was all about me. I had to care about them the right way, make all the decisions about how they would learn and behave, structure things the way I thought was best, be non-assertive lest I hurt their feelings, pity their positions in life.

When I made the shift to thinking, "I have the power that a teacher has," I recognized the other half of the equation: they have the power that children have. This led me to listen to them better. I allowed them to make appropriate decisions about their learning. I drew clear boundaries. Children didn't run on the desks any more. They listened when that was good for the group and talked when it was helpful. They didn't run around in the halls or go to the bathroom every five minutes. I had figured out that I was a teacher who could make a difference in kids' lives by assisting them to be self-disciplined—not by letting them do whatever they wanted at any time. Mostly I just changed my attitude.

I didn't have to worry anymore. Neither did the kids. I was there to help them. They were there to develop and learn. We could work this out. Although it took some time for them to believe in the shift, they eventually did. We had a great year. I was re-hired. The kids went to the next grade with their personal power intact and knowledge in their heads.

I didn't tell the kids about my attitude shift. But if it happened today, I would. I would say something like, "I have not been fair to you. I need to be the adult, the teacher in this classroom. I thought I was helping you by letting you do whatever you wanted. I wasn't. You know that things get out of control in this class way too often. I need to help you set better boundaries and be responsible people. What should we do to get started making this a place that's good for all of us?"

Other issues in school-age programs can trigger a pattern of power struggles between children and adults. These include

- Schedules that don't allow enough time for transitions.
- An environment that doesn't allow children to make choices.
- Child-to-staff ratios that are too high.
- Unclear expectations.
- Children or staff experiencing fatigue.
- Staff who are not allowed to function as individuals.
- Cultural, class, regional, or religious differences that are not understood or respected.

Are any of these issues present in your program?

_____

_____

_____

_____

_____

What can you do to minimize each one that you recognized in your program?

_____

_____

_____

_____

_____

Remember, one of the cool things about schoolagers is that you can talk to them. When situations arise that could lead to power struggles, you can say things like, "I don't argue with kids," or "I don't chase children." When I do training for school-age programs, I am glad when we have several sessions over a number of weeks rather than one session. Staff can bring their individual problems to class. We make suggestions. The person can come back the following week and tell us how the proposed solution worked, or didn't. I often suggest to participants that they say to a child who is darting off from some kind of confrontation, "I don't chase children." The staff person involved often does a lot of "Yes-butting" in response to the suggestion.

"Yes, but he may run out into the parking lot and get hit by a car."

"Yes, but if I walk away from her when she's mad like that she cries all day."

"Yes, but being tough with him is the only thing that works."

These are reasonable fears on the part of someone whose job is to care for children. However, after cautioning people not to use the technique if they are certain that "the child has no impulse control," I tell them to give it a try. Build in some safeguards in your own mind about what you will do if he doesn't come back, just in case. Then, keep your feet firmly planted and say, "I don't chase children." Next, remember that what you do is as important as what you say. Don't stand there watching to see what he will do with a look that says either, "I dare you to try," or "Oh, heavens, he is going to run to the next county." Instead, turn nonchalantly to another task or to another child. See what happens.

You may have to try it a couple of times. But no matter how sure the staff person was that her adult stance wouldn't work, in my experience ninety percent of the time it does. The staff person is usually astonished. The child may come back and do something else to cause a power struggle, but he will almost always come back.

Why do they come back? Because their purpose was not to run away. He or she wants to pull you into a power struggle. Who is in charge if an adult is chasing a child around? No one, really. The adult is looking foolish to everyone, including herself. The child is asking for attention for whatever his needs are in an inappropriate way that will not get his needs met. If he cannot get your attention by running away, he will try other things, and you will deal with them when he does. If he is just escaping your immediate reprimand by running into the next room, let him go. Catch him later and talk about whatever problem needs to be solved and what he might have to do to clean up whatever mess he made. But by not responding to the running away except by stating your position on the matter, you have de-escalated the situation. You have stopped the power struggle.

Schoolagers are smart and have language. Take advantage of that.

When you are trying on this new model and getting to feel comfortable in your new role as a competent adult, try this exercise: imagine the kids you are working with, in other settings. Depending on their age, they might have pajamas with feet in them or funny fuzzy slippers. Their parents might still read them stories before they go to bed. They may play with dolls or stuffed animals or little cars that they make noises for. Imagine images of them that remind you that they are indeed children and not the bigger-than-life people that I made of my first class.

Draw a picture now of the child that causes you the most discipline problems. In the drawing show him doing a nice childlike thing. Don't mock the child in the drawing. Think of him, instead, the way that you might think of your niece or nephew, child or grandchild, or yourself at that age.

Keep this softer image in your mind and heart when you have interactions with this child. See what happens.

This shift only works, of course, if the adult believes that children have their own power and allow them to use it. Kids sense immediately the adult who thinks that adults are in charge of everything, who feels that children need to be controlled at all times. And they make the adult's life miserable. They are masters at pulling adults into arguments by challenging their power. Before you make the shift, take this quiz. Please answer as truthfully as you can, considering each situation individually. You do not have to show your answers to anyone.

True or False.

1. _____ When a child says, "Why should I?" your typical response is something like, "Because I said so!"

2. _____ When at snack a child says, "Yuck, I hate this stuff," your typical response is something like, "Okay. Starve for all I care."

3. _____ If child says, "I don't like you," your typical response is something like, "I don't care if you like me or not. Just do what I say."

4. _____ If a child yells at you, you might put him on a time-out until he's ready to apologize.

5. _____ If a child calls another child "stupid," you might put him on a time-out until he's ready to apologize.

6. _____ If the kids are going outside and it's cold, you might say, "No one leaves this room until I see everyone's jacket on."

7. _____ If you tell a child that he broke a rule in the gym and he says, "Tough!" your response might be something like, "Out of this gym right now!"

8. _____ When the child responds to your statement above by saying, "Make me," your typical response might be something like, "I'll make you, all right!"

9. _____ If you plan an activity and the kids say, "This is boring," your typical response might be something like, "Well, you can do this or stare at the walls, your choice."

If you indicated "True" on more than four statements, you have some work to do. Don't be discouraged if you have nine "True" responses. Once you practice a little, new responses will become second nature. It isn't that difficult—you just have to do it. You decide that you are the adult guiding the kids. However, not everything they do is up to you to remedy.

If you had three or fewer "True" responses, please do the exercises and continue learning anyway. Maybe you get into power struggles with children using different words than the ones in the examples. Perhaps you really have no problems with power struggles. You can still reinforce your appropriate behaviors and maybe learn a couple of new things along the way.

You don't argue with kids, because you are the adult and don't have to. So, you are asking, what do I do instead? Let's think of some examples, knowing, of course, that each situation and each child is different. You are working on developing a relationship with each child, which will help you individualize your responses.

Please remember to keep yourself from saying, "Yes, but—"; give the suggested idea a chance. Think of variations for it that would fit your circumstances. If your response to a suggestion is, "That would never work with my kids!" then think of a way to make it work. If your response is, "I've tried that," then think of a new way to try it. What else might have to be changed in order for it or a similar solution to be successful?

1. A child responds, "Why should I?" to a request that you make.

Your response might be, "Because you are one of the nicest people I know and you like being helpful, don't you?" Please note: you did not deal with the fact right then that he spoke to you disrespectfully. That is one of the hooks that can drag you into a power struggle. Instead, you reaffirm what else you know about him. Your goal is to get the task done now, not to confront him on his manners. You may do that later, if it is a habitual problem. Or you might wait until he's finished the task and say, "Thanks a lot. That was really helpful. And, by the way, let's try to remember to talk kindly to each other. Okay? Thanks again." Or you might decide that with the task done, his language will work itself out over time, and just let it go.

exercise continued on next page

2. A child at snack says, "Yuck, I hate this stuff!" Your response might be, "That's why there's peanut butter, jelly, and bread. Right over there. Help yourself."

Again, you did not engage in conflict about this issue. You already have a system in place to give kids a choice. You use it and move on. Remember that kids are much more expressive about their likes and dislikes than adults tend to be. You may want to talk privately to the child later about the vehement response, but then again, even if no one ever tells him not to say that, he still probably won't say it when he is a dinner guest when he grows up.

3. If a child says, "I don't like you," your response might be, "That's too bad. You don't have to like everybody. But I like you. What can I do so that we can get along better?"

Please write down answers to the following questions and then discuss your answers with another person. Does it feel like something you could comfortably say to a child? Why? Why not? What do you think the child might say in response? What might your next response be?

_____

_____

_____

_____

_____

_____

_____

_____

Now can you and the person with whom you are discussing these questions think of another possible response to give the child?

4. When a child yells at you, you could say, "I'll talk to you later when you are more calm." And then you leave.

What might another response be that would not involve a power struggle?

_____

_____

_____

5. If a child calls another child "stupid" and you are not really close and not involved in the conversation, you could ignore it. If you are a part of the children's conversation, you can wait to see how the other child responds before you do. The other child may take care of it herself by saying something thing like, "What do you know?" and the rest of the conversation may go just fine.

How would you react if the other child just walked away?

_____

_____

_____

6. If the kids are going outside and it's cold, you might say nothing and let them decide what to wear or you might say, "Weather report: conditions are very cold outside. A jacket and mitten advisory is in effect."

How else might you deal with this situation?

_____

_____

_____

7. If a child responds to your reminder that he broke a rule in the gym by saying, "Tough!" you might wait to see if he is just blowing off steam and doesn't say or do anything else inappropriate. In the meantime, you can go on with the game.

How else might you handle the situation in a way that prevents a power struggle?

_____

_____

8. You tell a child that his turn at the computer is over and that he has to leave so that the next scheduled child can have his turn. He says, "Make me." One way you could handle the situation is to say, "We've agreed not to talk to each other that way here. I'll come back in a minute or so and we can talk about what's going on."

How else could you deal with this situation?

_____

_____

exercise continued on next page

9. If you plan an activity and the kids say, "This is boring," how would you respond?

_____

_____

10. Describe a power struggle that you have witnessed between a child and an adult.

_____

_____

_____

How could the adult have prevented the power struggle?

_____

_____

11. Describe a power struggle that you have had in the past.

_____

_____

_____

What is another way to deal with a similar situation that would prevent a power struggle?

_____

_____

_____

Remember that you can change your attitude. You are the older, more experienced person and they are the children. Once you own your power you can allow the children to have theirs. You will realize that you don't always have to teach them a lesson or correct everything they do in a punitive way. You can let some things go by and the world will go on and the kids will grow up to be good people. You will realize that it's not all about you—that the things children say and do aren't a challenge to your rightful power.

Practice replacing your automatic old reactions that led you into power struggles with children, with new reactions like the ones in the examples above. It's a little like learning a new language. At first you have to translate from your first language to the new language. With study and practice you soon speak fluently without having to think about it. Changing your attitude is hard work at times, but your important role in children's lives makes it worth the effort. You will also find that you can do your job more easily. You will be more relaxed, less frustrated, less angry. And you can observe the discipline problems decreasing dramatically.

Do Be Flexible

The school-age care program *on a U.S. Air Force base shares space with the adult recreation center. Before and after school, kids use the pool table, weights and exercise equipment, and basketball gym. Vending machines line the walls of one small room. That room and the machines are off limits for the kids. Staff don't want the kids to compete over spending money or to eat junk food.*

On La Toya's tenth birthday, she arrives after school with a pocketful of quarters. She says hello to Mona, the staff person on duty that day. Then La Toya and her three best friends hide and whisper in the book corner. "Do you think we can convince Mona?" her friend Whitney asks.

"Not in a million years," says Sue. "This is the Air Force, after all."

"Yeah," says Rachel, "but this isn't a matter of national defense or anything."

"She's pretty cool," La Toya says confidently. "And remember that big surprise party that we gave Mona for her birthday? She loved it! We know she's nuts about birthdays."

"It might be worth a try," Sue says hesitantly. "I just hope we don't get into trouble."

"Mona doesn't 'get people in trouble' like that," says Whitney.

"True, that's true," Sue concedes.

"I say we go for it," says LaToya, getting pumped. It is, after all, her birthday. "I'll do the talking. I am the birthday girl."

Mona can see that something is up. As they approach her at the snack center, she asks, "What's up with you girls? That looked like a pretty serious discussion you were having."

"Not exactly serious. More like exciting," Rachel pipes up.

"Shhh, I'm doing the talking, remember?" La Toya interrupts. "Today's my birthday. I'm ten."

"Happy birthday," Mona says. "I did remember because it's up on the birthday calendar. Not only that, you've reminded me every day for a week."

"So, well, we thought maybe we could do something special, me and my friends."

"What do you have in mind?"

"My mom gave me some money this morning to buy something to share with my friends. The only place I see my best friends is here 'cause we're in different classes, you know."

"Yes."

"And you say that there are some rules that can never be broken and others that are—how do you say it?"

"Flexible?"

"Yeah, that's it, 'flexible.' We were wondering if the vending machine rule could be flexible today."

"How could we work that out do you think?"

"We could go in there quietly. Close the door and promise never to tell anybody that it happened. For real, promise."

"I'll tell you what," Mona offers. "You can pilot this program."

There is silence while the girls think it over.

"My dad's a pilot. I don't think we're ready," Sue responds.

"In this case, to 'pilot' means to test out. You can test out whether you think having a birthday gathering in the vending room works. What would be good and what would the problems be if we changed the rule for everyone's birthday. If you think there are more pros than cons, we could bring the idea to the whole group and see what they think. So you try it out today and we'll talk about it tomorrow. Is that a deal?"

"Deal," says LaToya, eyes shining. "And thanks."

As they bounce towards the vending room, LaToya says to her friends, "Told you she's cool."

⑨ ⑥

What did Mona teach these girls? That consistency is not an end in itself. She had laid the groundwork earlier by letting them know that some rules are flexible. They are guidelines. Like the program's budget, they embody the principles that make sense at the time. But things come up. If there is no money in the budget for new outdoor play equipment, but a company is selling out its supply at cost, you may juggle the budget. You may choose to put off buying new carpeting, for example.

If the principle that the kids and Mona had set down, "No one gets hurt here," was in jeopardy, there would not have been any flexibility. If the girls had asked to go off base to the local convenience store, there would not have been any flexibility because that is a licensing issue. But the rule about the vending machines, on this day, could be flexible enough to meet the kids' needs. Therefore, she also taught them that she considers their needs. She strengthened her relationship with them. By making them "pilots" she taught them that often with privilege comes responsibility. That they needed to assess whether the rule could be flexible for the rest of the group as well, so that the issue would be considered more fairly for everyone.

How easily could there have been a power struggle? Mona could have said, "Rules are rules. Birthday or no birthday." They might have argued with her or gotten angry. When Mona wanted them to help clean up that evening she would be dealing with four pouting girls who would see no reason to honor her need to have a tidy center. If, on some other day, she was flexible with a different rule for other children they would object vehemently about unjust treatment. They wouldn't have learned to assess a situation, bring it to a group, and come to consensus.

However, her decision to be flexible was not based on simply avoiding an unpleasant struggle. That can be a danger for adults. Giving in just because it is easier is not being flexible. It is letting go of your rightful power. It is also modeling irresponsibility.

Mona was reasonable. She reviewed the rule for this situation. She remembered the reasons for the rule. Determining that the kids' nutrition wouldn't suffer if they had soda and chips one day, and that money competition wouldn't become an issue for this exception, she grabbed the opportunity to guide and affirm a relationship.

It might have been Mona's decision that flexibility was not possible in this case for a variety of reasons. But she would have discussed the reasons with the girls. The girls could have come up with their own reasons— without a power struggle or damage to the relationship.

Children need consistency. However, consistency for its own sake doesn't make sense and it is often a cause of power struggles. We can provide kids with consistency in rules, schedules, staffing, independence guidelines, and relationships whenever that makes sense and is possible. We also need to ask them and ourselves to be open to looking at the circumstances and making adjustments.

For example, it is important that children be able to count on staff stability. It would be destructive to set up a system in which staff rotated from group to group on a regular basis. But if a staff member is ill or has a meeting, you can tell the children why the person isn't there that day. They will adjust. If we examine our programs, I think we will be able to see that we ask children to understand inconsistencies quite frequently. It is only fair that we adjust with and for them when it is appropriate.

In *The Seven Habits of Highly Effective People* (New York: Simon & Schuster, 1989), Stephen Covey talks about "emotional bank accounts." If we never put anything into another person's emotional bank account, there is nothing to draw from. Let's say you have a friend who always wants you to listen to his problems, to call him frequently, to do him favors. But he never listens when you share, never calls, and is always too busy to do last-minute favors. You become less and less willing to be there for him. He has put nothing in the bank. He is overdrawn.

If, on the other hand, he isn't a good listener, doesn't like telephone calls, and is extremely busy, but he takes the time to send you e-mails, cooks you a great dinner once a month, clips coupons and sticks them in the mail to you because he knows you use them, he is putting "money" in your emotional bank account. He doesn't have to put in the same kind of assets that you put in his account. But he can now withdraw when he needs an empathetic ear at the end of a hard day at the child care center or needs you to pick up his cat at the vet.

Relationships work that way. Trust builds that way. We don't invest in other people just to get something back. We do it to be in relationship—to be fair and kind. Our relationship with kids can be no different. We ask them to follow lots of rules, to follow a schedule that works for the school district and their parents, to be aware of the community they are in (think of how little time kids have today to do things just because they want to), to eat what we provide, to speak respectfully to people they hardly know, and so on.

Those are all deposits that kids are making. They may not be making them for us personally, but the deposits make our work possible, or at least make it easier. We need to make deposits in their accounts as well. If we don't, they will become resentful and uncooperative. They will push harder to have power struggles. There will be more inappropriate behavior. Whenever there is a choice between making a deposit and being consistent for the sake of consistency, put something in the bank. It will yield a high rate of interest.

The consistency issue can bring about power struggles among staff, also. Often when I am training I hear things from staff like, "If we all just had the same rules for the kids, things would be much better around here. The kids get confused. One thing is okay in one room or with one staff person but different in another place or with another staff person."

There is some truth in these kinds of statements. The vital rules should be consistent: No one should get hurt. Everyone should be safe. Also, staff typically cannot control company policies, state regulations, district regulations, health standards, and the like. However, after setting aside the vital rules and those things that are out of our control, most of the things that we ask the kids to do are a matter of opinions and preferences, or maybe even the needs, of individual staff members.

Here is an example that might help illustrate the point. Sheila, who is blind, works in a school-age care program. She is a music specialist who teaches many groups at a large site. To help her know who is talking, the children say their names when they speak to her. For example, "This is Lupe. Where did you get that little instrument that looks like a guitar?" With other staff members, it is unnecessary for children to identify themselves before they speak, and it would be foolish in the name of consistency to make such a rule.

Another common misconception is that all staff need to have the same expectations of all children. I know of a site where two school-age care rooms are next to each other. The children are free to move back and forth between the two rooms. Pat believes that neatness is very important, so she keeps everything arranged carefully, labeled, and shiny. Cindy, in another room, doesn't think that the kids can have a good time or learn very much unless there are feathers flying, glitters shining, and paper scraps strewn everywhere. Can the kids adapt?

Of course they can. They adapt to the different expectations of the members of their households, the different expectations at home and at Grandma's house, of the teachers at school and the teachers at school-age care, of the dance teacher and the Sunday school teacher. And they need to adapt. They will always meet different rules and expectations. One boss will want one thing, and another something else. One friend will accept things from a friendship that others won't. They will have to learn the rules of different cultures. They won't act the same way in a synagogue as they do at a sports bar.

Instead of fighting to make expectations the same (and each person thinking that her standards are the ones that should be adopted), staff can build on their diversity. They can decide which ground rules must remain consistent and then figure out how to live and thrive with the differences. They can talk to the children about the value of the differences. For example, Pat might say, "You know, kids, you are so lucky to have a teacher like Cindy. She is so creative. I see the neat stuff that you make while you are with her. Maybe we could display some of it in this room to brighten it up a bit."

At the same time, the kids might hear from Cindy, "Hey, kids, let's label these different kinds of drawing tools so that we can find them more easily. That's a trick I learned from Pat. She's such a great organizer. We can decorate boxes and put markers in one, pastels in another. You get the picture."

We recognize that it is unsettling to children to have the adults in their home disagreeing with each other. It is also difficult for them to be around staff members who are tense with each other. Raised eyebrows, talking negatively about each other, arguing, slamming doors, saying to kids, "You may get by with that in George's room but not in here"—behaviors like these all add to the tension of the place that kids need to rely on when they can't be at home. Remember, that is how many children think about school-age care—it is where they have to be because their parents aren't at home. Even if they like it, there is some built-in insecurity. Think of the look on a child's face when his parent is an hour late. He is anxious, tense, even frightened. We need to make the environment as secure and relaxed as possible. Conflict over consistency breeds stress. It also teaches kids how to have power struggles instead of how to work situations out with others.

When we show children that we will remain consistent about what really matters (for example, that it is never okay to hit someone or to leave the site), we build their trust that we are there to take care of them. If we bend and are reasonable about reviewing other rules and procedures, we are more likely to get kids' cooperation when we enforce the things that must remain consistent. If we don't fight with them about all the little things, if we are not rigid, they will be less likely to challenge us when we do stick to the policies.

Take time now to review your rules and procedures.

Make a list of ALL the rules, procedures, and policies, spoken and unspoken, that you expect children to adhere to when they are with you.

_____

_____

_____

_____

_____

_____

_____

_____

_____

_____

_____

_____

Now put *F* next to the expectations that could be flexible depending on circumstances. Put *N* next to the rules that need to be in place consistently.

Then choose two N rules. Explain why consistency is necessary for each N rule.

N rule 1. _____

_____

N rule 2. _____

_____

Choose three F rules. Give an example of when you might be flexible about each of the three rules.

F rule 1. _____

_____

_____

exercise continued on next page

F rule 2. _____

_____

_____

F rule 3. _____

_____

_____

Even though there may be circumstances you cannot control that can make power struggles more likely, you can prevent power struggles and all the discipline problems they generate by remembering that consistency is not an end in itself and—that you are the adult and they are the children.

To complete this chapter, please take this open-book quiz:

1. What piece of advice did psychologist Ray McGee say was important for dealing with children?

_____

_____

2. What is a power struggle?

_____

_____

3. Why can't an adult ever win a power struggle?

_____

_____

4. Give an example of a power struggle.

_____

_____

5. How could the power struggle in the example you gave be avoided?

_____

_____

6. How does saying "I am the adult. They are the children." help prevent power struggles?

_____

_____

7. What is your rightful power as an adult?

_____

_____

8. What kinds of power should be nurtured in children?

_____

_____

9. Why and when is flexibility important?

_____

_____

10. Why and when is consistency important?

_____

_____

11. How can the flexibility issue set the stage for power struggles?

_____

_____

12. How can children be affected by power struggles among staff over consistency?

_____

_____

exercise continued on next page

13. What is one other issue that causes power struggles when you work with children?

_____

_____

14. What did you learn about yourself in this chapter that you want to work on? How will you change it?

_____

_____

15. What did you learn about yourself in this chapter that you like and want to keep? How does this characteristic help you avoid power struggles?

_____

_____

Please write your notes, thoughts, or stories here:

Chapter 17

It's All About Power: Don'ts

by Aneesa

No teacher has the right to cure a child of making noises on a drum. The only
curing that should be practiced is the curing of unhappiness. The difficult child
is the child who is unhappy. He is at war with himself; and in consequence,
he is at war with the world.

≈ A. S. Neill

Don't Argue with or Ignore Children

While arguing with children and ignoring children may seem completely different from each other, both impede children from learning the coping skills they need to be successful. Of course, the more successful children become, the fewer discipline issues we will have with them.

The very children who most need us not to argue with them—to stay out of the power struggles—are the children who are most likely to try our patience. We can sometimes feel our resolve to stay away from punishment and control weaken the minute they open their mouths. At times like that, it helps to remember that these children may even need to build new connections in their brains so that their behaviors can improve.

If we slip back into punishment tactics, like arguing with them, we slow down the possibility that they will be able to learn new behaviors. In the long run, we are causing more problems for ourselves as well as for the children. Arguments with children do not help build resiliency. Less resiliency means more behavior problems.

These children, whom we often call "difficult," are also the children whom we often want to ignore. Their behaviors don't seem to improve, so we feel hopeless. We are less likely to take them seriously when they complain about other kids' behaviors towards them or express dissatisfaction with us or the program. Part of us believes that they should feel fortunate that we allow them to stay in the program at all. As a matter of fact, if it were up to us alone, they might not be there. We may feel that they deserve whatever the other kids do to them. If they are acting appropriately, we don't want to jinx the situation by talking to them. We are also a bit afraid of them. So, we are prone to leaving well enough alone rather than inviting any possible confrontation.

The problem is that without entering into relationships with them by taking their concerns seriously, noticing their positive behaviors, or simply relating to them as we do with other children, we are not building their resiliency. We are not teaching them how to improve their behaviors. We are not helping their souls and possibly their brains to heal. The misbehaviors will not decrease if we ignore the children, or if we allow them to engage us in arguing. In fact, misbehavior is likely to increase as the children's pleas for help get louder and louder, as children beg for someone to notice that they are there and that they are in pain. If children don't get help, misbehavior becomes their way of being.

Remember that change is the ultimate goal in behavior guidance. A change in behaviors so that children can become competent and happy. A change in behaviors so that your job is less stressful and you feel more competent. Good teaching and healthy relationships allow for change. Both people learn, have insights, and get excited about the changes. Arguing with and ignoring children does not promote change.

Information on brain research and resiliency tells you to stay with the new relationship model of behavior guidance. In the relationship model you don't argue with or ignore children. Arguing with or ignoring children impedes—puts obstacles in the way of—a child's developing resiliency.

But what can you do when you find yourself about to argue with or ignore a child? Well, you want to help them change, and you're willing to change your own behaviors to do that. You want to help them be successful and increase their ability to cope, or their resiliency. Let's look at the six ways we discussed in chapter 7 that loving adults help children build resiliency skills:

Children move towards resiliency when adults

- help them tell their stories.

- help them develop self-worth and competence.

- teach them how to connect with others by forming relationships with them.

- teach them how to adapt to changing circumstances.

- help them learn to find alternatives.

- give them achievable responsibilities so they can experience success.

The following scenarios help us explore what it looks like when adults are able to help children be resilient in these six ways.

Adults help children tell their stories.

Ashley runs into the school-age care room. *"I just saw a bee as big as a bird," she tells Frank, her teacher.*

"Bees don't get that big," Frank says. "You have to stop exaggerating."

"It was coming to sting me."

"Ashley, it was not. There is no such thing as a bee that big."

"Yes, there is. I got stung by one that big the day my brother was born. I cried but nobody cared about it."

"I'm not listening to you if you keep telling lies," Frank says.

"You're just a stupid person, Frank. I bet if my dumb little brother told you, you'd believe him."

"Maybe I would if he tells the truth."

"I am telling the truth. Besides, you can't listen to my brother, 'cause he died the day he was born. Ha, ha, stupid. I fooled you!"

"Are you telling another fib? If you are, it's not funny!"

"Whatever," Ashley says, slamming the door as she runs away down the hall.

⊚ ⊚

Frank both argued with and ignored Ashley's attempt to tell her story. He was stuck in the old model of arguing with kids if their facts aren't right. He did not look beyond the literal meaning of her words to what she might be telling him. Therefore, Frank lost the chance to allow Ashley to tell him about a painful part of her life. He could have helped heal old wounds that are likely to spawn inappropriate behaviors.

Maybe Ashley does have a habit of exaggerating. Children who are reaching out for help with their stress often do. They sometimes feel that they need to do so to be heard. Nonetheless, Frank's arguing and inability to pay attention to Ashley's needs caused a series of misbehaviors. She called him names. She slammed the door. She ran away.

Her probable guilt about crying the day her brother died and her need to be recognized as a needy little child at a time when the focus was on her brother may have made that bee look as big as a bird. She tried in an unskilled way to let an adult know about her anxieties. Because she wasn't heard, she gave up and acted out.

Often when I am giving workshops or consulting, people say, "I listened to you, but what do you do when kids call you names?" If there is time to talk about the entire incident or the child and adult's history, we often find that the grossest misbehaviors often could have been prevented.

Ashley did not approach Frank with misbehaviors. What would have happened if Frank had thought about relationship-building and teaching in his response to Ashley? The incident might have looked like this:

Ashley says, *"I just saw a bee as big as a bird."*
　　"Wow! You saw a huge bee?" Frank responds.
　　"Yeah, and it was going to sting me."
　　"Are you afraid that bees will sting you?"
"No, I'm not just afraid. It really was going to sting me."
"I'm glad it didn't. Where was it?"
"Out on the playground, by the fence."
"Let's see if it's still there."
"I'm scared. I don't want to go."
"Bees can be scary. I'll be with you. Maybe we can chase it away or something. I won't let you get hurt."

"Okay."

Ashley and Frank begin walking to the playground. "Have you ever been stung by a bee?" Frank asks.

"Yeah. Once. It hurt."

"Was that here?"

"No, I was kind of little."

"How little were you?"

"Five years old. But I acted like a baby."

"Bee stings hurt. Did someone take care of you?"

"Nah. My mom was in the hospital. She just had my brother."

"I didn't know you had a brother."

"He died right when he was born."

"I'm sorry. So your mom couldn't help you. I'm sorry she couldn't be there. That must have been hard."

"Maybe. But I didn't have to act like a baby. My dad said so."

Frank puts his arm around Ashley. "It's okay to tell people that you are hurt. You needed somebody to take care of you too. I'm glad you told me about this bee."

"You are?"

"Sure. Now we can figure out what you can do when you see a bee so that you will be safe."

"Okay."

"You're a good kid, Ashley."

Ashley snuggles into Frank a minute. Then she dashes off in front of him. "The bee was right there. Right over there," she says.

In this scenario there is no name-calling, no argument, no disrespect. Instead, Frank helps Ashley to tell her story. Certainly all of Ashley's old issues are not solved, but they are less frightening. She didn't need to store them away one more time where they could fester. Frank and Ashley can talk about Ashley's life again sometime, after she learns how to keep herself safe from bees.

Adults empower children to develop a sense of self-worth and efficacy.

Six-year-old Gretchen *loves to dance and spin to music when she thinks no one is watching. When the after-school program planned a talent show, Gretchen's teacher, Rosela, asked, "Why aren't you signed up, Gretchen?"*

"I can't do anything right."

"It looks like you can dance to me."

"Everyone says I look stupid. Even my mom."

"I know a little about dancing," said Rosela. "We could work up a routine. It's all in the practicing. You can do it."

For a month Gretchen practiced with Rosela. At home, she practiced in her room with the music turned down low. When the big day arrived, Gretchen shivered with fear. When she got on stage, however, she practically floated. During the applause, Gretchen saw her mother standing, smiling and clapping.

Backstage, Rosela wanted to give Gretchen a hug, but Gretchen ran off, looking for her mom and throwing a "See ya!" over her shoulder.

≈ Jean Steiner and Mary Steiner Whelan

☺ ☺

The happy ending of this story might have never happened if Rosela had handled it differently. It might have never even begun if Rosela hadn't paid attention to the children in her care. If she ignored their informal play, if she didn't use her observation skills to note the children's interests, she wouldn't have known that Gretchen had an affinity for dance. Her ignoring behavior wouldn't have allowed her to say with certainty to Gretchen, "It looks like you can dance to me."

Notice that Rosela didn't argue with Gretchen's premise that "I can't do anything right." She simply stated her reality that she has seen and judged that Gretchen can dance. Gretchen knows in herself that she can dance. An argumentative statement would have been, "That's silly, Gretchen. Everybody can do something."

Rosela, instead, used her adult power by revealing her own strengths and offering to use them to help Gretchen. She guided Gretchen to realize the power she has in her dancing abilities without first taking her power away by discounting, or arguing with her.

It all paid off. At the end of the performance, Rosela didn't claim Gretchen's power as her own by insisting on a hug, or by saying, "Come here and give me a thank-you hug," or "I told you you were wrong," or "We showed your mother." She let Gretchen experience her own self-worth, enjoy her own accomplishments, and go to be with her mother, her strengthened self-esteem in tow.

Caring adults teach children how to build relationships.

"Okay, everyone, here we go. *The first annual Kid's Place volleyball tournament planning meeting is about to begin." Steph, the school-age care staff person, is excited about her tournament idea. She's worked hard on it. She got the local sporting goods store to sponsor the event. There are new volleyballs, a net, shirts, and trophies for prizes.*

"Everybody sit down and share your ideas about how you think this should work."

The kids toss out ideas.

"I think there should be only boys against boys."

Steph answers, "There will be no sexism here. There will be boys and girls on both teams."

"I think we should play the last game for our parents."

"That would be too complicated," Steph replies.

"Let's hire referees so that it's fair."

"Can't afford it. I'll be the referee," Steph says.

"Let's have it last all year!"

Steph replies, "Way too long. It will last six weeks."

Paddy, a child who often gives Steph trouble, begins to crawl on his stomach out of the circle.

"Get back here, Paddy. Do you have any ideas?"

"Cheerleaders," he mumbles.

"Cheerleaders? That won't work. I want everyone to play."

"I don't want to play. I want to be a cheerleader."

"Come on. I know you would rather play than be jumping around looking silly. You're just afraid."

"I'm not afraid of nothing. Especially not you. This volleyball idea is gross."

"Look, I've put a lot of work into this. The least you can do is sit up and be quiet."

"Can't make me. Can't make me play volleyball, either," Paddy says. Then, he stands up and does jumping jacks while he screams, "Rah, rah, rah! Cheer, cheer, cheer!"

Some of the other kids laugh.

"Get out of here. Go sit in the hall. You aren't going to ruin this for everyone."

◉ ◉

Poor Steph. She had great intentions. She put energy into her work and wanted the best for the kids. She just lost sight of the fact that the focus of her work is relationships with kids. Challenging and interesting activities are crucial to helping schoolagers, but the programming should enhance and strengthen connections between people.

Steph is teaching us something in this scene. Role-modeling relationship skills don't just happen during one-on-one encounters. During group interactions, children can observe how healthy interactions work. If their relationship skills are not strong or if relationships scare them, they can learn as observers. All children can experience the safety and comfort of connecting with each other in meaningful, fun, and respectful ways.

Those experiences didn't happen during Steph's meeting. While Steph was working with the whole group, she argued with and ignored the children's input. She diminished the children's value as people by rejecting their ideas. She used her power to deny theirs. From Steph, that day, the children learned that relationships can be controlled by the person with the most power. When they have the power they may imitate her. Before they have adult power they will try to take some of hers.

Hence, Paddy's inappropriate behavior. It is likely that Paddy reacts more quickly and strongly to power struggles than many other children do. Steph sees him as a "difficult child." Her style of taking control and not entering into a give-and-take relationship clashes with his needs to try to be seen as important or to be seen at all.

Paddy is acting out what the other children are probably feeling at some level. Perhaps the other children have more positive relationship experiences in their lives or higher self-esteem. Maybe some of them will also reject Steph's plans by losing interest in the tournament or not cooperating later.

The children in the group did not gain any skills in relationship building that will make them more resilient. They did not learn that taking the risk to voice their opinion is worth it. They only learned about being controlled. And the wonderful event Steph planned is already marred by discipline problems. We can almost hear her saying, "I'm just not going to bother anymore. I get nothing but trouble for my effort."

If Steph had more skills with children, she could have been one of the several invested adults in Paddy's and other children's lives. She could have been with them when they risk relationship again, when they meet difficulties, her trust and interaction could have helped them be resilient. Unfortunately, she won't be that person for these kids. It's too bad. I'm sure she wants to be.

Adults help children learn to be adaptable.

He's one of those kids. *You know, the kind that freaks if anything in his routine gets changed. His name is Daniel. His big hazel eyes will break your heart. His fears will frustrate you. His biting and screaming when things don't go his way will* frighten you. What can you do for him?

Daniel arrives after school. He always goes to the game shelf, gets the puzzle cube, and puts it on the snack table, the last place on the left side. Then he hangs up his coat and gets snack. He may or may not ever play with the cube, but he wants it there during snack.

One day he comes in and the cube is not there. "Where is it? Where is it?" he yells.

"Where is what?" Noreen, the staff person, asks.

"The cube. My cube. I want my cube."

Noreen answers, "It's not your cube. It belongs to everyone."

"Get it. I need it."

"No, you don't. You can eat snack without that cube this once."

"I won't." Daniel starts crying.

Noreen turns away, hoping the lack of attention will deter Daniel. Besides, she isn't sure what to do. Daniel goes over to his usual snack place. He kicks the chair over and hits the child next to him with his jacket.

Noreen says, "Stop that now. Sit down like everyone else. Enough now."

Of course, it is not enough now. The scene goes on as you can imagine until both Daniel and Noreen are out of control and a supervisor has to be summoned.

☺ ☺

Daniel is the child you argue with because you feel sorry for him, first, and don't know what else to do, second. Using the information from the first three scenarios, do the following exercise to sharpen your skills at finding alternatives:

Using your skills with children and your new way of approaching behavior guidance, describe how you could interact with Daniel in this situation so it would not escalate and so he would learn more about being adaptable. What would you say? What would you do? How do you think he would react?

_____

_____

_____

_____

_____

_____

_____

Discuss your solutions with others. With the information you gained from talking about it, how would you change or add to your solution to help Daniel?

_____

_____

_____

_____

Adults help children find alternatives. Are you the kind of person who sees one solution to a problem and can't be convinced that there might be alternatives? Or do you know someone who is like that? You, or that other person, need help developing problem-solving skills. We hear much about problem solving these days. It isn't all that complicated. If something doesn't work, think of an alternative. The process can be as simple or as complicated as you want to make it. But basically that is it—if you've tried and tried and it doesn't work, try something else. That's what we should model for children and help them to practice in their lives.

How do we model problem solving and looking for alternatives? First of all, we don't continue to use techniques that don't work with children.

"I put him on a time-out every day, but it doesn't help."

"I've tried ignoring him and tried convincing him, but neither one makes a dent."

"I made ten behavior charts, but none of them worked."

If you ever hear yourself talking like that, know that it is time to try something else. If you are talking like that to yourself, you are probably arguing with or ignoring this child from time to time.

There are few situations in life that are more frightening than thinking there is no alternative. Fortunately, that is rarely true. Even in something as scary as a terminal illness there are choices about how to live and how to die.

In the following exercise you will examine the ways that you can feel stuck in your own life. It will help you understand better how kids feel. It may also help you figure out why finding options is sometimes difficult for you, which may be making it harder for you to help kids.

Look now at your life. Is there anywhere that you feel stuck or at least feel that there are fewer alternatives than in other parts of your life? It may be your job or a friendship or a marriage or a money situation or your health or your appearance or wanting to paint your house.

Write down what the situation is.

_____

_____

_____

_____

_____

Next, write down the names of two or three people in your life who may have influenced you to believe that there are no alternatives in this situation.

_____

Write down the messages that each of these people gave you that keep you feeling stuck.

_____

_____

_____

_____

Write a note to those people telling them that you are going to solve the problem. That you are a problem solver now with the power to change things in your life.

_____

_____

_____

_____

_____

Think of two people in your life who are good at finding alternatives. Write down their names.

_____

What messages would they give you about problem solving in this situation?
Write them down.

_____

_____

_____

Write a note to one of these people, thanking them for helping you become a problem solver, and a seeker of alternatives. Tell them that you are going to figure out a solution to this problem, but don't give a solution yet.

_____

_____

_____

Now brainstorm alternatives that might help you solve the problem. Don't worry about whether they make sense or are realistic or are something you really want to do. Anything goes. Write down at least ten ideas.

_____

_____

_____

_____

_____

_____

_____

_____

_____

exercise continued on next page

No matter how much you want to say "yes, but," no matter how stuck you feel, choose from your list two alternatives that might work. Circle the two alternatives.

For each alternative you chose, write down the action steps that you are going to take and the dates on which you are going to take them in order to try these two alternatives.

_____

_____

_____

_____

_____

Write yourself a note. Congratulate yourself for being a problem solver. Talk about your fears and your hopes. Even if you feel that you are caught in a vise or going through a dark tunnel, tell yourself to keep writing until, at some level, you believe you will solve this problem.

_____

_____

_____

_____

_____

As in other areas of our caring for children, we cannot teach what we do not know and have not experienced. Empathy for the child who can't solve problems is easier to come by if we have gone through the hardship ourselves. Likewise, we are more likely to believe that children are capable of finding alternatives if we are capable ourselves.

You are working hard in this section. It is valuable work because it will help you to be able to stand by children enthusiastically when they do not believe they have options. Here's one more exercise to help you apply what you know about problem solving.

Now think of a child in your care with whom you argue or whom you want to ignore. Perhaps she has a difficult time finding appropriate solutions to her problems. Maybe she is stuck in a tunnel in which the only possibility she sees is destructive behavior. Write the child a letter. Tell her that you believe in her. Tell her about a time when you saw her choosing a different course of action. Tell her what you wish for her. Tell her how you are going to help her find alternatives and get unstuck. Tell her that you care for her. You may want to read or give the letter to the child.

_____

_____

_____

_____

_____

_____

_____

Now promise yourself that the next time you want to argue with or ignore this child you will find an alternative way to deal with her.

Adults facilitate successful experiences with children.

One of the women in my neighborhood *was outside playing with her five year old. He has some speech and learning delays. She saw him pulling up dandelions by their roots and tossing them around the yard.*

She asked him, "Do you know how to pick dandelion bouquets?"

"Sure," he responded proudly.

"Could you pick one for the kitchen table?"

"Sure."

He picked a handful of dandelions.

"Thanks," his mother said.

"Sure," he answered.

☺ ☺

Such a simple exchange. In order to have successful experiences, children need to have responsibilities that they can handle. For that boy the task was at just the right level of responsibility. The dandelion bouquet was a successful life experience. He told his mother that he was competent. He followed through and picked a bouquet. I imagine the flowers are in a glass on their kitchen table now.

The mother knows her child. She doesn't ignore him. She doesn't tell him to stop pulling up dandelions. If she had, he might have said, "I don't have to," and an argument might have started. Instead, she empowered him to be competent. The next time he faces a difficulty he will have more self-confidence that will help him to be resilient. He is more likely to know that he can be successful. After all, he can pick dandelions.

The ability to help children experience success comes from attending to them. You need to know what they can do, expect them to do it, and recognize that they did it. Don't ignore the unsuccessful child. Observe her closely. She will tell you what you can expect of her.

Make a list of three children you care for, who you believe would benefit from more successes in their lives (that's all children, of course, but some seem to need it more than others).

After their names write two responsibilities that you can give them that will help them to feel successful. Remember, they don't have to be huge .

Don't argue with or ignore children or you will impede resiliency—the ability to take on life's stresses and know that you will be okay. You can be the caring adult who makes the difference in a child's life. Or you can be one of many who, when all linked together, leave children with the skills and beliefs they need in order to bounce back—like a healthy person. By helping a child to be happy, rather than going to war with her, you will make a real difference that will be reflected in her changed behaviors.

Chapter 18

Cools:
Do's

by Aneesa

When children are born, they are free and should always be treated that way.

≈ Article I. United Nations Universal Declaration of Human Rights

Do Help Children Use Cools

What are "cools"? Cools are an alternative to corporal punishment, an alternative to time-outs, a way to help children take the time they need by themselves.

Twenty years ago, *I worked in an inner-city school in the eastern United States. I came from a progressive inner-city school in Minnesota. Because I had lived with poverty growing up, I was excited about the opportunity to continue to work with children whose families had limited income and resources. I was honored to work with families who wanted a better future for their children.*

On the first day of teacher orientation, I knew that I had landed in Oz. The principal brought me to her office for my one-on-one time. She had served in the Army in World War II. She told me that we could all survive in this school if we stuck together. "If we can do it in the trenches of Germany, we can do it here!" she said. I was shocked, but kept listening.

The principal told me how difficult the children were and about their families' inadequacies. Then she handed me my supplies for the year: four board erasers, four boxes of chalk, and a paddle.

"I won't be needing this," I said, giving her back the paddle.

"You're new here," she answered. "You'll need it."

"I'll quit first," I said and laid the paddle on her desk.

ⓢ ⓔ

Systems were encouraging corporal punishment twenty years ago, which is not *that* long ago. Then a shift began in society. It is evolving slowly. In some places, I hear, it is still okay to hit children in schools with their parents' permission. Historically, it has been a parent's duty in many religions and cultures to use the rod on children. "Spare the rod and spoil the child," those who questioned the practice were warned. In some cultures, physical punishment was meant to teach children compliance so they would not be judged insolent by those with the power to hurt or kill them.

Much of the belief system regarding corporal punishment has changed in the United States; not in every culture or religion, but, in most families and communities the use of corporal punishment is diminishing. People are sent to prison rather than publicly flogged. There is, of course, violence in many prisons, but that is an abuse of a system that our society otherwise agrees on. There is still capital punishment, but it is a long, involved process and is not recognized as the common way to deal with criminals. Using physical violence on your spouse is domestic abuse and a crime. Society's rules are changing—not everywhere, not in every case, but overall our society is moving in the direction of saying that violence against another person is not something we want woven into our country's way of life.

In the United States, when there are resources and time to study child development, physical punishment is proven repeatedly to teach children fear, to breed violence, to fuel anger and resentment, and to lower children's ability to believe in themselves.

For example, a study at the University of New Hampshire in 1997 concluded that, "when corporal punishment is used to reduce antisocial behavior of children, the long-term effect tends to be the opposite. If corporal punishment is replaced by nonviolent means of discipline, it could reduce the risk of antisocial behavior among children and reduce the level of violence in American society."

Guiding children to experience their own power, to make reasonable decisions for themselves, to be self-disciplined and responsible are stronger safeguards for their future well-being than physical punishment.

The University of New Hampshire conducted another four-year study, ending in 1998, that showed that refraining from spanking helps to increase a child's I.Q. It concluded that children are better off when they learn to control their own behavior rather than responding only out of fear of being hit.

As American society's beliefs have changed in the past twenty or thirty years, and as our knowledge of child development and psychology has expanded, corporal punishment of children has become unacceptable in institutions caring for children. People caring for children have had to replace that paddle with some other means of control. But the way we think about children—that punishment-control model this book has discussed—has not changed, and so many people still see control as the issue. One of the strategies that has emerged, something that has seemed to many people like a good idea, is the "time-out."

Time-outs do not teach a child to control herself. The time-out does not put an end to behavior problems. It is used as punishment. The child's need to assess a situation, to solve a problem, to be accountable for her actions, is taken away by the adult. That is no more useful than other forms of control and punishment. I believe that the time-out should not be a part of school-age care. So do many other people. As a result, some programs are saying that time-outs may not be used. This is a move away from a technique that has often become a punitive replacement for physical punishment. When we decide not to use time-outs anymore, we must be careful that we do not use them in a different form. Old habits are hard to break.

When I do consulting, staff members and directors sometimes tell me that they do not use time-outs. However, as I work on site, I often observe that they are used—sometimes under a different name, such as time-in, or simply by saying to children, "Sit over there until you can behave." Or the staff continues to threaten children with them. Or I find that the staff wishes they could use them because they believe that time-outs are effective. What often happens in this case is that the staff does other punitive things instead. That is because just eliminating time-outs, by mandate, does not change the way many teachers, like American society in general, rely on punishment and control to deal with children's behavior.

Eliminating corporal punishment didn't change this, and neither does just eliminating time-outs. Until we change the way we think about how to help children change their behaviors and learn relationship skills, forbidding certain techniques is not the entire answer. Corporal punishment, time-outs—one form of punishment follows another, and discipline problems continue to increase and intensify.

"But," you may be saying, "there are times when a child needs to be away from others." I call these times "cools." They are not a replacement for time-outs. They are for those times when a child needs to be free from the stimulation of the group. They are not about the fact that he threw a basketball at another child or tracked mud into the hall. Each of those things can be dealt with in many ways. Cools are about the child and what he needs.

How do we go about letting children know that it is all right and admirable to remove themselves from the scene? First of all, let all the children know about cools before they need one. Tell them that there will be instances when they might need to cool off or calm down, or be alone. Times when they can get themselves together so that, whatever the situation is about, they can come back and handle it on their own or with an adult's help.

Let them know that the cool isn't a punishment and it will not take the place of being accountable for any behaviors that need to be addressed. It is simply time to cool off or relax. They don't need to be out of control to take advantage of a cool. Maybe they feel sad, or want to think by themselves, or are frustrated, or mad, or overwhelmed, or just tired of being with so many people.

You can use examples from your own life. Talk perhaps about when you disagree with someone and feel yourself getting angry or crying. Tell them what you might do before you go back to deal with that person. You might take a walk or go to your room for a while, or splash cold water on your face, or listen to soothing music. You could tell them that you use some of the same techniques when a computer won't work for you and you want to give up or throw it out the window. Or when the pie crust won't roll out.

Or you might start getting crabby because you have a house full of company and you realize that you just need to be alone. Or you have been at work with people all day so you stop in a park to listen to the birds sing on the way home. Or you want to think about something and everybody's noise—the TV, phones, talk—interrupts your concentration so you put on your headphones and listen to music that helps you think.

After you give them examples and affirm their feelings by admitting that you have feelings that you need to control and times you want to chill out, too, you can lead a discussion. What kinds of things are helpful for them to do when they find themselves getting so upset that they can't do the task at hand? Be certain to tell them that having strong feelings isn't bad. It's what we do with them that makes the difference.

Guide them in beginning to recognize other feelings that are not as strong as anger, such as sadness, or irritation, or wanting to be alone, that might be clearer to them if they take a cool.

Do not tell them that you will not be using cools instead of time-outs, because you won't. They are a different thing altogether, because they are not primarily about a child's behavior, but about a child's needs.

Ask them how they might be able to get away for a while to deal with whatever the feelings are. They may come up with things like counting to ten, going outside, getting a drink of water, or bouncing a basketball. Guide them to remember how upset they get sometimes and ask them whether the coping techniques they listed, which you will have written down on a chart, will work for those times. They may generate more ideas, like running laps, pounding something, or throwing things. You can add techniques such as visualization, speed writing, reading, music, and working with clay, giving them some information on how to do them.

Ask the children to choose from the list one or two techniques they think will work for them. Tell them that the next time they get one of those feelings a cool might help with, they might try one of the techniques they have chosen. Tell them that if at some point in the future you think you see them struggling with those feelings, you might ask whether a cool would be helpful. Some children in the group will never need to take a cool, but normalizing it by presenting it as something that is not designed for certain kids will take some of the stigma away for those children who have more problems with control issues. It will also help all the children learn about dealing with emotions.

For those children who you know have major upsets, it is helpful to set up individual plans. Help them learn to sense when life is getting to be too much to handle so that they can take a cool before they are totally out of control. Have them describe to you how they feel when they start to lose control. One child told me that he felt like "hot oil is bubbling in my body." You can develop signals between you and the child—perhaps a raised eyebrow or a hand signal. You can help the child catch herself when you see her getting off track. Or the child can signal you and you will know that she is going to get a drink of water or going to the place where she has decided she can calm down. That place can be different for different children and at various times. Then, children can tailor the cools to their own needs and everyone will not have to be aware that the child is taking a break.

Cools are not a new substitute for time-outs. Time-outs are discussed in this chapter with cools so that you don't think that cools are a new version of the time-out. I want to address both issues so that there isn't confusion, not to connect them. I think you are getting that message. They are different in most ways. If you want to tell kids that you won't be using time-outs, that should be an entirely different discussion. You probably don't even need to announce the elimination of time-outs. They can just disappear.

Let's review what cools are:

- Nonpunitive.
- Controlled by the child.
- Established as a concept before the child loses control.
- Respectful of the child's needs—in both the long and short term.
- Not necessarily obvious to the entire group.
- Not followed by punishment.
- Decided upon in a calm manner.
- Chosen by the child rather than the adult.
- Not for a specific amount of time unless the child and the adult previously decided that that is a helpful strategy.
- Not in a designated place for every child.

There are times, of course, when the preventive measures aren't going to help. You will have a child who is raging, throwing things, swearing, or hysterical. At times you may even have to restrain certain children. But this should be a very rare event. Even when the child does lose control, you can remind him that he can calm himself down. You can tell him that he is a smart person, that there are techniques he can use, that you trust he will calm down soon. You can calmly repeat this to him even if he doesn't seem to be listening. Don't shout at him or make it a threatening command. Simply and gently let him know that you trust him and he can trust you. That your adult-child relationship is one he can depend on. You are the adult; he is the child. You have a relationship built on respectful daily interactions, and that relationship will carry both of you through this difficult time. The child knows that what follows this discussion will be problem solving and guidance, not lecturing or punishment.

A television news magazine show *recently did a feature on a child who had borderline personality disorder. They showed video tapes of his parents struggling with him—using complicated restraining positions, yelling, punishing, staying up most of the night because he refused to go to bed while they tried to hold him down or keep the door closed. They would try to make him eat his vegetables by holding his shoulders against the chair. He would escape and hide under the table. The parents were truly caring but had no idea what to do anymore. The TV producers brought in a psychologist to advise the parents. "Stay tuned for the surprising solution," the moderator said as they cut to a commercial.*

The psychologist told the family to give the child more power. "Let him decide when he will eat. Let him go to sleep when he wants to in his room. Put a TV with nonviolent videos in there if it helps him relax. Let him stand up and move around the room when you help him with his homework. Never, ever get in a fight with him. Tell him that he can control himself. Help him come up with ways to do that. He can let you know when he has had enough interaction. Time-outs won't work; they will just make him angry and leave you exhausted. This child needs to have more control over his own life, not less. You may not have what we think of as the all-American family that eats all their meals together and the children are in bed by nine o' clock, but you will have a happier family."

A short time after the psychologist helped the family set up the new program, the network interviewed the parents and taped a typical day in the home. The parents said that they didn't recognize their son as the same boy. They had to give up some things that they had always believed about control, but it was worth it. They were getting to know their son as a person, and he was getting to know them. The video showed a much more relaxed family living in a caring relationship. The boy had changed his almost animal-like behaviors to active, happy child's behaviors. He ate, slept, was involved in his homework and in life. The fact that the solution was for the parents to give the child more control, not less, awed the show's moderators. "Not even one time-out, much less spanking or yelling," one said to the other.

"Imagine that," said the other. "But it seemed to work."

"It certainly did."

When we deal with children who display the most difficult behaviors, it is easy for us to forget what we know about children. Because we often feel frightened, we think that we don't know what to do. But we do know what to do. We can deal with the children in the ways that work. We can help them stop to take charge of themselves, in a caring, assertive, and competent manner.

As we said, cools are helpful for children who don't have major behavioral issues. All children feel that they need to get their power back sometimes. Even the child who rarely acts out may be having internal struggles. He may be an introvert or shy and feel overwhelmed by the stimulating environment and being around so many people. It is difficult for these children, especially, to have to interact with peers and adult caretakers for up to twelve hours a day, as so many children now have to do. If these children's needs go unmet, they may become withdrawn or even depressed.

Monica is seven years old. *The school-age care staff usually describe her as "sweet" or "nice." They worry about her sometimes because her mother has remarried twice since Monica was born. There are four children younger than Monica in the blended family's two-bedroom bungalow. But her mother loves her and is involved in her activities. And the staff says, "She will be fine because she is such a good little girl and has an adult's head on her shoulders."*

One November day, Josef, a staff person, observes Monica while the children play on the playground. There is a two-foot cement block wall around a garden area. Josef watches as Monica repeatedly stands up on the wall and falls off. Afraid that she will hurt herself falling, Josef goes over to Monica to give her some tips on jumping.

"Get away from me. Get away from me," Monica says in a soft but angry voice. She climbs back up on the wall.

"I just wanted to see if I could help you learn how to make smoother landings," Josef says.

"Get away," she says again.

Josef inches a bit closer. "Why?" he asks.

Monica flings herself from the wall. She lands on her knees. They scrape the gravel and start to bleed. Monica cries. Josef sits next to her. He puts his hand gently on her shoulder.

Monica chokes on her own tears. "I'm so dumb, I can't kill myself."

Taking an invisible deep breath, Josef says, "You can't kill yourself?"

"No. I thought last night in my bed how to do it. I thought that I could jump off this wall today and die."

"Die?"

"Yeah, I'm tired of being stupid. I'm tired of all of the voices."

"Voices?"

"Babies' voices, teachers' voices, day care voices, Mom and Dads' voices, kids' voices."

"When do you hear these voices?"

"Home, school, everywhere. Listen to them right now."

"These are real people's voices?"

"Yes, like yours right now. I want to be alone. If I die I can be alone."

"Oh, Monica," Josef says, "I'm so glad you told me about this. We can figure this out. You don't have to die to be alone."

Monica struggles up, "Now my knee hurts," she sniffles.

"Let's start by taking that hurt away," Josef says.

The staff talks to Monica's mom. Monica starts seeing a child psychologist. There are many problems to unravel because of all the changes in her life. Certainly, just being around lots of people all the time is not the only issue. But the psychologist does say that Monica is a child who needs time to reflect on her own. She gets exhausted and anxious when she is around people all the time. Her mom changes things at home so that she can have alone times and some one-on-one attention.

The school-age program does the same. None of the other children know about the cools that Monica takes to stay healthy and happy. By the end of the school year Monica is cheerful and back into life. She even challenges adults occasionally. The staff now describes her as "a normal kid."

☺   ☺

Children like Monica are not who we usually describe as "discipline problems." Nor are children who have learning disabilities that may prevent them from picking up social skills that allow them to fit in easily, or who are extremely intelligent, or who for other reasons are different from what we consider the norm. They will also benefit from cools. They need emotional space away from the pressure of acting in ways that seem to them to come so easily to other children. They need room to be who they are and to be comfortable with their need to take that time alone. Although they don't typically come up in discussions of challenging children, without behavior guidance their behaviors are problematic to themselves and to those who work with them.

Cools are a concept that many children do not know about. In these times when kids are often in care with many other children most of the day, and then take classes or music lessons or play team sports, they are rarely alone. Often, those who care for the children do what seems like a quick fix to keep the group functioning. Remember that there are no quick fixes and that the job you are doing is helping individual kids learn about themselves and about how to become self-disciplined. Cools are one vehicle that can assist you.

Think of a child who you think might benefit from learning about cools. Write down her name.

_____

Write down what you might say to the child to introduce her to cools. Include some suggestions that are really possible in your setting.

_____

_____

_____

_____

_____

Talk to the child about cools. Get her ideas. Try out cools for two weeks. You will want a small notebook to take notes during those two weeks. At the end of two weeks (mark it on your calendar), write down what happened. How did the initial conversation with the child go? What ideas did the child come up with? How did she receive your suggestions? Did the child use any cools? If so, what happened? If not, why not?

_____

_____

_____

_____

_____

_____

_____

If the child used cools, have you noticed any changes in behaviors? Why do you think there were or were not changes? If the child didn't choose to use cools, did you notice any changes in behavior? Why or why not?

_____

_____

_____

What could you and the child do to make cools a helpful, or more helpful, choice for the child?

_____

_____

_____

Congratulate yourself for your care and effort. Whatever the results, the child knows that you are thinking about her and want to be helpful. Write down your own congratulations.

_____

_____

Do Use Reverse Cools

"I have a headache this big," *Nina tells Steve as they watch the kids in the gym. Then she yells, for the second time, "Stop bouncing those balls off the walls!" She sighs and says to Steve, "Looks like I have to go over there. They're just not listening."*

Steve watches as Nina wrestles the basketballs away from two kids. She pulls them to the side of the gym and gives them a talking to.

When Nina comes back, she says, "Too bad you couldn't make it to the party last night. We had a few and watched the game. Got to bed a little late, but…sorry, it looks like I have to go over there again."

Steve puts his hand on Nina's shoulder.

"Can you take some advice?" he asks.

"From you, yeah."

"Let me go over there while you take a break."

"Sure, thanks."

"And, Nina, weekends are made for parties."

"You're right. Thanks again," Nina says, her face a little flushed. "I needed that."

≈ Jean Steiner and Mary Steiner Whelan

You may never party, but there are other reasons for you to have days when you are the one who needs an occasional cool. I call them reverse cools, because instead of asking children if they want to take a break, we reverse our thinking about who has the problem. We decide it's us and we take the time to go away, physically or mentally, to get our act together. Nina had a power struggle with the kids over the balls. It didn't work. Next, she might have tried giving them time-outs. That wouldn't be the answer either. Instead, with her co-worker's help she got a Coke and remembered that today she had limited coping mechanisms. She returned more tuned into herself and the kids.

Some days for you it may be that you couldn't find your car keys and had to take a bus, or you have PMS or hot flashes, or you had a disagreement with your partner, or your cat threw up furballs as you left and they're still on the couch. Whatever the reason, we all have workdays when we are not up to our usual level of functioning.

On the way to work each day, right before you read your reminder paper that says, "I am the adult. They are the children," do a spot check on how you are. If you realize that you are tired or irritable, be on guard. Plan on some cools, mental or physical.

Here is a list of examples:

- If the children seem to be shouting at the top of their voices, take a cool by asking another staff person, "Are the kids really rowdy today or is it me?"

- If there is a certain child you can't deal with easily even on a good day (we all have some), stay away from her as much as you can. Take a cool away from her.

- Give the kids choice day or a self-directed project. You take a cool and clean out a closet or rearrange shelves while you keep an eye on things. Let the kids know that you need time to get the task done and will appreciate their support.

- Take drinks of water more often.

- Take your tired or stressed mind away once in a while so you can come back more relaxed and focused: Remember your last vacation, plan your next one, imagine the smell of the great leftovers you're going to warm up when you get home, think fondly of the book you're going to read.

The work you do is intense. You may think there is no way for you to work in a reverse time-out, but you can. I just gave you some suggestions. Here are some more:

- Put on music and dance with the kids.

- Have the kids paint to music. Join them.

- Blow bubbles.

- Have a contest to see which child can be quiet the longest.

- Tell a co-worker a joke. Ask a co-worker to tell you a joke.

- Eat baby carrots. Offer some to the kids.

- Have book-reading time.

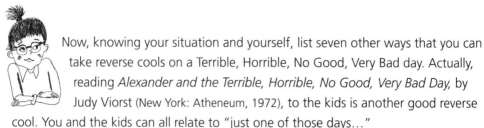

Now, knowing your situation and yourself, list seven other ways that you can take reverse cools on a Terrible, Horrible, No Good, Very Bad day. Actually, reading *Alexander and the Terrible, Horrible, No Good, Very Bad Day,* by Judy Viorst (New York: Atheneum, 1972), to the kids is another good reverse cool. You and the kids can all relate to "just one of those days…"

Your creative but practical list of reverse cools:

1. _____

2. _____

3. _____

4. _____

5. _____

6. _____

7. _____

Instant Calming Steps

Another helpful cool technique to remember and to teach the children is the list of instant calming sequence steps. It is helpful to practice them by yourself and with the children before a tense situation occurs. Then, when an unexpected difficulty pops up you can say to yourself or the child, "Start doing the calming steps."

Instant calming steps:

Step 1. Uninterrupted breathing—keep breathing in a regular pattern.

Step 2. Positive face—relax those face muscles from the forehead down. Smile if you can and if it's appropriate.

Step 3. Balanced posture—put your shoulders back. Pretend there is a string attached to the top of your head and the ceiling.

Step 4. Wave of relaxation—let all the tension in your body flow out of your fingertips.

Step 5. Mental control—focus on anything, the flowers on the shelf, the bulletin board, the flag, without too much thinking.

Robert K. Cooper, Health & Fitness Excellence—The Scientific Plan
(New York: Houghton, 1989)

Remember to use your creative ideas when you need them. Reverse cools make much more sense and will feel much better to you and the kids than putting kids on time-outs, or whatever, because you are experiencing a less-than-perfect day.

It is interesting to apply the characteristics of a cool as listed on page 284 to reverse cools.

Reverse cools are:

- Nonpunitive.

- Controlled by the person who needs them. Adults control reverse cools. They decide when the reverse cool is over.

- Established as a concept before the person loses control. In this chapter you learned to assess yourself on the way to work each day. You know some techniques that you can use when a reverse cool is desirable. You know that a reverse cool is a tool that you can use to help you act appropriately.

- Respectful of the person's needs—in the long and short terms. Reverse cools respect your needs both in the short term—for the day or part of the day when you can't handle as much—and in the long term—when you won't feel incompetent or guilty because you lost control with a child.

- Not necessarily obvious to the entire group. No one, except perhaps another staff person if needed, will know that you are taking a cool unless you want them to.

- Not followed by punishment. What's there to punish? In a reverse cool you decide to take care of yourself before or as you catch yourself acting in ways that you don't want to. You help the children and the other adults by removing yourself when you need to.

- Suggested in a calm manner. You don't beat yourself up or get angry at yourself when you take a cool. You say calmly, "I want some time to reduce my stress and get reorganized. I will give myself that time today, or right now."

continued on next page

- Chosen by the person who needs the cool. You, as an adult, always choose when you will take a cool. This is developmentally appropriate. As an adult you know yourself and have developed strong coping mechanisms. Children are still learning and developing so they, at times, need guidance from an adult to know that a cool is an option.

    At times, you could listen to the children's clues. They might say things like, "You're crabby today." Do a self-check to see if you need to think about that vacation for a minute or walk around the playground once or some such thing.

- Not for a specific amount of time. A reverse cool only needs to be as long as you want it to be. There might be times when you wish the reverse cool could last for hours. But that is another developmental issue. We as adults can often get ourselves together more quickly than do children. We have more practice and we understand our responsibility to get back to our work.

- Not in a designated place. There is no need to have a reverse cool chair for adults as there is no need to have a time-out chair for a child. Either would be punitive, would tell the whole group what is only the individual's concern, and might not meet the person's needs at that time. If what you, or a child, need is to walk or listen to music alone, then sitting in a particular corner wouldn't suffice.

If we can prepare for our needs and have techniques available to meet them, we are respecting ourselves and those around us. It is not our "fault" that we need a cool. It is not the child's "fault" that she needs a cool.

It can be difficult to change our beliefs about the need for punishing or controlling children with time-outs, just as it was to change our society's beliefs about corporal punishment. But if we see ourselves and children's needs as similar, it may be easier to make the shift. We are all in a developmental process. Children need more guidance from us to learn self-discipline. That's why we are there to help. They will learn more quickly and our jobs will be easier if we develop a system that respects our own and their rights to be in charge of feelings and how to deal with them.

You are working on that by doing this book. Children are fortunate to have you in their lives.

Describe a time when you behaved with children in a way that you wish you hadn't.

_____

_____

_____

How did you feel during and after the incident?

_____

_____

How could you have handled it differently?

_____

_____

_____

How might you have felt then?

_____

_____

_____

What did you learn in this chapter that you think will be the most valuable in your future work with children?

_____

_____

_____

Chapter 19

Cools:
Don'ts

by Vicki

...you will never put me in a corner anywhere. I would build myself a round room first so there would be no corners.

≈ Juanita Jewel Craft

Don't Use Time-Outs

Which of these institutions in the United States is receiving funding at a higher and higher rate each year: schools or prisons? That's right, prisons. ("During the 1990's states assigned higher priorities to other [than educational] programs, particularly corrections." Federal Reserve Bulletin, 1996.)

Why is this a problem? Right again. Because prisons don't work. The majority of people in prison have been there before. Some have been in and out many times. According to the U.S. Bureau of Justice Statistics, 1997, "Fully 94% of all state prisoners have either been convicted of a violent crime or been previously sentenced to incarceration or probation."

Why don't they work? Because people don't learn anything positive there. We as a society put people in prison and then let them out. They haven't, for the most part, learned new skills or worked on the roots of their behaviors. What people do learn in prison often further entrenches them in the behaviors and beliefs that got them there in the first place. They learn to be resentful, to be more angry, to seek revenge, to try not to get caught the next time, to relate to people who are destructive, to accept that they have no self-control and are bad, not to trust. The more times they go to prison the more clearly they learn those lessons.

There are heinous crimes for which a person needs to be removed from society—perhaps for a long time or forever. But there are many more people who could become an asset to themselves and the world if they were rehabilitated.

Time-outs are like tiny prisons.

With one sweeping motion, *Keith sends the half-finished 500-piece puzzle of a peaceful country scene flying around the room. He has been arguing with Joey about whether they should do all the sky pieces first or put in whatever pieces they want to. When Joey doesn't see it his way, Keith explodes, yelling, "Try to put it together now!" Bits of cows and corn and sky sail everywhere.*

Janelle, the staff person, says, "Time-out, Keith. Get on that chair over there and think about what you've done. Maybe, when I'm good and ready, you can get up."

Keith picks up a handful of pieces and throws them up in the air. He gives the chair a push, turns it around, and sits in it backwards.

Joey refuses to pick up the pieces. "I didn't do it," he states firmly.

"No, you didn't," Janelle says. "But it wouldn't hurt you to help."

She starts picking the jagged bits off the game shelves and the floor. Joey leaves. A few kids help Janelle.

A bigger crowd watches Keith. After sitting in the chair for a few minutes, he slides down and starts kicking whatever his feet can reach. The attendance sheets fall off the sign-in table, a child passing by gets kicked in the shins, a bucket of Lincoln Logs spills across the tile.

As he kicks, he shouts at Janelle, "I don't care if you make me sit here. I like it. It's fun to watch you crawling around like a dog looking for puzzle bones."

Some kids laughed. "Who are you laughing at?" he asks them. "Oh, you've never seen a dog before?"

More laughter.

Janelle looks up, raises her voice and says, "Look, mister, you're never getting off the chair that way. You can be sitting there when your dad comes. We'll see what he does about it."

Keith's dad rules Keith with ridicule and spankings. Keith says, "Nobody can hurt me. Who cares?"

But he gets quiet. While he sits there he's thinking, I'm gonna punch that Joey kid in the mouth tomorrow. I'll get him. In the bathroom when no one's looking.

And then that teacher tries to be all buddy buddy with me. Not any more, chick. You and your stupid communication club. I'm not gonna talk in that thing anymore unless it's swearing.

And then, I'm not coming to this place anymore. I'll tell my dad I'm stayin' home. He won't care. He can use some of his money for other stuff.

Janelle picks up the last puzzle piece she can find. She glances at Keith. He's quieted down at last, *she thinks.* Maybe he'll come to his senses. I don't know when he'll learn. He's on a time-out more than he's in. I hope it's sinking in that it's not worth it.

Keith is thinking, My dad's gonna beat me for messing up. I hope he beats her up too. He's tough enough. It don't matter what I do now.

He inches off the chair. With one foot touching it he stretches his body out so that he can reach the markers. He scribbles large black lightning bolts on the tile.

"Back on that chair, Keith," Janelle says.

"My toe's on it."

"You know what I mean!"

"What do you mean? I'm on it."

Some of the kids start chanting, very quietly, "Go Keith. Go Keith."

Janelle hears them but pretends she doesn't. Keith says to them, "You guys are totally rad. We can start a gang or something when she lets me off this thing."

"I'm getting the supervisor if you're not up on that chair in two seconds."

"Good, maybe she'll kick me out!"

"You're not going to be talking so smart when your dad gets here."

"What did the troublemaker do now?" Keith's dad comes into the room behind Janelle.

Janelle starts to give him the details.

"It doesn't matter," his dad says. "He'll get what's coming to him tonight. Grab your stuff, all of it this time. I'm not waiting while you come back in because you forgot that ridiculous Batman backpack."

He lectures Keith as they walk down the hall. Janelle watches from the doorway. Keith looks over his shoulder. He gives Janelle a dirty look and mouths a swear word.

"It's hopeless," she thinks. "If they don't learn at home there's nothing we can do about it."

◉ ◉

Janelle is not a bad teacher. She really hopes that Keith's behaviors will improve. She is using the methods she knows to try to teach him how to behave appropriately. What Janelle hoped Keith learned and what he actually did learn are obviously two different things. Janelle hoped that he would be punished into realizing that his behavior was wrong. But he already knew that. She hoped that somehow the thought of having to be on time-out would teach him a lesson and that the next time he wanted to do something wrong he would think about that and not do it. Even though time after time that wasn't what happened. She hoped that his father's discipline would scare him. It did, but he learned to give up rather than reform.

What did Keith actually learn? What people in prison learn. Try the exercise below to spot all the things Keith learned from this interaction.

Go through the story and put the appropriate number from the list below next to the sentences that illustrate what Keith learned. You may use each number as many times as you think is necessary. You may also put more than one number on each sentence. For example, put a 1 on the sentence that begins, "As he kicked, he shouted at Janelle..." Here are the things Keith learned:

1. To be resentful

2. To be more angry

3. To seek revenge

4. To try not to get caught next time

5. To relate to people who are destructive

6. To accept that he has no self-control and is bad

7. Not to trust

Keith demonstrated his learning in many ways. He said and did many unacceptable things. But he might not have if Janelle had dealt differently with the situation. After the puzzle-throwing incident, the other behaviors stemmed from the time-out. Janelle and Keith tangled themselves up in a huge power struggle. Time-outs are often a jumping-off point for power struggles. And remember, an adult can never win a power struggle. So, in addition to not learning how to control his behaviors, Keith ended up being the hero to some of the kids in the group. He also went home to more punishment. Janelle knew that this might be the case, and when she went home that night she probably felt bad about that. She just didn't know what other choices she had.

Fortunately, you have the opportunity through this book and other resources to acquire other skills. You already have.

Go through the story again. Write a description of three ways Janelle could have handled the situation before or after the puzzle scattering.

1. _____

_____

_____

2. _____

_____

_____

3. _____

_____

_____

Keith's story is a powerful one. However, even when we think we are handling a time-out much better than the staff person in the story, children often suffer some of the same consequences. Even if there is a new name for the time-out, it is a controlling and punishing tactic. Being told, in whatever way, that you are not good enough to be a part of this group right now does not feel good. It feels shaming and shame leads to acting out or withdrawal, not to self-esteem. Even the most benign time-outs do not assist children in learning skills to control their own behaviors, to manage their own feelings, or to clean up their own messes. A time-out certainly does nothing to enhance your working relationship with a child.

So, before you think of using a time-out again, remember Keith. No child deserves even a shadow of that kind of experience.

You will be able to prevent incidents such as this one from happening to you and to the children. You will guide children so that they do not have to rebel. Rather, you can help them rebuild their ability to relate.

Don't Use Corporal Punishment

Never, ever, use corporal punishment. Anything that an adult does to physically hurt a child is corporal punishment. Hitting is the example that we think of quickly. However, added to the statement that you can never, ever, use corporal punishment are these warnings. Pulling a child's hair is corporal punishment. So is pinching his cheeks, holding his face tightly in your hand to get him to look at you, yanking him by the arm, pushing him into a chair, shoving him against a wall, squeezing his arms, snapping your fingers on his head, forcing him to stay in a chair by pushing down on his shoulders, or tugging at his ears. None of these actions is ever appropriate.

In the last chapter we talked about our society moving away from corporal punishment as a useful vehicle for behavioral change. We still have a long way to go in that direction. And some of us are frightened because we don't know what else will keep the criminals off the street, or our families together, or our children in line so that they are safe from outside forces.

That many of our children are threatened by outside forces is not imaginary, historically or in the present. This was true, for example, in the days of slavery when African-American children could be punished by the slave owners or his managers. Or Native American children could be kidnapped. Or Irish children could be ridiculed. It has continued to be true for many oppressed people in this country when facing a world full of prejudice and discrimination. Children of color, particularly boys, continue to die from police brutality.

Of course we want to protect our children as forcefully as we can, even if it means hurting them to make them behave.

Oprah Winfrey spoke to this issue on her show in October, 1997. She said, "I know that it's [corporal punishment is] part of the tradition and it's part of the race. But I say this as a Black American in this country: If we want to change Black history, we need to think of a new way of disciplining our children, because this is passed on from the slave master. And I believe that it is up to this generation to break that chain. And I know it's difficult."

Remember a time when you were a child and an adult punished you physically. Briefly describe the incident.

_____

_____

_____

_____

How did you feel before and after the incident? About the person who hurt you? About yourself?

_____

_____

_____

_____

What was the adult trying to teach you? Do you think you needed to learn it? How else could the adult have taught you the same thing?

_____

_____

_____

_____

All of us want to keep what is good from our history. Corporal punishment is not good. And besides, hurting children in order to teach them anything is not effective. It induces anger, encourages the use of violence as an acceptable tool, and teaches that power can't be shared and that children can't control themselves. And it hurts.

Think of the last thing you did that someone might judge inappropriate. Maybe you broke a dish, or shouted at your partner, or made a sarcastic comment, or gossiped, or ate too much, or went back to smoking, or drove too fast. Imagine that whoever didn't like your behavior walked across the room, saying, "This is for your own good," and hit you across the backside with a belt, or a hand, or slapped you.

What is the first thing you feel as you imagine this scene? Pain. Physical pain. It smarts or aches or burns or stings or throbs. It hurts. It is not okay to hurt people. It doesn't make sense. If we were ever hit by anyone, we don't want to hit others. If our fathers hit our mothers, we don't want to hit. If slave masters hit our ancestors, we don't want to hit. If our partner hits us, we don't want to hit. If our brothers or sisters or the bullies at school hit us, we don't want to hit. Because we know that it hurts, and we don't want anyone else to have to feel that pain. It is not okay to inflict pain—not because we lived through it or are good people today. Not for any reason. The people who hit us might love us. They may think they are helping us, but they aren't. They are hurting us—outside and in. So why would we hurt children in order to teach them to be kind, or respectful?

I recently heard Fred Rogers speak. He was talking about the amount of violence that children see on television, in the movies, on video games. He said that the message we need to send to children is, "There are better ways of dealing with bad people than hitting and shooting them." (Keynote address, NAEYC conference, Toronto, November 1998).

You are not a bad person because you did whatever that last inappropriate thing you remembered was—because you broke a dish, or made a sarcastic comment, or whatever. The children you deal with are not bad people. But even if you were or the children were, there are better ways of dealing with the problem.

If you believe that corporal punishment destroys rather than teaches, you are in disagreement with many parents.

Children who are accustomed to physical punishment at home may test you because they know that you cannot or will not hurt them. Stay out of power struggles with these children. Keep sending them the strong message that together you will be able to solve problems without hurt.

"Cory, why do you think you keep swearing here? *Do you swear like that at home?" I ask, frustrated by parent complaints and my own inability to stop Cory from using words that a six year old shouldn't know.*

"I don't talk back at home."

"Well, then, why do you do it here?"

"'Cause you don't smack me. My dad smacks me in the mouth."

≈ Jean Steiner and Mary Steiner Whelan

◉ ◉

Cory's dad would probably tell you that he hits Cory because "it works." But it doesn't. Cory takes his swearing elsewhere and keeps his anger in until it erupts. The life-long lessons you teach children about not hurting others do work. They seem to take longer and require more thought than corporal punishment. But that is our job and our gift to the children.

When I have conversations with physically aggressive children about why they hurt other children, they say things like, "for fun," or "I like to," or "I don't know." If I have a strong long-term relationship with the child and we are in a private setting, I sometimes ask, "Does anybody hurt you?"

More often than I wish, especially with boys, the response is, "Yeah. My dad hits me."

"I'm very sorry," I say. "I wish nobody ever hurt you. Do you want to hit your kids when you're a dad? Do you want to hurt your kids?"

I've never had a child answer anything but a sincere, "No."

"You are practicing every day what you will be when you are a dad," I say. "If you want to be a nice dad you have to start practicing right now. If you want to be a kind man you need to learn how to be a kind boy. Do you know what I am talking about?"

"I do," the child usually says.

"Please tell me what I said in your own words so that I know that I explained it right."

Almost always the child understands. And almost always there is a noticeable change in behavior.

We often have to talk to children about their truths, and sometimes those truths include violence. Even though our society is beginning to place value on reducing the violence against people, we have a long, long way to go. Children often live with violence because individuals still practice it.

You will be teaching children that despite the fact that they see violence in the media, and perhaps in their neighborhoods or homes, it isn't right. You can provide the life-altering experience that shows them another way.

You can't lead them to that learning if you hurt them. It happens in school-age programs that children get hurt by adults. I hear about it and see it. You are physically and emotionally hurting children if you engage in any of the actions listed at the beginning of this section. And you are destroying any progress you may have made with the child through a positive relationship. Remember, you never want a child to look at you the way Billy looked at me. You never want a child to say or think, "you are just like the rest of them."

If you ever do hurt a child, and it can happen to any of us in our stressful work and with the beliefs that are a part of each of us, apologize. Say "I'm sorry," as soon as you catch yourself. Go back again later, when you are both calmer. Say, "I had no right to hurt you. I think it is the wrong thing to do. Please forgive me. It will not happen again. Is there anything I can do to show you how sorry I am? Will you forgive me?" You should not say "…but I had to do something because you were so out of control." No excuses. Just repentance. You will be teaching a powerful lesson.

Take a minute to think of any ways that you have physically hurt children in the past. Forgive yourself. If you still work with the child, plan to talk to him. Whether or not you have ever hurt a child, write a pledge to yourself that you will make every effort that you can to never to hurt a child in the future.

I pledge…

The closing exercise for this very serious chapter is to reflect on the positive nature of your work. By reducing punitive and hurtful practices you restore balance to children's lives, even though you may not witness the impact you make. I hope reflecting on this poem written by a child care worker helps to bring balance to your life.

We sow the seeds on the other side of the water,
and never see the harvest turn to flower.
Yet we dance in the colors of the day
and know the power of the bursting bud.

We teach the children to sing
Though we will hear the song but faintly
Falling away across the water.
And the loud applause will not sound for us
Only the soft stirrings of peace in the children's hearts
And the thunder of the ages in their veins.

≈ Linda Rhody

We are a richer people and our world is a stronger, more compassionate place because you dedicate yourself to the love of children.
Peace.

Chapter 20

Feeling Groovy: Do's

by LaNaya and Zahkyia

Nobody has ever measured, not even poets, how much the heart can hold.

≈ Zelda Fitzgerald

Do Allow Children to Express Their Feelings

Feelings, nothing more than feelings..." (Morris Albert). So the song goes. It is not true in a way. Unless someone taught us not to know that we feel, we react emotionally to what happens to us. Even if we don't recognize the feelings, they are there. The song might say, "Feelings, such essential feelings..." It isn't as melodious, but it is more accurate.

Children who are in our care come to us with bushels of feelings. In our efforts to provide interesting activities, to adhere to schedules, to keep things on an even keel, and to deal with large groups effectively, we often don't allow space for children to learn how to express themselves. Children are sometimes in institutional care for twelve hours a day. If the people working in the institutions ignore or discourage emotions, children learn to stifle them. They don't learn how to cope emotionally. They don't learn that feelings give us energy, release tension, are an organic and rich part of who we are.

Ignoring children's emotional lives leads to discipline problems. Buried emotions can bubble to the top like lava or the layers can solidify like limestone deep in children's souls. In either case they cause discipline problems. The lava can erupt and cause aggressive, disruptive behavior. The limestone hardens the heart and causes loneliness and depression.

We are often better at accepting children's positive feelings than the negative ones. We want children to be happy, grateful, and excited about life. These kinds of feelings we label "positive." And we certainly are right to want children to be joyful. But we sometimes believe that is all childhood is about. As a society, we wrap childhood up in a package of pastel ribbons and papers. The package contains innocence, cuteness, and laughter. "They're only children," we say. "Let them enjoy childhood while they can." We buy them cartoon-figured clothes, tickle them under the chin, and read them silly stories. None of that is necessarily wrong, but it is only a part of what childhood is about.

Children have the same complex set of emotions that adults have. To not recognize children's complexity is disrespectful. They deserve to be taken seriously, and not to be assigned to a package that allows us to glow with naive pleasure. That naiveté doesn't allow children a full range of expression. Children resent us for dismissing their complicated natures. And they show it by their actions, even though in many cases they couldn't name what is bothering them.

As Kathleen Norris, novelist and children's activist, says, "To children, childhood holds no particular advantage." They are busy doing the hard work of becoming people. Watch a toddler. If we romanticize him, we describe him as "darling" or "so cute." And he is that. But look at him again. This time attend to the work that the child is doing. He is learning to walk, to balance, to speak, to explore others' reactions, to express emotions, to make sense out of the world. Life is intense even though the toddler deals with it in small chunks dictated by his short attention span.

Ask any good toddler teacher what reaction a toddler has if he feels that someone is making fun of him, or thwarting his important tasks, or not taking him seriously. The reaction is often an outburst. Hence, the "terrible twos" label and the accompanying temper tantrums. At times the reaction is withdrawal or whining or refusal to move. His world, his childhood, is where he lives, grows, and learns. It is a tough job.

The same is true of the schoolagers. They may have mastered walking, speaking, and some of the balancing, but they are still working on development. Their work is vital to them. They want adults to honor their work and accept all parts of it. If we don't, they will often react with "inappropriate" behaviors. The behaviors actually are appropriate, in that they reflect the child's unmet needs.

Among those unmet needs is the expression of emotions that we don't label as positive. We label anger, sadness, frustration, and disappointment as "negative." This label says that there is something bad about those feelings. However, the truth is that there is no such thing as a bad emotion. Emotions just are. It is what we do with them that determines whether we remain healthy and treat others responsibly. If we are healthy we most likely will act in socially acceptable ways.

And, yet, many school-age programs do not allow emotional expression, especially expression of negative emotions. Adults also often try to control positive emotional expression that seems excessive to them. If a child laughs too hard and too long or shouts with exuberance, adults may say, "That's enough silliness, now," or "Pipe down."

Emotions and Culture

Acceptance of various kinds of emotions is in part culturally based. For example, the Inuits have a game in which a group divides up into pairs. Each person tries to make the other person laugh. The twosome that laughs the hardest wins. They are talking here about rolling around on the floor, tears streaming down your cheeks, side-grabbing laughter. Some Scandinavian cultures express very few emotions. Many Latin countries and some African countries historically give expression to emotions in a very open way. Many Asian cultures are more reserved. My German grandmother didn't want anyone to smile in photographs, and my uncles didn't talk much at family reunions.

Some cultures openly grieve with wailing. Others appear stoic. People in some cultures frequently touch each other with hugs and kisses. Other cultures are not comfortable without a certain amount of physical space between people. Of course there are great variations among people within the same culture. We cannot and should not stereotype or expect all people from one background to be the same. How boring that would be! And we cannot label people's ways of expressing themselves emotionally as belonging to one group. But we can look for, appreciate, and respect cultural differences.

We do not all have to express our emotions to the same degree or in the same ways. On the other hand, just because ways of being are rooted in a culture does not mean that they are healthy. We need to examine our own cultural patterns and decide which ones we want to keep and which ones we want to change.

When we work with children from cultures different from our own we want to respect cultural ways. We need to assess our comfort level to determine if our reaction to children's emotions is based only on our cultural norms. Are we somewhat frightened by the freedom some children have to express themselves in words and body language simply because we grew up differently? Or, are we pushing children to be more expressive than they are only because that is what is expected in our culture?

As adults we must seek out more information about cultural differences. At the same time we need to challenge patterns that seem to be harmful to children. Being respectful and proactive at the same time may feel like walking a tightrope. But learning and risking make us better teachers for the children.

Without knowing it, until we meet a situation that causes us to analyze our standards, we judge certain behaviors as appropriate for different economic classes. We would be most comfortable if everyone's standards were the same as ours. But they aren't and that doesn't make them wrong.

What would your family's reaction be if you or a brother or sister of yours chose to marry someone of a different economic status? There might be comments such as, "He's such a stuffed shirt," "She is so boisterous," "He is so crude," or "She doesn't know how to let down and have a good time," or "She just doesn't know how to socialize with our kind." Many comments would be editorials on emotional expression. When we work with children, we need to be aware of these perceptions.

Emotions and Gender

Gender can also play a role in our expectations regarding emotions.

Petri skids into first base *and gets one of those stinging scrapes that have little stones in them. He tries to stop crying. Taking big gasps of air, he sobs, "Boys don't cry. Boys don't cry."*
"Well, I cry," says Ali, the teacher, cleaning out the wound as gently as possible. "And most of the guys I know are smart enough to cry when things hurt. You're a smart guy, so let all that hollerin' come out."

≈ Jean Steiner and Mary Steiner Whelan

Ⓢ Ⓔ

Traditionally, it is more acceptable for girls to express emotion than for boys. That is beginning to change, albeit slowly in some places. The macho image of never expressing emotions is, however, still with us. We may be getting somewhat more tolerant of boys' crying and being gentle. Just ask young men who are in the dating scene now. One of the things many of them feel they must do to be accepted is to be sensitive, to cry during romantic movies, for example.

However, I still hear adults telling boys not to be sissies or not to act like girls. Emotions expressed by crying or giggling may be accepted from girls but not from boys. If boys use the dress-up clothes to get dressed like girls, or if they like to dance or sing silly songs or play with dolls, or if they are sympathetic with others, we often send them messages, loudly or silently, that these are not male behaviors. It is difficult to teach boys that there are other ways to handle their emotions in a world where football players smash each other, and TV and video heroes shoot and beat on each other.

Men pay a high price for remaining emotionally silent. Heart attacks, alcohol abuse, ulcers, workaholism, and cancers can be rooted in stifled emotions. Others pay a price, too, when men become violent or overly competitive or controlling. We want today's boys to grow into healthy men who can enjoy the fullness of their emotional lives, and who contribute richly and really to healthy relationships, work places, communities, and their families.

Kimberly slams her locker door shut. *"I hate this stupid place,"* she says. *"I have no idea why my parents send me here."*

Doreen, the school-age care staff person that afternoon, asks Kimberly, "Have a problem, do you?"

"That Roberta person teacher in the morning has a problem."

"Oh, what's her problem?"

"I was playing in the building corner this morning. Minding my own business, really. I made a huge block building, and I decided to implode it like I saw a building doing on TV last night. I told the boys my plan. They busted in and caused the explosion before I could. I got really mad at them."

"Then what happened?"

"Missy, missy Roberta comes over and says, so sweetly, 'Can I see you, Kimberly?'"

"And then?"

"So I go over, and she says, 'That's what happens when you try to do boy things. You might want to try doing more girl things. You like art, don't you?' So then I said, 'I like art and I like imploding buildings. Is there something wrong with that?' And she said, 'See, when you try not to be the young lady you can be, that's just what happens. You get loud and angry. Being mad isn't very attractive, you know. You're getting older. Boys like sweet girls. Take my word for it.'"

"So, what did you say to that?" Doreen asks.

"Nothing, I just walked away. Then she said, 'See, that's just what I mean. That's very unattractive.'"

"Do you think it's okay to be a girl and to be loud and to get angry?" Doreen asks.

"Yeah, I do."

"So do I. Let's think of some ways that you can deal with people who don't agree."

❂ ❂

You help children be who they are. Not who others think they should be. At the same time, you teach them to deal with the real world. It is sometimes more difficult for staff members in school-age programs to accept girls' expression of strong emotions than it is to accept boys' expression of softer emotions. That may be because most school-age care staff people are women. The culture that forms in school-age care is, therefore, more female than male. Women staff have to be especially careful that they don't impose on girls the sanctions on powerful emotions that our society has imposed on them.

It is okay for girls to get angry, to be competitive, to be assertive, to be powerful. The result of not expressing those emotions is sometimes manifested in whining, frequent crying, manipulation, and cuteness. These behaviors are socially more acceptable for girls than expressing strong emotions directly, forcefully, or powerfully. Unfortunately, expressing emotions in these roundabout ways also keeps girls from gaining personal control over their lives.

The long-term costs to women for keeping powerful emotions in check include depression, eating disorders, anxiety, certain cancers, and the acceptance of abuse and destructive control by others. We want girls to learn to be in charge of their lives and to grow into women who are mentally and physically healthy. Women who can make positive contributions to relationships, workplaces, communities, and their families.

Helping Children Express Their Emotions

All these variables make the job of helping children express their emotions a complex one. We need to be aware of the children's and our own emotional lenses. We can then see as clearly as we are able what is respectful, and how we can guide children's healthy emotional development. The effort is essential both to our commitment to guide children and to build an environment with fewer discipline problems.

Write down some of the unwritten rules (please make them as specific as possible and give examples if you can) about emotional expression that you learned because of…

your culture

_____

_____

_____

your gender

_____

_____

_____

your economic class

_____

_____

_____

exercise continued on next page

Then write down how you think two of these rules will bring challenges to your work
with children.

_____

_____

_____

_____

_____

_____

Then write down how you think two of these rules will enrich your work with children.

_____

_____

_____

_____

_____

There are many ways we can encourage children to get in touch with
their emotions and to express them in healthy ways. One of the most valuable techniques is guessing, and giving children the chance to correct you.
Schoolagers really like to be right. You can often help them get to the emotional underpinnings of their situation by guessing about what the trouble
is, or what they are feeling. The guessing should be a sincere attempt to
understand the child. If you use it as a manipulative tool to get at information, the child will feel unsafe and won't let you in to help. Children will
judge your sincerity by your tone of voice, which is that of a wondering
question, not a probing or interrogating one, by your body language, if it
is relaxed and nonthreatening, and by your words, which are kind and not
judgmental—words like, "probably," "I imagine that…," "Could it be…,"
and "I wonder if." This story gives some examples of this technique:

 **You watch Alexis**, *alone, kicking stones on the playground. Usually she plays actively with her friends.*

"What's up?" you ask. You make a guess.

"Nothing," *she answers giving a rock another soccer kick.* The child dodges.

"You're really giving these rocks a good kicking. Are you lonely?" You make a more specific guess.

"Uh, uh." Child corrects you.

"Bad day at school?" You make a guess.

"Not at school." The child corrects you.

"Somewhere else? You seem upset." You invite the child to correct you.

"I guess. My dog Shrimpy died last night." The child gives you information.

"I'm sorry. That must make you sad." You make a guess.

"A little. But mostly I'm mad." The child corrects you.

"Mad about what?" You ask for information only the child has.

"Shrimpy was hit by a car. My mom and dad let animal control take her away. I didn't even get to say good-bye." The child gives you the information.

"You really wanted to see her one more time?" You guess.

"Of course I did. She was my best friend. Would you like to have your best friend die and people don't even let you say good-bye? Wouldn't you hate those people?" The child gives you more information.

"I'd probably be angry." You accept the child's powerful emotion without saying that it's okay to hate.

"I'm more than angry. I hate them." The child reiterates the emotion wrapped up with revenge.

"I hear what you're saying. I'd be angry and sad. Very sad. What did you and Shrimpy do together?" You teach the child that two emotions can exist at once. You seek more information that only the child has. You don't ask her to understand her parents' point of view. You don't argue with or contradict her. You attend to the child.

"I don't know. Stuff. I was sad, but my mom told me that no crying will bring her back. And if I kept crying she'd never get me another dog." The child feels safe enough to trust you with another feeling.

"Do you still feel like crying?" You don't say the parents are wrong. You stick with the child's feelings. You make another, this time more educated, guess.

"Sort of." The child tests the safety issue.

"It's okay to cry here. Do you want me to stay with you and talk or would you like to go inside for a while and be sad alone?" You reassure. You offer two ways for her to be sad.

"I want to be alone, I guess." The child chooses. She experiences control in the midst of what she thought was an unacceptable feeling.

"Okay. Norm is in the art room. You can be in the quiet corner there if you want. Tears can help people feel better. Norm will understand. Do you want me to write him a note telling him what's going on?" You tell her how she can meet her need of being sad alone. You offer to help her.

"I can tell him. Do you think he'll tell my parents that I'm sad?" Feeling power in the situation, she says she can handle it herself. She checks out the safety issue again.

"Not if you ask him not to." You reassure.

"I'll go in." She feels strong enough to accept the option.

"All right. And I'm sorry, Alexis. It's sad when you lose a friend. You are feeling things that are okay to feel—even if they hurt. I bet Shrimpy was a neat dog." You affirm her feelings.

"She was. See ya."

You can almost hear the relief. Thanks to you, Alexis will not live with the anger and the sadness all bottled up. She will not throw a rock at someone or think that sadness is bad.

⊚ ⊚

Guessing is one powerful tool used in this story. The other is reflective listening, sometimes known as active listening. Reflective listening is a skill that takes time to develop. It means that we reflect what the child says back to her without judgment. At times, you extend the reflection to invite the child to express more feelings.

One example of reflective listening in this story is the question, "You really wanted to see her one more time?" You reflected the child's statement, "I didn't even get to say good-bye."

You changed the wording somewhat without telling the child what to feel. You did not go down the your-parents-are-awful-people street. At the same time you didn't deny the child's feelings towards her parents by saying something like, "You don't hate your parents. They were just doing what they thought was best for you." A statement like that would shut down communication. You knew that the child was stuck in anger at her parents. The anger covered her emotions of sadness and loss, which was where you wanted her to go. You wanted to help her recognize the sorrow so that she could do the necessary grieving.

Like guessing, reflective listening has to come from sincere intentions. The child will know if you are just probing with a new technique. Another caution when using reflective listening is not to parrot. That is, not to always say back the child's exact words. Think of how annoying it would be for you if someone repeated everything you said.

For example:

You say, "I don't feel very good today."

Your friend says, *"You don't feel very well today."*

"No, my stomach hurts."

"Your stomach hurts."

"And my head is throbbing."

"And your head is throbbing."

"It could be stress, I suppose."

"It could be stress, you suppose."

"I suppose it could."

"You suppose it could."

By now, your head really would be throbbing. (There are some proponents of reflective listening who encourage parroting. I think that it can be used in small doses but is insulting if it's used consistently.)

Reflective listening

- Affirms that you are listening.

- Affirms the speaker's feelings.

- Helps the speaker find more information within herself.

- Doesn't give advice.

- May present options.

- Stays focused on the speaker. (No long stories about when your dog died when you were six years old.)

- Strengthens a relationship through the expression of mutual understanding. (For example, "I would be angry.")

- Is used to help the speaker to vent or problem solve, not to trap the speaker into revealing information.

- Is empathetic—not overly sympathetic. (For example, not "Oh, you poor, poor thing. What will you do without your dog— you'll be lost.")

- Allows the speaker, through empathy and options, to know that she has the power to deal with the situation at hand.

Go back through the dialogue with the child about her dog.
Underline all the examples of reflective listening that you find.

Other ways to help children become aware of their emotions:

- Model appropriate responses to your own emotions.

- Give children the opportunity to disagree with you.

- Allow children to make choices about what they want to do based on how they are feeling. ("I am grouchy today. I don't think I want to play the laughing game.")

- Discuss feelings as a group after a field trip or a special event. ("How did you feel when we visited the nursing home?" "I felt sad." "How did you feel when the African dancers put on those masks?" "I felt scared.") Although not all children will want to share their feelings during these discussions, it is helpful for them to know that others had similar feelings. It is also useful to begin discussions about topics that raise feelings resulting from lack of experience or from prejudice. You can then talk about where some feelings come from. You can dispel myths and be that life-altering instrument in children's lives once again.

- Read stories that are about feelings, and stop to ask questions. "I wonder how Grace feels when she sees her mother coming to school. What do you think?"

- Have the children read to the other children and think up questions as they read.

- Have the children draw and paint to various kinds of music. Ask them to draw the feelings or a picture representing the feelings they experience during the music. Ask them to give a title to the artwork based on emotions they felt while drawing. You might provide them with a list of emotions to broaden their knowledge beyond sad, mad, and happy. Ask them to sign the art as an artist does so that they take ownership of their feelings. "Frustrated and Hopeful, by Damon."

- Make up board games in which pieces move when a scenario is read and the child names the emotion that the character in the scenario might experience. Admit more than one correct answer. Provide a list of possible answers that can be used during the game.

- Play charades with emotional themes so that the children will act out feelings.

- Read *Kids Like Us,* by Trisha Whitney (St Paul: Redleaf, 1999), and use *persona dolls* as she suggests to help kids develop their feelings vocabulary. Whitney notes that many children do not have the words to describe their feelings: "Many times children will be able to use the words *sad, mad,* and *happy* to describe emotions. Sometimes *good* and *bad* is the extent of their feelings vocabulary." In this case, a teacher's first task is to help them learn to identify what they are feeling. You can use the list below to guide you; remember that older school-agers can learn even more complicated and subtle words to identify their feelings.

Feeling Words for Five to Eight Year Olds

from *Kids Like Us,* Trisha Whitney

upset	satisfied	thoughtful
mad	confused	calm
surprised	interested	stressed
frustrated	anxious	jealous
excited	angry	bored
worried	furious	dreamy
loving	outraged	embarrassed
let down	irritable	grateful
proud	patient	curious
disappointed	impatient	wild
happy	depressed	cautious
grumpy	unsure	sorry
bossy	pleased	hurt
sad	frightened	cheated
silly	afraid	generous
lonely	terrified	sympathetic
scared	nervous	confident
friendly	guilty	greedy

All the techniques that we discussed are tools to help children get in touch with their feelings. However, the most important instrument in helping children express their emotions is you. Put aside your fears of dealing with emotional children. (Remember: You are the adult. They are the children.) Most of us slam a door occasionally or cry or get excited. Children are no different. There is no need to be afraid or to tell them that emotions are to be locked away.

Shift from thinking, "Children should be seen and not heard," to "Children who are heard are healthier and cause fewer discipline problems." Children are still learning to deal with their feelings. As with many other issues, if children don't learn to feel safe with you as they learn, they may not learn anywhere. If children do not learn the appropriate ways to demonstrate their feelings, they will act them out inappropriately. You are the key, and you are capable. Go for it!

You may now choose to do one of the following four activities in the space below.

1. Make a list of five charade topics that could help children act out emotions. Tell how and why each topic would help the kids.

2. Write a dialogue between an adult and a child that demonstrates guessing and/or reflective listening.

3. Remember a time in your childhood when your emotional expression was not accepted by an adult. What did you learn that is still a part of your life today? Write down your memories. Share them with a friend.

4. Write a persona doll story that introduces a feeling word and tell the story to some children (maybe even your own children, or a neighbor's children, or your nieces and nephews).

_____

_____

_____

_____

_____

_____

Do Notice Children's Positive Behaviors

Why is noticing positive behaviors an issue in behavior guidance? Noticing positive behaviors encourages more positive behaviors. It tells a child that she is capable. It lets a child know that she counts, and that she is not taken for granted. She learns that her positive behaviors get attention, and that she doesn't have to act out to get attention. When you notice positive behaviors, you affirm that she is going in the right direction, that she is developing healthy habits. You validate her efforts when you see her improve in an area that is difficult for her. You are also building a positive environment.

Why does "noticing positive behaviors" appear in this chapter along with a discussion of emotional expression? Children feel safe in a setting in which others acknowledge them. Secure children feel free to express their emotions. They trust that people accept them for who they are. Shamed children, those who are constantly criticized, learn to bury their emotions. They fear blame so they hide themselves and their feelings. The feelings come out in other ways. The result of feeling shame may be grandiosity, passive-aggressive behavior, denial, refusal to accept responsibility, belligerence, or many other problematic behaviors.

If you encourage children to learn more about and to express their emotions, but don't recognize their positive behaviors, their accomplishments, and their beauty, then they will not trust you. They will not feel that they can have an open relationship with you or with others. They will become emotionally challenged, not emotionally competent.

Emotional expression does not happen in a critical environment. Nor does it happen easily in a neutral environment, a setting in which adults take no notice of children's positive choices. Children have no way of knowing, then, what the adults are thinking. They get no adult feedback. In your role as the adult working with children, you have power just because you are the adult. You can use it to help children feel their own power by noticing who they are and affirming their positive behaviors.

Many of you grew up in places where no one told you that they loved you or that you excelled or were okay at something, even though they probably did love you and maybe even recognized your strengths. This is part of the "spare the rod and spoil the child" syndrome, which is still present in many homes, schools, and school-age care programs. Adults fear that if they compliment or recognize children's positive actions, the children will become complacent, spoiled, or egotistical.

However, human development doesn't work that way. If people don't receive approval, they become anxious. They are never certain whether or not their actions are acceptable. They become afraid that they are never good enough. They continue to try to receive approval, often in inappropriate ways. Or they give up and assume that, no matter what they do, it won't matter.

Have you ever had a boss who never or rarely gave you positive feedback? How did you feel in that environment? Unappreciated? Nervous that you weren't performing the way you should? Less motivated to do a good job? Were you less likely to form an open, honest relationship with that boss? To share your weaknesses and strengths so that you both continued to grow? Although your relationship with children is not that of boss and employee, there are similarities. Children often react in the same way as you would in a setting devoid of positive feedback.

A friend of mine worked in a school-age care program in which the supervisor asked staff members to write brief positive notes weekly to each child. She gave them planning time to do it and even a cute form. One staff person, Zoe, never managed to get it done. She complained that it wasn't necessary and that she didn't have time. Zoe also brought complaints about the kids' behaviors to staff meetings and the teachers' lounge. She didn't understand why she always got the "bad" kids.

At one staff meeting, the supervisor reminded staff to write the notes. Zoe responded, "You want to know why I don't do those notes? Most weeks I can't think of a positive thing to say about most of those kids."

Imagine the kind of environment those children entered every day. No positive energy. Nothing to draw validation from. A teacher who couldn't think of a single positive thing to say. How did the children respond? By closing down and acting out. There was no relationship with this teacher that they could trust. Criticism filled the air. Any emotional expression probably met with Zoe's critical commentary.

"Why do I always get the bad kids?" Zoe asked. You can answer her question. Because she thought they were "bad." Because she gave them no reason to be different. Because they weren't noticed for their positive traits, and because they had no help expressing their emotions, the children spat out feelings with resentment and shame.

The happy ending to that story is that Zoe's supervisor worked with her. She helped her shift her attitude about behavior guidance. She taught her how to act as if the children had redeeming qualities. Zoe wrote her notes weekly. The supervisor would sit in her room each day and teach her how to observe the children and give them positive attention. She taught her how to be less fearful of the children's emotions. It was a struggle for Zoe, who came from a very large, rigid family, where there was no room for individuality or empathy. But she learned a lot. In a couple of years she didn't get the "bad" kids. She enjoyed her job more and got those notes written every week.

Noticing positive behavior nurtures emotional expression. In such a positive atmosphere, children can test who they are, receive feedback, and thrive. They are less likely to act inappropriately. Discipline problems diminish. That is why an openly positive environment and emotional expression are linked. And that is why they are both elements in behavior guidance.

Here's the trick, though. Noticing children's positive behaviors is not the same as excessive praising. It does not interrupt a child who is intent on a project or interfere with a child's imaginative play. It does not single a child out in front of her peers. If it does any of these things, it will not nurture positive relationships or help children express their emotions honestly and directly.

You already know about excessive praise and the ways that it makes children dependent on adult approval and doesn't teach them how to make their own judgments. Let's take those other dangers one at a time.

First of all, noticing does not interrupt a child who is intent on a project. Children have the right to be engrossed in an activity without adult interruption. For example, Katrina is doing beadwork. She took time to do a design and to choose colors. She is now beginning to string. You are impressed with her concentration on the task and its details. Especially because her attention span is often short. You could go to her and say, "You are really concentrating on the task and its details. How did you come up with that design? Why did you chose those colors?" But before you do, read on.

Many of us are involved in projects that we enjoy. I will use writing as my example. Today I spent a couple hours reorganizing some of the writing in this book. Then, I spent another difficult hour trying to overcome the "I just can't write today" syndrome. For the last hour or so, for some unexplainable reason, the writing has been going well. I am clipping along, able to concentrate and get the words from my head to the keyboard.

What if my daughter, who is in the other room, came to my desk right now and said, "Mom, I've been meaning to tell you how impressed I am that you've been working on the book for so long. I know how hard it was for you to get started. How did you come up with the idea to write it anyway? Tell me about what you're working on now."

How would I react? Part of me would think, how nice of her. But at this moment a stronger reaction would be, "Why now? There goes that streak I was on. Why couldn't she interrupt me when I was looking for an interruption." I might answer her quickly and somewhat sharply. If I were a child I might say, "None of your business," or "Leave me alone." I would not feel positive about being noticed; I would feel annoyed.

However, if tonight at dinner she made the same comments and expressed the same interest, I would appreciate it. I would feel proud of myself and loved by her.

Now back to Katrina and her beadwork. She might have feelings similar to mine if you interrupted her work. In addition, if concentrating is a challenge for her, you will not have helped her to stay focused on her beadwork! After she puts the beadwork away for the day, your comments would be welcome. You could add another question to help her identify her own feelings. A question like, "How do you feel about your work?"

If you handled it that way, respecting her involvement with her project, that would be noticing—giving her feedback on positive behaviors. If she hadn't noticed them herself, you helped her to notice. If she did, you reinforced her positive feelings about herself. You affirmed her right to feel "proud," or "satisfied," or "okay," or however she might express her feelings.

Second, noticing doesn't interfere with children's play. When my son, Kevin, was a young child, he created marvelous play fantasies. Sometimes I would join him. I remember one day when I started to play with him. I'm not certain that I really asked him if I could. But he let me be part of his imaginary world. His bed was an ocean. The pillows were islands. A toy truck was a boat. Blocks served as rafts. Popsicle sticks were people.

Kevin and I sank the ship, rescued the people on rafts, chased the sharks away. We had a great time—for a while. All of a sudden Kevin said, "This is a bed, not an ocean. I don't see any boats or sharks. This is just my room."

For half a second, I wanted to say to him, "I know. But we were pretending."

Fortunately, I understood his message before those words came out of my mouth. His message was, "This is my world. I've let you in as far as I want to. Now it is time for you to leave."

So I said, "You're right, this is a bed and this is your room. I've got to finish the washing. See you later."

"See you later, Mom," Kevin said.

I closed the bedroom door on my way out. As I walked down the hall I could hear the sharks splashing in the ocean again.

Kevin taught me a valuable lesson. Children need space and privacy to play—to be imaginative, to try on new roles through dramatic play, to figure out their worlds on their own. Ever since that day at the ocean—I mean in Kevin's room—I have been more observant of children at play and less interfering.

As school-age children, we spent lots of time alone in our rooms or yards or at the park. I know I imagined myself to be a movie star or a teacher well beyond the age that people would suppose. My best friend Trisha and I played movie star and teacher on the front porch. We required few props. Our imaginations kept us busy for hours. We would act out our roles with much drama. If an adult came near us, we quit playing. We probably wouldn't have ever played again if an adult had seen us and said, "I'm so happy that even at your age you are able to use your imaginations."

Children in school-age care programs have few opportunities for privacy. They are with supervising adults most of the time. Part of your work is to establish an atmosphere that encourages and protects privacy. One of the ways you do that is by leaving children alone when they are playing and you can see that they are living in their imaginative world. They may be working out emotional issues on their own. Without this kind of time, children become anxious and may act out their anxiety in inappropriate ways. And so, when you notice children's positive behaviors, be sure you are not interfering with their imaginative play.

Finally, noticing positive behaviors does not single out a child in front of peers. Schoolagers hate to be embarrassed. And they find many things embarrassing. Most parents know that even walking down the street with their older school-age child embarrasses him. Whose opinion are schoolagers most concerned about? You're right. Kids their own age. So if a child is doing an activity in an especially capable way or if he is kind to someone, do notice. Do tell him about it. But before you make a public announcement, ask his permission.

"Jason, I saw you help Sam clean up that paint that he knocked over. That was very thoughtful."

"Thanks. It wasn't anything much."

"Do you mind if I thank you during peacetime discussion this afternoon? That kind of thoughtfulness helps keep the peace."

"No, don't do that. The kids think that I'm a big enough nerd as it is."

You noticed the child's positive actions but you did so privately. It's good that you did. Because if you had stopped the group and drawn attention to Jason's helpfulness, you would have embarrassed him. He would have felt that his somewhat fragile image with the group was damaged. He might have stopped doing random acts of kindness rather than feeling encouraged to do more. He also wouldn't have shared with you that he considers himself a nerd. Now that he has, you can help him in various ways to work on self-esteem issues. You will also be even more sensitive to his needs. Because you are, your relationship with Jason will strengthen and he will let you help him more. He is less likely to withdraw or act out to try to overcome his perception of himself as a nerd.

Now that we have the precautions in place about noticing children's behavior without praising excessively, interrupting or interfering, or singling children out, we can talk about some of the best ways to notice positive behavior.

Ten ways to notice positive behaviors:

1. Write a note to each child at the end of every week. The notes should give specific feedback. Rather than saying, "George, you are a great kid," say, "George, you took a risk this week when you agreed to read the book to the class. Congratulations!"

2. Write surprise notes to a child when you observe a positive behavior.

3. Give a thumbs-up sign from across the room that you and the child recognize as, "Well done!"

4. Offer words of encouragement at unexpected times. When a child is doing something as simple as petting the pet bunny, you can say, "It looks like the bunny likes the way you pet her." Note here that you did not say, "I like the way that you pet the bunny." The child is not petting the bunny to please you. And, you want to keep from taking power away from the child.

5. Casually mention a positive behavior after the fact. For example, later in the afternoon, you might be walking down the hall with the child who built the great tower with the blocks. You may not have said anything about his building earlier. Now, on the way to the gym, you say, "Great tower." Depending on the child and his reaction, you might stop there. Even if there is no outward response, the child received the message. Inside he stores it in a corner where a negative message used to live.

   If the reaction is positive or if you think that the child is ready to start expressing his own pride, you might also say, "Did it take a lot of work?" or "What gave you the idea to put all those pillars in it?"

6. Have the children keep journals. At the end of each day or each week, as they sign out, they also write a positive thing about themselves.

7. Have a Child of the Week. Draw the names out of a hat. Have a quiet conversation with the child and ask how he might like to celebrate, without anyone spending any money, his week. Kids could write affirmations for him. He could bring in family pictures. He could make an autograph book that all the kids signed. Whatever he and you together think of to honor who he is.

continued on next page

8. Set up situations in which children can be helpful to someone. Let them help younger children, the custodian, the cook, the aide with special needs; lead a project for children in the hospital; be the can counter for the food shelf drive; work on a car wash for school supplies for children in a poorer country.

   And then write them thank-you notes.

9. Have children draw names and write one note a week to another child about something they saw them do that was positive.

10. Keep your eyes open and talk to the child as you would a friend when you see positive behaviors.

You will make some amazing discoveries about yourself, the children you work with, and the power of positive change, as you establish an environment that accepts and honors children's emotional expression and notices their positive behaviors. I hope that your work will be more full of joy and meaningful moments than ever before. I know the number of discipline issues will decrease, and that the children will be happier, healthier people.

The following scenario will help you practice.

Reggie is nine years old. She has brilliant orange-red hair, crooked teeth, and a screeching voice. She and her two friends—Annie, quiet but smart and tricky, and Maxine, buoyant and verbal—are, according to the staff, "older than their years." They frequently break the rules, lie to cover for each other, talk back to staff, and say words that they shouldn't know.

You are the staff person. You have worked hard for the entire school year to form relationships with each of the girls. Some days you think you've made some progress, and some days you don't.

Of the threesome, Reggie is the toughest, on the outside. You suspect that she has some serious emotional problems. But her mother won't take her to a counselor. Reggie's mother believes that Reggie's father sexually abused her daughter and the fact that Reggie sees him every other weekend is the problem. She says that as soon as she can get sole custody from Reggie's father, things will be all right.

Annie comes from an upper middle-class home. Her parents are both surgeons. She has a nanny at home after the school-age care program. Quincy is the third nanny this year. Annie rarely sees her parents, who expect her to be good and get excellent grades.

Maxine lives with her grandmother, Ella, and three cousins. Maxine's mother is away at college. She got a scholarship to a college out of state. She thought that Maxine would be better off staying with her grandmother for a few years. Maxine's cousins' mother is a crack addict. She is in and out of the house. Ella is warm and loving but runs a strict house. She wants her four granddaughters to finish school before they have babies and to stay away from drugs. She says that she isn't going to be as lenient with them as she was with her daughters.

Because the three girls in your program don't live close to each other, and go to three different schools, they spend time together only at the program. They do manage to make the most of it.

Now, you are going to practice responding to the girls in a way that allows emotional expression and notices positive behaviors while guiding them towards appropriate behaviors.

Begin by describing some systems that you would have in place regarding the girls and the group in general. Do you have signals, such as a certain word or gesture that each girl is familiar with that tells them you are noticing that maybe it's time for them to monitor their behavior, for example? Do you have places for children to be alone? What do the children know about how you respond to swearing or emotional out-bursts? What else would you like to say about the girls and your history and relationship with them?

_____

_____

_____

_____

_____

_____

_____

_____

_____

exercise continued on next page

This is a typical afternoon with the three girls.

Maxine arrives first. She bounds into the room, shouting, "What's that stinky smell? It better not be snack. If we're having that rotten cheese for snack again I'm going to puke!"

Write down what you would say or do:

She then goes to the closet and hangs up her backpack and coat. She goes to the snack table. "It is that bad old cheese." She picks up a piece and rolls it into a ball.
    Reggie arrives next. "Hey, Reggie, look what I made for you. A cheeseball," Maxine shouts across the room. Reggie comes over and looks at the cheese.
    "Do you expect me to eat this [swear word]?"

What would you say or do?

Annie arrives. Her friends tell her how bad the cheese is. She wraps all of theirs up in napkins and puts it in the wastebasket. "That's a good one," Reggie says.

What would you say or do?

The girls move to the gym. Reggie gets jump ropes for her friends. Then she invites a first grader to play with them. Things go well until Annie trips over the rope and skins her elbow. She begins to sob uncontrollably. "Call my mom. I'm really hurt. I want my mom now."

What would you say or do?

_____

_____

_____

Reggie stays with her friend Annie. She looks at you and says, "Call this girl's mother now."

What would you say or do?

_____

_____

_____

Maxine leaves the crisis scene with the first grader. Maxine then begins swinging the rope around over her head. The first grader asks her to "play nice."

What would you say or do?

_____

_____

_____

Reggie and Maxine work together on a mural. They try to put it on the wall but it rips. They decide to leave it on the floor.

What would you say or do?

_____

_____

_____

The crisis ends. It is a Friday. Reggie's father is supposed to pick her up at 5:00. At 4:40 she uses a bathroom pass. She doesn't return. A custodian brings her to the room. He found her under a stairwell.

exercise continued on next page

What might the conversation between you and Reggie sound like?

_____

_____

_____

_____

_____

_____

The day finally ends. When you're thinking about the day, you decide that on Monday you might do some follow-up work concerning some of the day's events.

What situations would you follow up on?

With which girl(s)?

When and how would you do it? Why?

_____

_____

_____

_____

_____

_____

_____

_____

Discuss your answers with another adult who worked with this chapter. Ask if that person can think of any other approaches you might use to make the program respond to the girls' needs. Also ask for feedback on how you dealt with each situation.

That exercise was a lot of work. Pat yourself on the back. The next time you work with schoolagers, you will bring new insights with you. Lucky kids!

Please write your notes, thoughts, or stories here:

Chapter 21

Feeling Groovy: Don'ts

by LaNaya

Slow down. You move too fast. Gotta make the morning last. Just kickin' down the cobblestones. Looking for fun and feeling groovy.

≈ Simon and Garfunkel

Don't Always Correct Children's Behaviors

Slow down. You move too fast. Allowing children to express their emotions and noticing their positive behaviors, thoughtfully and respectfully, requires time. Because lack of time is often an issue, it sometimes seems faster to simply correct children, snap our fingers, and make them get to it. We may believe that it is our role to point out children's behaviors whenever they don't do it "right."

Of course, there are situations when correcting children's behaviors is necessary, like when someone is getting hurt. But it is not imperative to do so as often as we may think. Also, we don't always save time when we operate on the "Because I know better" system. Children will often react to this behavior-management style with inappropriate behaviors that take lots of time to deal with. Not only is slowing down our reactions to children's imperfect behavior good for children, but in the long run it can be a timesaver.

Describe to yourself what you would say to the child in each of these scenarios.

1. *Hao is playing by himself in the sandbox. You can hear him saying to himself, "This place stinks. There's nothing to do. It's for babies."*

2. *Candyce and Kora are angry at their mutual friend, Hannah. You're not sure why, but it has something to do with Hannah not calling Kora at home last night. Candyce sided with Kora and now the usually stable friendship triangle is wobbly. As Hannah walks towards the other two girls in the block corner, Candyce says, "Here comes Hannah. Pretend that you don't see her." They purposely turn their backs to her.*

3. *As you walk a group of kids to the gym, Marc bounces the basketball off the hall wall. He does it once and then tucks the ball back under his arm.*

4. *Patrice helps you in the kitchen. You are gathering the makings of ants-on-a-log. The children will make their own for snack. You go to the refrigerator to get the celery. When you turn around, you see Patrice eating a few of the raisins out of the bowl.*

5. *Carlos is gluing feathers to a design. You see him use the end of one of the feathers to pick his nose before he glues it to the paper.*

What would you say to the child in each of these scenes? If you said, "Nothing," you are choosing wisely.

There is no reason to point out the children's behaviors in the above scenarios. No real harm is being done. No one is being injured. Someone might argue that Hannah's feelings are being injured. But you know these girls and are pretty sure that they will work out their problems soon. You keep watching and soon the girls are talking again. Children need to have the opportunity and the time to work out their own conflicts when possible.

It is well worth taking the time to decide if a behavior can be ignored. You are in the business of building a positive environment and allowing children to develop a sense of safety and freedom.

When we were children, there probably was not always someone around to correct our every move. Even as adults, we sometimes do things that not everyone would find acceptable. When my friend Kathy and I were little girls, we would have giggly backyard discussions about sex. We didn't know that much about it at the time. Our sessions were actually ways of trying to normalize and decode something that we found a bit scary.

As an adult, I am known to eat ice cream directly from the carton with a tablespoon. A good idea? Maybe not. Am I a bad person? No. Would I do that when I am serving guests? No. (At least not if they're watching.) Maybe you occasionally slam a drawer when you are angry or bang a pan on the kitchen counter when you are frustrated. Perhaps you cry when you feel hopeless.

Children in school-age care need to have freedom to express their feelings too, even if like you and me and every other adult, they don't always do it in the best, most skillful way. They need to be able to relax and have spontaneous expression even if there are adults present at all times.

Pointing out children's behaviors whenever they don't meet our standards is in many ways asking for trouble. Too many admonishments build a negative environment. Do you have a relative or friend who constantly points out your every flaw? If you do, you know that there are times when you would rather not be with her. And, when you are with her, you might want to tell her to mind her own business. There is not an easy flow in the relationship. You end up defending against the criticism. You say things that you wish you hadn't. Power struggles ensue. Or you might close up, walk away, dismiss the person as well as anything she has to say.

Constant criticism does not make another person respect your feedback or cause changes in their behavior. (I have a friend who has been nagging me about the ice cream thing for twenty years.) If an adult over-corrects children, they tend to pay little attention to what the adult says or wants. Even when the situation is serious the children will react defensively or ignore the adult's opinions. They no longer attempt to discern the value of the adult's comments. They may become belligerent the moment they are with such an adult. The adult has given up all of her power by abusing it through excessive criticism.

The group of children with such a staff person may not all respond overtly. But a culture of negativity emerges. The children are not happy, have discipline problems, are disrespectful, and are often bored. This charged atmosphere is obvious to others who interact with the group.

I was the director for a time of a child care center that cared for children two and a half to twelve years old. The youngest children's teacher had a negative outlook on life. She complained, criticized, and felt victimized. On a personal level, other staff and I talked to her about her attitudes.

Her class of little children was unruly. When other adults or children came into her room, her class would call them names, throw things, sometimes even bite. Other staff members and I tried to help their teacher figure out ways to deal with the children's incorrigible behaviors.

One day I attended a workshop on staff development for directors. The trainer spoke clearly about the impact of our own attitudes on children's behaviors. "Children learn well through osmosis. They are sponges who soak up our moods and our beliefs about life."

I suddenly realized what was going on in the the young children's room. The teacher's personality problems and the children's behavior problems were not two different issues. They were the same issue. I went back to the center the next day and had a meeting with the teacher. I told her about what I had learned at the workshop. "It is not in the children's best interests to have a teacher who approaches life as critically as you do. You have two weeks to change your behaviors, to do an attitude adjustment. Let me know if I can help. If you don't change, you will have to find another job."

She didn't. She didn't seem to try. Through her negative lens, the issue probably looked like another personal persecution. Perhaps she had grown up with overly critical adults. But I couldn't fix that for her.

I fired her and hired a new teacher. Obviously one of our main criteria was a positive attitude. The new teacher didn't have to be a cheerleader, just positive. We found an intelligent, gentle teacher who approached people and situations in calm and positive ways. In a month, the children in her group acted in calm and positive ways. Theirs was the first room that I would choose to show visitors because the atmosphere was warm and cooperative.

Adults' negativity often manifests itself in overcorrection, and school-agers react to it the same way those little children did. The most gifted school-age care teacher I know does what looks like magic with children. Children with the most difficult behaviors respond favorably to her. I worked with her for several years. When I observed her, I would try to figure out her techniques so that I could teach them at workshops. I did pick out some useful tips. However, as I continued to watch her, I remembered that workshop I went to and the young children's classroom. I realized that what this school-age care teacher *did* wasn't the source of her magic. It's who she *is* that makes the difference.

Here is a story about her:

Shannon, the after-school teacher, *shoots baskets, plays out-field, and ties fishing flies with the kids. She makes them laugh and is their listening friend. One day, she is putting away the equipment and hears three girls, huddled in the corner of the yard, talking in their "I'm your best friend. Don't tell anyone" voices.*

"I'm going to be a tattoo artist someday, for real. My parents will just flip," says Anastasia.

"I'll probably have three kids or something boring," sighs Gretel.

Leaning against the tree, Brook says matter-of-factly, "I'm not going to be a grownup. I'm going to be like Shannon."

≈ Jean Steiner and Mary Steiner Whelan

◉ ◉

Actually, Shannon is one of the most grown-up people I know. What Brook is saying is that Shannon does not fit the stereotype that some children have of adults, especially those adults who supervise them. She is their friend—their adult friend. She plays. She listens. She laughs. She joins them in their world and makes it a more comfortable, accepting place. And she expects them to act as her friend. When she gives feedback on their behavior it is as an adult friend. It is not critical. Instead, it is careful, respectful, and important.

We can learn specific behaviors from Shannon. But we need first to check our outlook on life. If it is negative, a thousand techniques won't help. Because we may continue to criticize children in an attempt to control what we view as a world out of our control—a world that does things to us. We feel, then, powerless and fearful. We use critical, controlling power to hide our fear.

Children cannot flourish in an atmosphere like that. Somewhere in their souls they know that the criticism is not coming from a place of concern and caring. Instead, it is being used to meet the adult's needs. The more the children react by acting out, the more fearful and powerless we feel. We control more by blaming, sometimes even disliking, the children we work with. And the cycle continues.

We bring children our many gifts. We also bring them our whole selves. There is a bit of the controlling, critical person in all of us. Our job is to move our outlook and behaviors down the spectrum from overly-critical, or wherever we find ourselves, to hardly-ever-critical. That movement will take personal work in practicing noncritical reactions and behaviors.

What are some of the specific behaviors that Shannon and other quality school-age care staff exhibit that help them become less critical? How do they manage to correct less and relate more? They do the opposite of policing children. They interact with children. They talk to them about everyday things in the children's lives and some things that are appropriate about their own. Jerome Bruner, educator and child development expert, says that 80 percent of conversations that adults have with children are about what they are going to do next or about changing their behavior. We wouldn't be very responsive to a friendship that operated that way. Respectful relationships show interest in each other and have free-flowing talk.

Successful staff play with children. They join them in jump rope and basketball, checkers and mancahali, hiking and biking. They don't join in to be like children but rather to be friendly. They are interested in the kids' music, dreams, confusions and successes. They joke, sing, paint, act spontaneously. They are *there*, not somewhere else in their heads. That's how they get to know the kids. That's how they know what to do next when a discipline situation occurs. Successful teachers don't overreact to situations. They stay calm and in relationship even during the tough times. The following is a list of some of the elements that successful staff use when they interact with children:

- humor
- positive language
- appropriate touching—a hand on the back, a high five
- ability to walk away from behaviors that are not perfect but are harmless
- kind humor
- listening more than talking
- skill teaching—children respect the person who can teach them how to shoot a basket or construct a sentence or knit a scarf
- fairness
- calmness
- sense of humor about themselves
- clear directions of what will happen when—long before it happens, again shortly before it happens, and very shortly before it happens

- honesty
- openness
- nonsarcastic humor
- quiet voices
- respect for children's ideas
- allowing children to make plans
- introducing children to new ideas and activities
- respectful treatment of coworkers
- serious attention to children's concerns
- refusal to accept disrespect
- matter-of-fact rather than overly reactive orientation
- excitement about learning new things and about children's interests
- and, once again, humor

Add five behaviors to the list that you think are helpful when working with children in a positive way.

_____

_____

_____

Which behaviors do you think you could practice more often? Why?

_____

_____

_____

Which of the behaviors do you feel you use frequently? Why?

_____

_____

_____

If we are busy trying to relate more positively with children, we will eventually break the habit of overcorrecting. It is difficult to do, especially if we had families, teachers, and other adults in our lives who were overly critical of us.

A helpful tool might be to imagine a pet mentor perched on your shoulder. Only you can see and hear her. The mentor's role is to remind you when you are thinking a negative thought or are about to say something negative to a child. It might say, "Calm now. Be calm," or "You don't want to say *that*. What can you say instead that will be positive?" or "Ignore that." Or as you're walking into a room it might whisper to you, "Look at how those kids are laughing with each other. They are pretty neat kids, aren't they?"

If you slip and correct a child needlessly or harshly, your mentor will gently remind you that you need to try to undo the negativity that you have put into a child's world. "Tell him you are sorry," the mentor will say, or "Tell him a few good things about himself." Use the following exercise to get to know your mentor better:

Name your pet mentor. I am naming my mentor Stack after a dear friend of mine who was a teacher for forty years. She had a way of gently but firmly letting me know if I was on the right track. She also let me know how capable I was.

Next draw a sketch of your mentor. Give it a personality that will allow you to feel comfortable with it looking over your shoulder. When I was growing up, the nuns taught us about guardian angels. I talked to mine often and didn't feel so alone during scary times. I always envisioned her as looking something like Peter Pan.

Now, write your mentor's name next to the sketch. Then, under your mentor's picture, write some of the things you think she will want to tell you sometimes about being positive and not overcorrecting children. Have fun and listen!

My name is...

Here's what I'd like to tell you...

Chapter 22

Who's in the Picture: Do's

by Zahkyia

A mind that is stretched by a new idea can never go back to its original dimensions.

≈ Oliver Wendell Holmes

Much of this book is about new ideas. You've shifted models, looked at yourself and your work in new ways, practiced new skills in the exercises, and implemented new attitudes and practices in your work. You even have a pet mentor perched on your shoulder!

This is the final chapter. It discusses the last do's: Do reframe children's behaviors, and do use conflict resolution. There are no don'ts to correspond with these final do's. If you can reframe children's behaviors and teach them conflict resolution in respectful ways, you have learned much of what this book has tried to teach. There will soon be no need for you to spend time thinking about don'ts because you will have eliminated them from your daily practice. You will, instead, work on perfecting the do's and being a positive influence on children's development. So, we will end the book as you will continue your work—on a positive note.

On with the last do's! They will take concentration and energy. The concepts in this chapter may stretch your mind and will help you to enable the children to stretch theirs. Stretching doesn't have to hurt. Isn't one of the best feelings in the world waking up in the morning and taking the time to stretch before you get out of bed? I hope this chapter is that kind of stretching. It will take some effort, but it will help you to feel strong and relaxed about the work you do each day. I know you will be thoughtful and enthusiastic in examining these do's and deciding how to practice them in your work.

Do Reframe Children's Behaviors

We all guess at what makes the kids we work with tick. A typical staff discussion about a child who chronically misbehaves produces a list of reasons for his behavior based on some evidence, mostly circumstantial, and on psychology, intuition, and experience.

For example, let's say that one of the children in your program, Jessica, comes storming into the room every day after school. She shouts (sometimes inappropriate words), knocks things over, tosses her school stuff around, takes other kids' snacks. And that's just her entrance! The rest of the afternoon doesn't get any better.

You and other staff members, concerned about the behaviors and Jessica, try to figure out what is going on. You decide that Jessica acts in these ways because her mother drinks, her father usually doesn't show up when he says he will, she has attention deficit disorder, and she was in a foster home when she was a baby.

You then decide how you will intervene. A whole series of behavior modification begins, with rewards, consequences, and so on. Most of it doesn't work.

Part of the problem is that you are beginning from a place, although well intended, that says there is something wrong with the child and her family. You believe that you need to fix the child with great effort. You really don't think it's possible. The child will absorb these attitudes. Most people usually live up to what others think of them. If you believe that a child is defective and that the situation is hopeless, so will she. And your conclusions are just guesses! There is no solid proof that any of your speculations have bearing on the child's actions when she enters the room.

It is imperative that we take children's lives seriously, of course. We need to be aware of their histories and struggles. You are to be commended for putting in the extra thought and effort necessary to try to understand a child. And, no doubt, life's circumstances do influence children's behavior. But remember, when you do that you are still in the land of guesses. Reframing suggests that you tuck the information that you have about the child away and just look at the behaviors for a while.

Another part of reframing is isolating one behavior we want to help the child change. In the other guessing system, we often set out to change the child. We believe she is broken, so we have to fix her. If we do, we believe, all of her behaviors will improve. The task is overwhelming and ineffective. Certainly, we want to continuously send the child positive messages, bolster self-esteem and confidence, let her know she is lovable. That is what we want to do for all children anyway. It is unrealistic to think that if we guess correctly about the root causes of the child's behavior, we will know how to heal the child.

Choosing one time of day, or one behavior, to reframe lets us focus on a more manageable goal. It feels more doable to us and to the child. Most likely, the success in one area will have some positive effect on other behaviors. That is just a bonus.

In the case of Jessica, you decide to focus on her entry into the room each afternoon. Before Jessica comes in the next day, you come up with some new guesses about her behaviors. This time your guesses are positive reasons why Jessica bounds (not "storms") into the room. You remember what L. Tobin says, "All misbehaviors have or can be imagined to have some positive function. . . . It is the art of wishful thinking, a play of thoughts and words that can turn a discouraging event into a dynamic new beginning" (*What Do You Do With A Child Like This?* [Duluth: Whole Person Assoc., 1998]). So, you take a couple of positive guesses about Jessica's behavior—things that you can at least imagine could be true.

"Jessica is happy to get to our program and is glad to see everyone," is the new frame that you choose. You reframe Jessica's behaviors. You take it out of the dismal, dusty frame of dysfunction and hopelessness. You reframed it in the bright, shiny frame of enthusiasm and connectedness.

The next day, Jessica comes into the room the way she usually does. Only on this day she is in for a surprise. You don't greet her with the expected string of commands such as, "Quiet down," or "Go in and out of the room quietly five times," or "Have a little respect," or "What do you think you're doing?" Instead you go over to her and say, "Jessica, you are always so excited when you get here. You have lots of energy and enthusiasm." You do not have any sarcasm in your voice because you believe what you are saying and you know that sarcasm hurts. If she is calm enough you might put a friendly hand on her shoulder as you walk away. That's all you say or do. And you say it the next day and the next.

I can almost guarantee that there will be a change in her behavior. Why? Because you are now sending the message that she is okay. You are not saying that she is out of control or sick. You are encouraging her, asking her to see herself in a new light, perhaps expressing her own truth. Instead of her critic, you are now her ally.

To be an ally you will have to allow her the freedom to disagree with your opinion. If you say, "It looks like you are excited to be here," and she says, "No, I'm not," what do you do? You follow through as you've learned to respond in other chapters in this book. You don't get angry because you reached out to her and she responded negatively. You don't get into a power struggle by saying, "Yes, you are." You might say, "Think about the possibility and we'll talk about it on Thursday."

You give her the chance to express her feelings. You do not deny her feelings but you give her a chance to think about it. You probably don't sit down right at that moment and discuss the differences between your new viewpoint and hers. Reframing her behaviors will probably take the child by surprise. She may react in a defensive way by saying, "No, I'm not." When children are seen differently than they usually are, they get a little scared. Give her time to get accustomed to being seen in a positive way. Rather than take the issue on right away, you can say something like, "Well, when I see you coming into the room in a hurry and talking a lot, I think that could mean that you are excited to be here. I know for sure that it means you have energy. Think about it, maybe you are glad to get here."

The other possibility is, of course, that you are guessing incorrectly. Give the child an opportunity to tell you that. After a few days of reframing, you can sit down informally with her and have a conversation. "I am glad to see that you have lots of energy. I am happy to see you. I'm wondering what you think."

Remember, you need to believe that the way you have positively reframed the behaviors is possibly true. You cannot be lying or manipulating. That would be both disrespectful and ineffective.

You don't want to be a phony who follows the child around gushing over lots of her behaviors. Take on one behavior at a time, in a low-key manner. Have discussions with the child, observe what is happening. As she begins to believe that you really do see her in a positive light, her behaviors will begin to change. As they do, you can add begin to reframe other parts of the day or other behaviors. You might say, "You like sharing snacks, don't you?" You can ask her, privately, how she would like to share snacks with others. Maybe she could be the snack distributor. Maybe she can just start to be accepted and accepting. You and she can be very happy about that.

Learning to reframe children's behaviors can take some practice. Try reframing the following behaviors. Write down what you would say to the child involved after you have reframed the behavior. The more you practice, the easier it will get.

1. Samuel is always teasing Don.

You say... *"I think you are trying to have fun with Don because you want him to feel like one of your friends."*

2. Freddie always butts in at the beginning of the line.

You say...

_____

_____

3. Linda tattles on other children.

You say...

_____

_____

4. Ken draws on the wall.

You say...

_____

_____

5. Kasha talks during reading time.

You say...

_____

_____

exercise continued on next page

6. Cassie talks back.

You say...

_____

_____

7. Give an example of a child's behavior that you have been thinking of as negative.

_____

_____

Reframe it. What would you say to the child using this new frame?

_____

_____

8. Reframe the same behavior a different way. What would you say to the child using this new frame?

_____

_____

What would you say to the child if he or she didn't agree with you?

_____

_____

9. Discuss your reframing words with a colleague. Ask that person to share reframing language with you. What did you learn from the discussion? Summarize what you learned below:

_____

_____

_____

_____

Reframing opens up the opportunity to children to match their behaviors with the positive connotation that you put on them. They are often surprised at your new attitude and will often surprise you with theirs. It can really be fun and is certainly interesting.

Of course, the children may need to solve a few problems and figure out other ways to express their positive intentions. You don't give them those solutions. You have opened the dialogue on the subject by pointing out to them the hidden positives in their behaviors. Let them do the figuring out as much as possible. You are there to support and affirm. So, you don't follow your statement to Jessica with, "Please learn to express your enthusiasm more quietly." That may be hard to do. Just remember how interesting it is going to be to see how Jessica reacts to the new messages.

We hope she will react in positive ways. Her behaviors will start to change because you reframed that one habit and gave her a new way to look at herself. You and she will begin to have a more connected relationship. She will talk to you about some of her emotions. Maybe one day when she is helping you to prepare snacks, you will say, "How are things going? You seem a little sad today." She may mention something about being scared because her mother drinks, or lonely because her father isn't in her life. You will hear about the very things that you guessed were bothering her.

You will have created a safe zone in which she is not judged to be bad. Feeling safe, she will begin to be able to express her feelings and start to work on them in healthy ways. Reframing will help get the results that you have been wanting. You just have to start at a new place.

Reframing is also going to change the "ecosystem" of your program. You are familiar with the ecosystems in nature. If one thing in nature is changed, such as an animal becoming extinct or its environment polluted, other parts of nature are affected. If you could stand outside of your program and observe it as though it were a movie, you would see that just as in nature, there is a certain balance. Children and staff members take on roles that tend to balance each other out—your program is an ecosystem. If the roles change because of reframing, the system may be out of balance for a while. In her book *Peoplemaking* (Palo Alto: Science and Behavior, 1972), psychologist Virginia Satir talks about the family mobile. Each member plays a role to keep the mobile in balance. If one of the family members changes her role, by stopping an addictive behavior, for example, the whole mobile wiggles and jiggles until balance is restored. You might find the same thing happening in your program.

Other children may try to stop Jessica from changing. They may say something like, "Oh, you'll always be trouble." They may put pressure on you to treat her the way you always have. They may feel jealous or simply threatened by the imbalance. Another child may assume some of Jessica's behaviors to regain the balance. Be aware of these possibilities. As the issues arise, address them with the individual children. Don't make a class announcement that "Jessica is really trying to be a better girl. Let's all try to help her." That would make Jessica feel unsafe and broken again. The new balance that eventually results from Jessica's changed behaviors will be healthier for everyone. It will be based on caring relationships and on valuing all the children.

Another outcome of reframing can sometimes be that you take another look at the program's role in enabling negative behaviors. You decided that Jessica is enthusiastic when she comes after school rather than disruptive. You may begin to take a look at the fact that your room's ecosystem doesn't allow for a display of energy right after school. Maybe other children come in with pent-up energy, too. Jessica is just speaking for all of them. You might then decide to do some restructuring that allows children more activity at that time.

Perhaps a couple of children often disrupt story time. You might say to yourself, "They are telling me for the rest of the class that story time is too long, or the books are boring or whatever." Maybe your system is out of balance and some children are reacting to the discomfort. Instead of trying to make the children fit into a system that is out of balance, you might change the system to fit their needs.

Whew! I told you this concept was a bit complicated. But it's something like riding a bike. Once you learn you'll never forget. Also, just as it isn't productive to try to ride a bike in a blizzard, there are times when using reframing isn't effective. There will also be times when you use reframing and it doesn't work. But please do try it. It can be very exciting. Take a risk. Nothing bad can happen from trying.

You have stretched your mind. Before we go on to conflict resolution, stretch your body until you feel some energy come back.

Do Use Conflict Resolution

C.J. holds the block *in shooting position. He is about to blast a fellow first grader with his fake gun when Cody, the staff person, walks in. Cody starts to give C.J. his lecture, which goes something like this:*

"C.J. who are you shooting?"

"A bad guy."

"Oh, I see. Do you think that that bad guy lives somewhere, like in a house or an apartment or something?"

"I suppose."

"Do you think that maybe other people live with him, like his mother and father, or sisters and brothers, or his kids?"

"They could."

"And do you think that after you kill him those people will feel sad?"

"Yeah."

"And C.J., do you think because you are aiming a gun at him and you kill him that some people might think you are a bad guy?"

"They might."

"Well, we want to think of other ways to solve problems here. That's why we don't play killing games and don't have toy guns. We want to practice other things, not hurting people."

"I know."

"So turn your gun back into a block, okay?"

"Okay."

That's how the conversation usually goes. C.J. has heard it all before. This time, before Cody starts, C. J. puts his hands on his hips, rolls his eyes and says, "Face it, Cody, there is such a thing as bad guys."

❧ ❧

Our society teaches children every day that the way to deal with conflict is through violence, power, and control. If you try to teach kids about conflict resolution, you are swimming against the strong current of popular culture. Video games, TV, the nightly news, some sports, and heroes tell kids that might is right and problems are easily terminated through violence.

You can be a life-altering person for a child. You will teach in many ways that even though there might sometimes be such a thing as bad guys, violence is not the solution.

Kids cannot solve their problems the way that the media teaches them. They cannot go around your program shooting or blowing things up (although, tragically, there are instances when such things do happen). However, they can bring the attitude with them. They can hit, call names, swear, kick, push, shove. It is up to you to give them alternative ways of solving their conflicts.

The first step in being effective in helping children to deal with conflict is not to be afraid of conflict yourself. Conflict will happen. It is part of life. It is certainly part of school-age care programs. School-age children, in groups, learning socialization and self-actualization, are bound to be in conflict at times. A community of children who feel free to exchange ideas and express opinions will have differences of opinion and principles. An atmosphere that does not allow children to do this is also inhibiting their ability to stretch their minds.

I once taught in a progressive little preschool in Connecticut. I really didn't know a great deal about preschool children at the time. Fortunately, the head teacher, Chaing, was experienced and wise. At the end of one particularly busy morning, she helped me clean up the classroom. I was a bit embarrassed because it seemed like such a disaster.

Blocks were baking in the oven in the housekeeping area. Dress-up clothes were in the reading area. Miniature farm animals sat on the art table. Rhythm instruments, that the children had been playing for the fish, rested now in the science area.

"I'm sorry things are such a mess," I said.

"Oh, I was just going to compliment you," Chaing said. "A creative classroom always allows children the freedom to experiment with new ideas. The result is just a different kind of order."

I used her wisdom to change my attitude. Order that is artificial and exists for its own sake, that doesn't allow for creativity and choices, is stifling, not reassuring. So it is with conflict. If children are not allowed to disagree, then they do not have the freedom to make choices, to creatively experiment with ideas.

Rather than be upset with conflict, reframe it (you're good at that now). Instead of letting your muscles all tighten and anger rise to your forehead, say to yourself, "Boy, I'm good. The kids are experimenting with their principles again. Here's a chance to help them learn how to get their needs met, be caring, and move on. I can't wait to help them."

There are different ways to deal with conflict. Each of us learned a somewhat different way in our families, schools, and communities. Take a minute to describe here what you learned about conflict as a child. Give a specific example or two to illustrate your points.

_____

_____

_____

_____

_____

_____

_____

_____

How has that learning affected you as an adult?

_____

_____

_____

How do you think what you learned and how it affects you helps or hinders you in helping children with conflict resolution?

_____

_____

_____

What do you want to remind yourself as you approach a conflict situation with children?

_____

_____

Conflict resolution is a popular topic these days. There are books and seminars, even international conferences about it. Those are all good signs that there is something of a movement brewing to give us alternatives to the old "might makes right." However, all the academic talk might lead us to believe that conflict resolution is too complicated for us to understand, much less to use in our programs.

Conflict resolution is not mysterious. We have talked about several components of conflict resolution throughout this book. Listening, flexibility, respect, and empowering children are all part of conflict resolution. You do not have to be afraid that if you don't follow the steps of a particular conflict resolution model perfectly, you will be harming children or even just doing it incorrectly.

Conflict resolution simply means what the words say. There is a conflict, a fight or disagreement. The fight ends. It gets resolved—"brought to a successful conclusion," as one dictionary says. A successful conclusion is one in which all participants have been heard and have listened; there is a plan to solve the problem that works for everyone involved; and if there is a person or persons who were in some way injured, there is reparation.

Conflict resolution is an alternative to continuous fighting. If a conflict does not get resolved, it continues, or it pops up again in a new way. Conflict resolution has a successful outcome because it is nonviolent. It is not solved by more verbal or physical harm. Children learn how to ask for help in working through a problem. They learn to share the real feelings that are at the base of the conflict. They feel confident in their ability to resolve differences peacefully. As the kids become familiar and comfortable with conflict resolution, they will use it or request help using it when conflicts begin.

I am not going to recommend one way of using or teaching conflict resolution. There are many resources available for that. Please refer to the resource section for some possibilities. The same conflict resolution technique or model doesn't work in every situation or setting. It can be helpful, however, to adopt a basic model that the children can learn. You can choose to use other approaches to resolve conflicts when appropriate.

A simple example of a possible model of a conflict resolution process is this ABCD model:

A. Always stop right now.

Ask to work it out somehow.

B. Become communicators. Tell your part. Share the feelings in your heart.

Brainstorm things to do.

C. Choose a plan to do.

D. Do it.

> Rebecca Janke and Julie Peterson, *Peacemaker's ABC's for Young Children:*
> *Teacher's Conflict Resolution Guide Using the Peace Table*
> (Marine-on-the-St. Croix: Growing Communities for Peace, 1995)

That's pretty easy. Let's use an example to practice the basics outlined here.

A school-age care program *operates after school in a rural town. They have only a small space and a few supplies. The kids know each other pretty well. They are like a big family, with all the advantages and disadvantages that brings. The staff and kids are familiar with the ABCD conflict resolution process.*

One day, Montie and Jamel begin to play checkers. Soon they are hitting and yelling at each other. Alisson, the staff person, goes over to them.

A. *"ABC's," she says. She puts her arms between them to separate them. They stop hitting but continue to shout.*

"The first step is to stop right now, remember?"

The kids exchange a few more words. Then Jamel says, "I want to work it out."

"Okay," says Alisson. "How about you, Montie?"

"All right, but it's his fault."

"I'm glad you both want to work it out. Let's sit down over here and get started."

B. *"The next step, as you know, is that we communicate with each other. You each tell your part including your feelings. Are you each ready to do that?"*

"Yeah."

"Yeah."

"Okay, then. Jamel, please tell your part," Alisson suggests. She has a sense that Jamel is more calm at this point than Montie. Asking who wants to start might begin a power struggle over the wrong issue.

"I wanted the black pieces. They all match. The red ones we use poker chips for because some are missing. Montie grabbed them away from me. I hit him on the arm and yelled some junk at him. That's it."

"Montie, tell us your part."

"So, because he decides that he should get the black ones he should just get them? He's always taking stuff and acting all big and stuff."

"Remember, Montie, just tell us about your part."

"He...I wanted to talk about who gets the black pieces. I asked him before the game if we could talk about it. He said sure. Then he just took them to his side. So I grabbed them away. He didn't keep the bargain so why should I? Then he hit me so I punched him back."

"Do you both agree that's kind of what happened?"

Jamel answers, *"Yeah."*

"Montie?"

"Yeah, I guess."

"When you say, 'I guess,' I wonder if you want to add something else to the facts."

"No. Yeah, it's right."

"Okay, Montie, it sounds like you had some feelings going on when Jamel didn't talk to you about the pieces."

"I was mad. Like, he's supposed to be my friend and then he can't even talk to me about stuff."

"How did you feel about what Jamel did to you?"

"It like hurt me. You know. People around here think I'm stupid. I thought he liked me. But when he wouldn't talk to me and just took the pieces, I thought oh brother, he thinks I'm dumb, too. So he can just take things away from me."

"Jamel, what were you feeling?" Alisson asks.

"Honestly?"

"Yes, honestly."

"I was feeling mean. I had a fight on the school bus and this creepy kid took my cassette and pulled it apart. It's the only cool music I've got. Other kids have lots of music and other good stuff. I was mad and I didn't want to be nice to get the good pieces."

"How do you feel because you don't have as many things as some other kids?" Alisson asks.

"Lazy, no good, like I'm ashamed 'cause my family's sort of poor. So I felt embarrassed because Montie's a rich dude and I'm not. So I just skipped the talking part."

"But you're Montie's friend?"

"Yes."

"Talk to Montie," Alisson says.

"I shouldn't get mean to you about it, Montie. It wasn't your fault. But you could have helped me out. You could have said something before you grabbed them. You could have reminded me that I made a promise." Jamel says.

"That's true. But that doesn't mean that you could hit him, does it?" Alisson reminds him.

"No. I'm sorry Montie. And I don't think you're stupid. I didn't even know that you thought you were stupid."

"I'm sorry too that I wasn't a better friend and shouted ABC's at you or something," Montie says.

"What about Jamel feeling like he's no good? Did you know he feels that way?" Alisson asks Montie.

"No."

"What do you feel when you hear your friend saying that?"

"I get tears inside."

"Tell Jamel."

"I'm sorry you feel like that because you're real good to me as a friend," Montie says.

"Thanks," says Jamel.

"What do you want to do about the problem now?" Alisson asks.

C. "We could take turns. I want Montie to go first. Because I wasn't fair and I want him to know that I'm his friend. Then maybe I could have the black pieces the next game," Jamel says.

"Is that okay with you Montie?" Allison asks.

"That's okay."

"Is there anything else you want to say to each other?"

"No."

"No."

"Do you both agree that this is a good plan?"

"Yes."

"Yes."

"Give each other a sign that you have resolved this conflict and that you care about each other."

D. *The boys give each other a high five and start to pick up the checker pieces.*

◉ ◉

Not all conversations go exactly like this one, of course. The children may not get to the source of their problems as quickly as did the boys in this story. But it does demonstrate a basic conflict resolution process.

Please notice the adult's role in the story. What does she do? She helps the children stay on task. She keeps things moving. Most importantly, her sensitivity, focus, and relationship with the children guide them to the component of conflict resolution that is complex. She goes with the kids to "...the awareness of the method of truth..." that Carol Gilligan talks about in *In A Different Voice: Psychological Theory and Women's Development* (Cambridge: Harvard UP, 1993). Of course, the children don't know that's where they're going. Alisson may not even know it. But this is the heart of conflict resolution. The reason that conflict resolution is so valuable isn't only that the conflict stops. It is why the conflict stops and what people learn through the process that creates long-term changes. The changes that Gilligan talks about will result in fewer discipline issues and in long-term changes in the children that affect them for the rest of their lives.

What is the "method of truth"? The first step in conflict resolution is the acceptance of the facts. The children agreed on what happened. What happened, not whose fault it was or why it happened, just the facts. That is accountability. It is the first step on the way to the truth that will make a difference.

The next, more intense, difficult to get to, and vital truth is each child's viewpoint and feelings and the other child's ability and willingness to understand and care.

Statements such as

"It like hurt me,"

"I'm ashamed,"

"I didn't know you felt stupid," and

"I get tears inside,"

indicate that the kids are getting to the crux of the matter. There is dialogue and understanding rather than blame and judgment. The conflict will stop and resolution will happen. Because, in large part, Alisson facilitated a process that helped the boys feel safe. They told their own, and listened to the other's, truth.

In the simple ABC conflict resolution model, B is "become communicators." Communicating is challenging, lifelong work. Montie and Jamel have a good start because at least one adult in their lives is guiding them. She is teaching them how to solve differences without violence. She also led them to "the restorative activity of care." She assisted them in strengthening their relationship, in learning how to be empathetic, and in expressing their care for each other.

What happened here is much deeper and more permanent than what occurs when children are just told what to do. When we simply order children to stop the conflict, they do not learn how to stop on their own in the future. They do not acquire the skills or experience the power of communication.

Understanding others and being understood, compromise, and caring are tools for life. In some instances the understanding and caring are not personal. The participants may never like each other. But they can learn to understand each other and care about the good of the community and themselves. They can learn to settle differences in ways that repair damages and lessen the number of future conflicts.

If children are not involved in the process, the conflict's basic issues do not get resolved. So, the conflict will probably erupt again. And before it does, the bad feelings of the previous battle will have had a chance to fester.

Old resentments add fuel to future disagreements, just as in an old relationship in which issues are not really resolved, today's fight over who takes out the garbage is also about who didn't care enough twenty years ago, just as wars at the borders of a country are about turf issues that are hundreds of years old. Being guided to find the truth of facts and motivations, and learning how to participate in restoring care, will serve the children well throughout their lives.

You have a great responsibility here. You also have a chance to be part of a dynamic, life-changing, fascinating process. Participating with children as the insights flash and the connections click is a high akin to an actor giving a great performance or a scientist having a curative breakthrough in research. You are practicing your profession. You are crafting your art. You are changing lives for the better.

And you are doing so despite the push towards violence that our children experience. This is especially true for boys. Although things are changing at some levels for very little boys and for men, the elementary and high school age boy is still under tremendous pressure to be tough. In his book, *Real Boys: Rescuing our Sons from Myths of Boyhood* (New York: Random, 1998), Dr. William Pollack says that boys are taught that they may express only anger and frustration. Caring emotions have to be shoved inside. Boys in this age group have high rates of depression that often go unnoticed. The depression can be displayed as aggression. Also, boys are not expected to discuss their emotions, so if they withdraw it goes unnoticed. Michael Gurian, author, cites statistics from a recent federal study showing that boys are four times more likely to commit suicide than girls. They are also diagnosed 10 times more often with attention deficit and hyperactivity disorder (ADHD). In the sad incidents of children murdering people, it is almost always a boy child who is the perpetrator, and usually the victim is a boy, as well. The boy is usually described as a quiet, kept-to-himself kind of kid who maybe recently exhibited some behavior changes. Boys commit more crimes than men and are 15 times more likely to be victims of crimes than girls (Nicholas K. Geranios, Associated Press 27 September 1998).

Helping boys feel safe enough to engage in conflict resolution will help them recognize and diffuse buried emotions. It will also help build a generation of male partners, fathers, co-workers, world leaders—people—who are comfortable with a range of emotional expression, and who can listen, and care, and live happy, healthy lives.

There is no doubt that girls, too, will benefit from your lessons in conflict resolution. You will usually find, however, that the process is easier for them. They will be relieved to find that the emotions and truths that they are often aware of have a place in resolving conflicts and that caring can be a powerful tool.

Your role as an adult is essential in this kind of conflict resolution. There are conflict resolution techniques that have the children go off on their own to solve their problems. The problem with that approach is that children are just learning these skills. They need a guide to facilitate their learning. There are, of course, times when the conflict is minor and the children can shake it off with a short discussion on their own, but for situations that call for true conflict resolution, an adult is vital to the process. If we as adults get into a relationship conflict, or a work conflict, or an international conflict that is not easily resolved, we often call in a counselor who is skilled in mediation. We cannot expect children to need any less. (There are times when older children can be trained in peer mediation, but even then the training should be extensive and the children should know that an adult is available for consultation.) Conflict resolution is certainly an area in which you are the adult and they are the children.

If possible, do the following exercise with another adult. You are going to write an example of conflict resolution.

First, describe a conflict between children that you have witnessed or that you imagine. Talk about it together until all the details are on paper.

_____

_____

_____

_____

Next, describe a possible conversation between the children and the adult that will result in conflict resolution. Remember the ABC's and the "method of truth." Talk with each other about what you think might work. You could even role play the situation with each other and see if that gives you any new ideas.

_____

_____

_____

_____

_____

_____

Congratulations. That was a difficult task. Keep practicing until you can say to yourself or your partner, "I get it!"

This is the last do. I put it here for a purpose. Conflict resolution sums up much of what we discuss in this book about behavior guidance. When you can comfortably and skillfully assist in the conflict resolution process, you have probably internalized the other do's and don'ts.

The children with whom you work are fortunate that you have taken the tasks in this book seriously and that you will bring new knowledge and skills back to their program. You have done personal work that was sometimes difficult, you have shifted models, discussed your beliefs with others, practiced new skills, and examined past practices, rejecting some and enhancing others. You are to be honored for the work that you have done in the process of completing this book. You are to be honored for the intelligent and heartfelt work that you do with children each day.

Remember early in the book when we discussed a definition of behavior guidance? We said that by the end of the book you would have your own definition. One that only you could write based on your life experiences, the children with whom you work, what you know intellectually about children, and how you feel about them. It is time now for you to write that definition. It may change through the years as you and the school-age child care field develop, as we all learn more about child development. But take some time now to write a thoughtful definition that describes what you think behavior guidance is.

My definition of behavior guidance is…

Congratulations on a job well done. It has truly been a learning experience for me to join you on this journey that will impact the lives of thousands and thousands of children, one at a time. My thoughts and hopes are with you daily as you make a difference for each of those children. The world will be a different place because you care, because you think, and because you practice your craft of guiding children. Peace.

Resources

Resource Books

Behavior Guidance

Dodson, Fitzhugh. *How to Discipline With Love: From Crib to College.* New York: Signet, 1978.

Dreikurs, Rudolf, and Vicki Soltz. *Children: The Challenge.* New York: Duell, 1964.

Faber, Adele, and Elaine Mazlish. *How to Talk So Kids Will Listen and Listen So Kids Will Talk.* New York: Avon, 1980.

————. *How to Talk So Kids Can Learn at Home and in School.* New York: Fireside, 1995.

Ginott, Haim G. *Between Parent and Child: New Solutions to Old Problems.* New York: Macmillan, 1965.

Gordon, Thomas. *P.E.T.: Parent Effectiveness Training: The Tested New Way to Raise Responsible Children.* New York: New American Library, 1975.

————. *Discipline That Works: Promoting Self-Discipline in Children.* New York: Penguin, 1989.

Kohn, Alfie. *Punished by Rewards: The Trouble with Gold Stars, Incentive Plans, A's, Praise, and Other Bribes.* Boston: Houghton, 1993.

————. *Beyond Discipline: From Compliance to Community.* Alexandria: Association for Supervision and Curriculum Development, 1996.

Kurcinka, Mary Sheedy. *Raising Your Spirited Child: A Guide for Parents Whose Child Is More Intense, Sensitive, Perceptive, Persistent, and Energetic.* New York: HarperCollins, 1991.

Molnar, Alex and Barbara Lindquist. *Changing Problem Behavior in Schools.* San Francisco: Jossey-Bass, 1989.

Tobin, L. *What Do You Do With A Child Like This?: Inside the Lives of Troubled Children.* Duluth: Whole Person Assoc., 1991.

Conflict Resolution

Carlsson-Paige, Nancy. *Best Day of the Week.* St. Paul: Redleaf, 1998.

Carlsson-Paige, Nancy, and Diane E. Levin. *Before Push Comes to Shove: Building Conflict Resolution Skills with Children.* St. Paul: Redleaf, 1998.

Friends School of Minnesota. *i to i: Integrating Conflict Resolution into the Elementary School Community: A Training Video.* Minneapolis: Friends School of Minnesota, 1995.

———. *Conflict Resolution Training Manual.* Minneapolis: Friends School of Minnesota, 1995.

Janke, Rebecca Ann, and Julie Penshorn Peterson. *Peacemaker's ABC's for Young Children: A Guide for Teaching Conflict Resolution with a Peace Table.* Marine-on-the-St. Croix: Growing Communities for Peace, 1995.

Kreidler, William. *Creative Conflict Resolution: More Than 200 Activities for Keeping Peace in the Classroom.* Millwood: Kraus, 1990.

Kreidler, William, and Lisa Furlong. *Adventures in Peacemaking: A Conflict Resolution Activity Guide for School-Age Programs.* Hamilton: Project Adventure, 1995.

Attention Deficit Disorder—ADD

Cohen, Michael W. *The Attention Zone: A Parent's Guide to Attention Deficit Hyperactivity Disorder.* Washington: Taylor, 1998.

Fowler, Mary. *Maybe You Know My Kid: A Parent's Guide to Identifying, Understanding, and Helping Your Child with Attention Deficit Hyperactivity Disorder.* Secaucus: Carol, 1990.

Hallowell, Edward M., and John J. Ratey. Driven to *Distraction: Recognizing and Coping with Attention Deficit Disorder from Childhood through Adulthood.* New York: Simon, 1994.

Observation

Martin, Sue. *Take A Look: Observation and Portfolio Assessment in Early Childhood.* Don Mills, Ontario: Addison-Wesley, 1999.

Programming

Bergman, Abby Barry, and William Greene. *The Complete School-Age Child Care Resource Kit: Practical Guidelines, Materials, and Activities for Implementing a Quality SACC Program.* West Najack: Simon, 1995.

Cooper, Robert K. *Health and Fitness Excellence: The Scientific Action Plan.* New York: Houghton, 1989.

Edwards, Carolyn, Lella Gandini, and George Forman, eds. *The Hundred Languages of Children: The Reggio Emilia Approach to Early Childhood Education.* Norwood: Ablex, 1993.

Harms, Thelma, Ellen Vineberg Jacobs, and Donna Romano White. *School-Age Care Environmental Rating Scale.* New York: Teachers College, 1998.

Koralek, Derry G., and Debra D. Foulks. *A Trainer's Guide to Caring for Children in School-Age Programs.* Washington: Teaching Strategies, 1995.

Koralek, Derry G., Roberta L. Newman, and Laura J. Colker. *Caring for Children in School-Age Programs.* 2 vols. Washington: Teaching Strategies, 1995.

Northwest Media, Inc. *Including All Kids!: Including Youth with Special Needs in School-Age Care.* Eugene: Northwest Media, 1997. Video and leader guide.

Oehlberg, Barbara. *Making It Better: Activities for Children Living in a Stressful World.* St. Paul: Redleaf, 1996.

Oser, Andrew. *Joy of Sports: Star Program: Life Success Skills through Physical Activities for Children Ages 5-8.* Discovery Bay: Front Row Experience, 1996.

———. *Star Power for Preschoolers: Learning Life Skills through Physical Play.* St. Paul: Redleaf, 1997.

Rohnke, Karl, and Steve Butler. *Quicksilver: Adventure Games, Initiative Problems, Trust Activities, and a Guide to Effective Leadership.* Dubuque: Kendall-Hunt, 1995.

Roman, Janette, ed. *The NSAC Standards for Quality School-Age Care.* Boston: National School-Age Care Alliance, 1997.

Development & Theory

American Association of University Women Educational Foundation. *The AAUW Report: How Schools Shortchange Girls.* New York: Marlowe, 1992.

Ames, Louise Bates, Frances L. Ilg, and Sidney M. Baker. *Your Ten-to Fourteen-Year-Old.* New York: Dell, 1988.

Bender, Judith, Barbara Schuyler-Hass Elder, and Charles H. Flatter. *Half a Childhood: Time for School-Age Child Care.* Nashville: School-Age Notes, 1999.

Elkind, David. *The Hurried Child: Growing Up Too Fast Too Soon.* Reading: Addison-Wesley, 1981.

Gossen, Diane C. *Restitution: Restructuring School Discipline.* Chapel Hill: New View, 1993.

Gurian, Michael. *A Fine Young Man: What Parents, Mentors, and Educators Can Do to Shape Adolescent Boys into Exceptional Men.* New York: Tarcher-Putnam, 1998.

Musson, Steve. *School-Age Care: Theory and Practice.* Reading: Addison-Wesley, 1999.

Pollack, William S. *Real Boys: Rescuing Our Sons from Myths of Boyhood.* New York: Random, 1998.

Support

ldwin, Sue. *Lifesavers: Tips for Success and Sanity for Early Childhood Managers.* Stillwater: Insights, 1996.

y, Stephen. *The Seven Habits of Highly Effective People.* New York: on, 1989.

Jean, and Mary Steiner Whelan. *For the Love of Children: Daily ations for People Who Care for Children.* St. Paul: Redleaf, 1995.

Sociology

Garbarino, James, Nancy Dubrow, Kathleen Kostelny, and Carole Pardo. *Children in Danger: Coping with the Consequences of Community Violence.* San Francisco: Jossey-Bass, 1992.

Hamburg, David A. *Today's Children: Creating a Future for a Generation in Crisis.* New York: Random, 1992.

Kotlowitz, Alex. *There Are No Children Here: The Story of Two Boys Growing Up in the Other America.* New York: Doubleday, 1991.

Kozol, Jonathan. Amazing Grace: *The Lives of Children and the Conscience of a Nation.* New York: Crown, 1995.

———. *Savage Inequalities: Children in America's Schools.* New York: Crown, 1991.

Maeroff, Gene I. *Altered Destinies: Making Life Better for Schoolchildren in Need.* New York: St. Martin's, 1998.

Mercogliano, Chris. *Making It Up As We Go Along: The Story of the Albany Free School.* Portsmouth: Heinemann, 1998.

Psychology

Coles, Robert. *The Moral Life of Children: How Children Struggle with Questions of Moral Choice in the United States and Elsewhere.* Boston: Houghton, 1986.

Gilligan, Carol. *In a Different Voice: Psychological Theory and Women's Development.* Cambridge: Harvard UP, 1993.

Glasser, William. *Reality Therapy: A New Approach to Psychiatry.* New York: Harper, 1965.

Miller, Alice. *Banished Knowledge: Facing Childhood Injuries.* New York: Doubleday, 1990.

———. *Drama of the Gifted Child: The Search for the True Self.* New York: HarperCollins, 1997.

———. *Paths of Life: Seven Scenarios.* New York: Pantheon, 1998.

Satir, Virginia. *Peoplemaking.* Palo Alto: Science and Behavior, 1972.

Other Resources

Child Care Information Exchange
PO Box 3249
Redmond, WA 98073-3249
Phone: 1-800-221-2864 or 1-425-883-9394
Fax: 1-425-867-5217
Web Site: www.ccie.com

Child Care Information publishes a magazine and offers resources and workshops for directors.

NSACA: National School-Age Care Alliance
1137 Washington Street
Boston, MA 02124
Phone: 617-298-5012
Fax: NSACA, 617-298-5022
Web Site: www.nsaca.org

NSACA has national- and state-affiliated organizations for school-age care professionals. They offer national and local conferences, sponsor local training and workshops, and publish national and local newsletters.

eaf Press
J. Syndicate Street, Suite 5
l, MN 55104-4125
1-800-423-8309
onal Call: 1-800-641-0305
0-641-0115
al Fax: 1-651-645-0990

e catalog of quality resources including carefully selected cific materials.

School-Age Notes
P.O. Box 40205
Nashville, TN 37204-0205
Phone: 1-800-410-8780
Outside of the U.S. call: 1-615-279-0700
Fax: 615-279-0800
Web Site: www.schoolagenotes.com

School-Age Notes publishes a monthly newsletter with ideas, strategies, tips, and activities. They also publish books and have a catalog of resources.

Please use the following pages
for your notes, thoughts, or stories.